TAM
ST. P

JOSHUA LAWR

VINOY PARK
CITY OF ST PETERSBURG

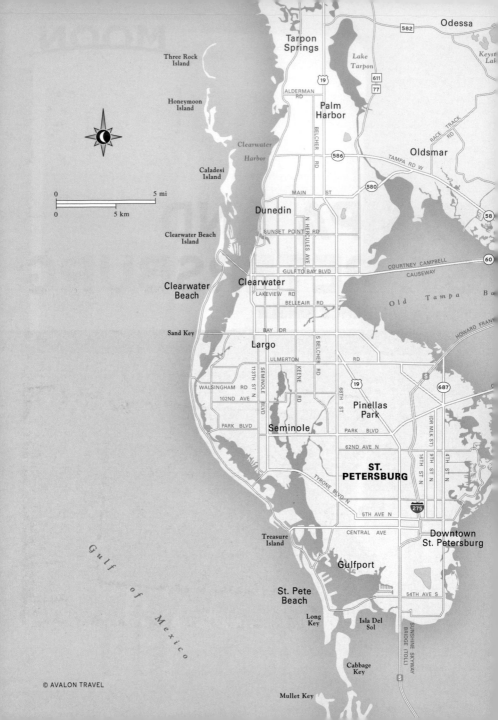

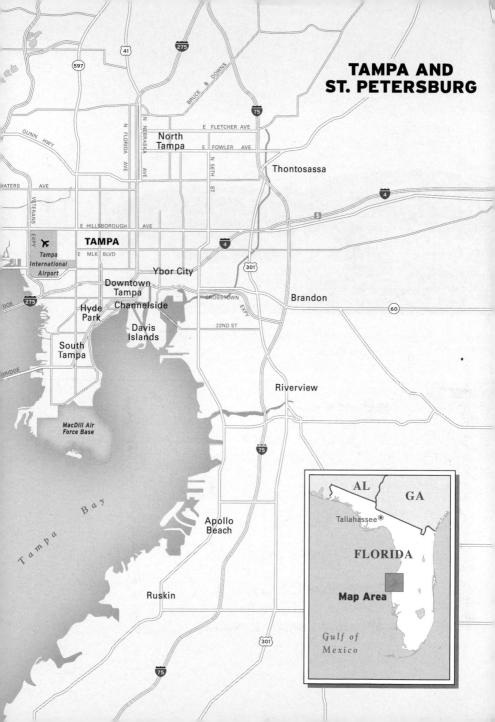

TAMPA AND
ST. PETERSBURG

Contents

DISCOVER

Tampa and
St. Petersburg

It's no wonder that Tampa and St. Petersburg have undergone explosive growth in recent years. The cities' vibrant economies are attracting job seekers in droves—and there's a reason they're choosing to settle here.

Tampa, with its refreshing bay and sunny climate, is more than just a place for business. Though it doesn't have any of its own beaches, there's plenty to keep you busy—from lively and historic Ybor City to the thrills of Busch Gardens and spring training with the New York Yankees. Tampa is looking as stylish as ever with new scenic parks and walks, trendy restaurants and hotels, and revitalized arts institutions.

Across the bay, St. Petersburg adds sand and surf to the mix. Dazzling white sand, turquoise waters, and gorgeous sunsets define the city and its miles of Gulf Coast and barrier islands. Just a few steps from the beach, there are equally

---

Clockwise from top left: The Vinoy Renaissance Resort & Golf Club in St. Petersburg; a boardwalk on St. Pete Beach; Myakka River State Park; a cruise ship in the Port of Tampa; Dunedin; Clearwater Beach.

dazzling art displays and upscale boutiques, like the Salvador Dalí Museum and the Chihuly Collection at The Morean Art Center. There are few places that offer this kind of sophistication so close to paradise.

Both cities excel in variety—from beautiful beaches to urban sophistication and family fun. Tampa and St. Petersburg pack the best of Florida into one pocket of paradise.

Clockwise from top left: Universal Orlando Resort; Clearwater Marine Aquarium; paddling on the Crystal River; Cinderella's Castle at Walt Disney World in Orlando.

Planning Your Trip

Where to Go

Tampa

Tampa is a huge **port city**—the largest leisure and industrial port in the Southeast—that fronts **Tampa Bay.** Though there aren't any beaches, there's a perfect convergence of **warm weather,** affordable accommodations, **professional sports, kids' attractions,** and **upscale shopping** that seems to suit every taste.

St. Petersburg and Pinellas County

Easygoing and relaxed, the city of **St. Petersburg** exerts its pull with a vibrant downtown of pastel art deco buildings and cultural attractions like the **Salvador Dalí Museum,** the symphony at Ruth Eckerd Hall, and theater at American Stage. But on the Gulf side of the peninsula, **Clearwater Beach** and **St. Pete**

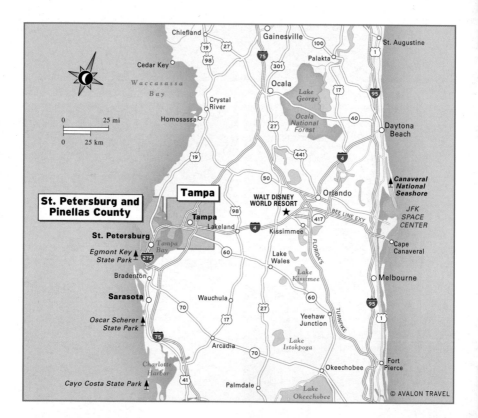

the Tampa skyline

Beach are welcoming shores of Gulf water lapping at white sand, backed by restaurants, souvenir shops, and boogie-board-and-bikini stores. Caladesi Island, Honeymoon Island, and Fort De Soto Park are all favored Pinellas beaches.

Day Trips

Orlando attracts millions of visitors annually to **Walt Disney World, Universal Studios, SeaWorld,** and many other family-friendly attractions.

The Nature Coast includes Homosassa and Crystal River, both famous for their **tarpon fishing** and **manatee habitat.**

Sarasota has been recognized as **Florida's cultural capital.** There are theaters, art galleries, and museums like the **John and Mable Ringling Museum of Art.** A chain of narrow barrier islands, including **Longboat Key** and **Siesta Key,** sits offshore to the west.

Clearwater Beach

When to Go

In Tampa and St. Petersburg, the peak visitor season is **winter** and **spring,** with most people visiting from January to April, which means higher room rates during those months. If you're visiting in March or April, be aware that these areas tend to get crowded during **spring break** as well. Less people visit from **September to December,** when the weather is pleasant and nearly vacant hotels offer their lowest room rates of the year. Be aware however that **hurricane season** runs from late summer to early fall. It's best to avoid the **summer** if you can, which brings hot, humid weather and surges of visitors on summer break.

The Best of Tampa and St. Petersburg

Day 1

After flying into **Tampa,** start the day with lunch at **Pelagia Trattoria,** an upscale Italian restaurant in the **Renaissance Hotel,** just southeast of the airport. After lunch, rent a boat and spend the rest of the afternoon cruising Tampa Bay or make reservations for a sunset sail with **Olde World Sailing Line.** Have a nice seafood dinner at an outdoor fireside table at **Oystercatchers** at the Grand Hyatt or head to **Shula's Steak House** at the Westshore if you want a sizzling-good steak. Finish off the evening with wine and dessert at **Armani's** rooftop bar, also in the Hyatt, with the best views of Tampa all lit up at night. Spend the night at the **Grand Hyatt Tampa Bay.**

Day 2

Start the morning with Cuban pastries at **La Segunda Central Bakery** in **Ybor City.**

Spend the morning exploring the historic and artsy Cuban district. If you're in Tampa during spring training, see the New York Yankees play at **Steinbrenner Field,** just east of the airport. Otherwise, walk along **Bayshore Boulevard** and enjoy the historic homes and shops. Have dinner at the Japanese-inspired **Water Sushi,** a late-night hangout that has live music almost nightly. Consider sneaking across the street for some heavenly dessert at **The Harry Waugh Dessert Room at Bern's Steak House.** Stay another night at the Grand Hyatt.

Day 3

Wake up and drive half an hour over the W. Howard Frankland Bridge to **St. Petersburg** for breakfast at **Skyway Jack's Restaurant.** Spend the morning fishing on the **Skyway Bridge** or shopping in **Downtown St. Petersburg.** While

St. Petersburg waterfront

downtown St. Petersburg

Siesta Key Beach

in Downtown, visit the **Salvador Dalí Museum,** intriguing both inside and out. Catch an evening baseball game with the **Tampa Bay Rays** at **Tropicana Field,** with the required dinner of ballpark hot dogs and cold beers. Alternatively, enjoy seafood and waterfront views at **400 Beach Seafood and Tap House,** within walking distance of **The Vinoy Renaissance Resort & Golf Club,** where you should stay for the night.

Day 4

Have breakfast at the Vinoy, then drive half an hour either to the lively **St. Pete Beach** or to the more isolated **Fort De Soto Park.** Have some fun in the sun before enjoying a sunset dinner at

The Hurricane in St. Pete Beach. Stay the night at the **Sirata Beach Resort.**

With More Time

If you have time for a day trip, get on I-75 and take the hour-long drive south to **Sarasota.** Spend the morning shopping at the luxurious **St. Armands Circle** before popping over to **Marie Selby Botanical Gardens** for a short tour through their fabulous orchid exhibit. Take the John Ringling Causeway, Highway 789, over Sarasota Bay. Drive to **Siesta Key,** and spend the rest of the day on **Siesta Key Beach.** Have dinner at **Ophelia's on the Bay** and stay at the **Turtle Beach Resort.**

Best Beaches

Venice Beach

ST. PETERSBURG

- **St. Pete Beach** (page 74): This long, wIde beach is a favorite of families and European travelers. There are plenty of family-centric resorts along this stretch of coast, which offer a great variety of activities and amenities to keep everyone entertained.

- **Clearwater Beach** (page 74): Go to this urban beach surrounded by seaside hangouts and hotels during the day to find the epicenter of oceanfront activity around Tampa. Sunsets from the beach pier are phenomenal, and by night the beach transforms into a fun spot with a nice mix of family activities and beach bar nightlife.

- **Fort De Soto Park** (page 75): Take a break from the city and explore the seven miles of pristine, preserved beaches at this beautiful park. You can also camp, hike, fish, launch a boat, and explore the historic fort on the southwest tip if you get tired of lounging and swimming.

- **Honeymoon Island and Caladesi Island Beaches** (page 75): These exceptional barrier islands located off the coast of Dunedin are only accessible by ferry. Both are preserved state parks with beautiful white beaches.

SARASOTA

- **Siesta Key Beach** (page 142): This beach always draws praise for its superior white sand. It gets crowded in the summer, but the exceptional size of this beach leaves sun seekers with plenty of spots to spike a shade-supplying umbrella or spread out a supersize beach towel.

- **Turtle Beach** (page 143): Tucked among villas and a residential district, this family-oriented beach has excellent picnic facilities and is much less crowded than the more popular Siesta Key Beach to the north on the island, yet it still has that special sugar-white sand that makes this barrier island a big draw for beachgoers.

- **Venice Beach** (page 144): This beach is famously regarded as the place to go to hunt for fossilized sharks' teeth. The very convenient location close to the heart of Venice makes this beach just a bike ride from most of the popular inns and villas. A great beach for families, it has nice picnic pavilions and shower facilities.

Family Fun

Day 1

Tampa really knows family fun. Spend a day riding roller coasters, exploring recreated African savannas, and splashing down log-flume rides at **Busch Gardens.** It's a park for all ages, with a mix of exciting coasters and cool animal attractions. Stay the night at the **Holiday Inn Express New Tampa,** only three miles from Busch Gardens, and you'll get free ice cream in the evening, breakfast included in the morning, and access to a nice heated pool to keep the kiddos entertained after the park closes.

Day 2

Drive for about an hour over the bridge on route 60 to **Clearwater Beach** for some sun, sand, and surf. For something extra special, take a pirate cruise with **Captain Memo's Original Pirate Cruise.** Later, check out **Sunsets at Pier 60,** a festival that runs every evening with crafts, magicians, and musicians. Pier 60 also contains a

covered playground for the little ones. Grab a casual dinner at the **Beach Shanty Café** before turning in at **Frenchy's Oasis Motel or East Shore Resort.**

Alternatively, spend the day at **St. Pete Beach,** with an optional excursion to **John's Pass Village & Boardwalk** for a pirate ship or dolphin cruise. In the evening, take the kids to see the Tampa Bay Rays play ball at the **Tropicana Field.** If you don't gorge yourself on hot dogs, have a casual seafood dinner at **The Hurricane.** Stay in St. Pete Beach at the **Sirata Beach Resort** or **TradeWinds Island Grand.**

Day 3

Start heading north along the coast on U.S. 19 and drive the 73 miles (1.5 hours) to **Homosassa** or **Crystal River.** From mid-October to the end of March, you'll find hundreds of **West Indian manatees** swimming in the warm waters of Kings Bay in the Crystal River

Clearwater Beach

Gone Fishin'

You can fish for some species year-round in Florida, but most species generally run during specific months. The peak fishing season for much of the Tampa area is April to October. In South Florida, the peak season runs October to March.

TAMPA

Snook, spotted trout, redfish, flounder, pompano, and sheepshead are some of the most popular fish to catch in the flats and waters around Tampa Bay. May is the peak season for Tarpon, and anglers come from all over the world to Tampa to try and catch this fish that fights like the devil. Alternatively, book a charter or take your boat offshore to catch kingfish, grouper, cobia, tuna, and amberjack, to name just a few.

fishing boat in Tampa Bay

If you're fishing from shore, visit Upper Tampa Bay Park, Ballast Point Park, or E.G. Simmons Park. For more access to the great fishing in Tampa Bay, rent a boat with Tierra Verde Boat Rentals, or take a charter with Tampa Fishing Charters, Capt. Chet Jennings Fishing Charters, or Tampa Flats and Bay Fishing Charters.

ST. PETERSBURG

The favorite fishing spot here is the Sunshine Skyway Bridge, where you can catch kingfish, Spanish mackerel, grouper, sea bass, redfish, flounder, and more. The North and South Piers total more than two miles of fishing bridge bliss. Other excellent fishing spots are Fort De Soto Park, John's Pass Beach, and Madeira Beach. Pier 60 in Clearwater is also a good bet.

THE NATURE COAST

Redfish and speckled trout are abundant in the shallow waters along the Nature Coast. The area is not very well marked and can be hard to navigate without a guide, but the fishing in this area is legendary. Cobia, mackerel, grouper, and snapper are the usual suspects when fishing offshore here.

Some top fishing spots include Chassahowitzka National Wildlife Refuge, the Crystal River, and the Homosassa River. For guided fishing trips, Captain Rick LeFiles or Captain William Toney in Homosassa will welcome you aboard their boats and take you to the finest fishing holes in the region. You can also rent your own boat at MacRae's of Homosassa.

SARASOTA

There's not much need to go offshore when the inshore fishing for snook, redfish, trout, pompano, and bluefish around Sarasota is so good. The narrow and winding mangrove channels in this area give inshore fly-fishing and light-tackle trips a wilderness backcountry feel. Offshore trips mostly target grouper, amberjack, and snapper.

Top fishing spots around Sarasota are Myakka River State Park, Siesta Key, Longboat Key, and Venice.

and the Blue Waters area of the Homosassa River. **Manatee Tour & Dive** or **Captain Mike's Swimming with the Manatees** will take whole families out for snorkel trips. If you find yourself and your family along the Nature Coast when manatees aren't in season, there are still good reasons to get wet. Drive to **Weeki Wachee Springs** for a fantastic Mermaid show and kid-friendly rides, or go **scalloping** if it's July 1-September 10. Stay at the **Plantation on Crystal River.**

Day 4

From Crystal River, drive for 89 miles (1.5 hours) along Highway 44 and the I-75 Florida Turnpike to **Walt Disney World,** comprising four distinct parks: the Magic Kingdom, Epcot, Disney Hollywood Studios, and the Animal Kingdom. Spend the day visiting the most popular one, the **Magic Kingdom,** making sure to ride the phenomenal **Space Mountain,** an indoor roller coaster that zips and zooms through the stars along a dark and thrilling space adventure. If you're on a budget, have a quick and tasty lunch inside the park at **Cosmic Rays Starlight Café.** If you're with kids or want to splurge, dine like royalty and have a dinner feast with a princess at **Cinderella's Royal Table.** Continue the Disney fun and stay at the **Disney's Grand Floridian Resort,** a fun Disney-themed Victorian-style resort that's just one monorail stop away from the Magic Kingdom.

With More Time

It's better to spread Disney World out over two days. Continue your adventures in the Magic Kingdom or visit one of Disney's other parks. My suggestion is to spend the day at **Epcot,** learning about the future of technology at **Project Tomorrow** and having fish and chips at the delicious **Yorkshire County Fish Shop.**

Spend another night in Orlando. In the morning, drive one hour on I-4 back to Tampa to catch your plane home.

St. Pete Beach

OYSTERS

The oysters that grow about a hundred miles north of Tampa in Apalachicola have become world famous as a result of the huge numbers that grow in the area, and because people say they taste better than any other oyster in the world. While in Tampa, or particularly if you're traveling along the Nature Coast, try them and you'll understand why so many are willing to travel so far to taste them.

- In Tampa, eat fresh oysters raw on the half shell, baked, stuffed, or Rockefeller style at **Oystercatchers,** or have a fried oyster sandwich at **Brocato's Sandwich Shop.**

- Near Sarasota, head to the islands and shuck those tasty treats at the **Siesta Key Oyster Bar.**

- In Crystal River, go to **Charlie's Fish House Restaurant.**

GROUPER SANDWICH

The grouper sandwich is a staple on the Gulf Coast for lunch or dinner after a day at the beach or out on the boat. The recipe is simple: Take a huge, flaky slab of grilled, blackened, or fried grouper and put it in a chewy bun with some premium cheese, fresh tomato and lettuce, and maybe a slather of tartar sauce, and you've got one supreme sandwich.

- In Tampa, go to **Skipper's Smokehouse, Oystercatchers,** or **Brocato's Sandwich Shop.**

- In St. Petersburg, head to **The Hurricane.**

SHRIMP

Anytime you visit the Gulf Coast, no trip should be complete without eating as much shrimp as possible. You can get them fried, in sandwiches, on salads, and even on pizzas around here, but the best way to eat shrimp is boiled in spices, peeled, and dipped in cocktail sauce with perhaps a bit of lemon and horseradish.

- In Tampa, get your shrimp fix at **Charley's Steakhouse and Market Fresh Fish, Oystercatchers,** or **Eddie V's Prime Seafood.**

shrimp in a seafood bouillabaisse

- In St. Petersburg, head to **400 Beach Seafood and Tap House;** on St. Pete Beach, try **Bongo's Beach Bar and Grill;** on Indian Rocks Beach, go to **Lulu's Oyster Bar and Tap House;** in Clearwater, grab some peel-and-eat at **Cooters Restaurant and Bar.**

CUBAN FOOD

Ybor City in Tampa is the hub of all things Cuban. Do not visit without eating a Cubano, a sandwich with Cuban bread (which has thin flaky crust and a soft interior), a mountain of roast pork and Genoa salami (salami being a strictly Tampa twist), swiss cheese (some say emmentaler), sour pickles, and spicy mustard—then warmed and flattened in a special hot press. Other Cuban staples include mojo chicken, ham croquettes, *ropa vieja*, mojitos, and my favorite, *guayaba y queso,* a flaky pastry filled with guava fruit and cream cheese.

- For the best Cuban food in Tampa, head to the **Columbia Restaurant.** For something more casual, take home boxes of sandwiches, Cuban bread, and delicious pastries from **La Segunda Central Bakery.**

© Disney

Above: Dumbo's Flying Elephants at Walt Disney World. **Below:** The Pier in St. Petersburg.

Tampa

Look for ★ to find recommended
sights, activities, dining, and lodging.

Highlights

★ **Florida Aquarium:** This 152,000-square-foot aquarium focuses on Florida's relationship to the Gulf, estuaries, rivers, and other waterways, with a strong environmental message (page 25).

★ **Ybor City:** Once known as the Cigar Capital of the World, Tampa's Latin Quarter offers visitors historic shops by day and the city's best nightlife and dining (Cubano sandwich, anyone?) when the sun goes down (page 28).

★ **Bayshore Boulevard:** These five miles of sidewalk are bordered on one side by the wide-open bay and on the other side by Tampa's fanciest historic homes (page 29).

★ **Busch Gardens Tampa:** This theme park is an unusual mix of thrill rides, animal attractions, and entertainment (page 29).

★ **Spring Training:** See the New York Yankees train at George M. Steinbrenner Field or watch Tampa's own Rays at Charlotte Sports Park (page 39).

★ **Tampa Theatre:** Ornately decorated to resemble an open Mediterranean courtyard, this theatre features 1,446 seats, 99 stars in the auditorium ceiling, and nearly 1,000 pipes in its mighty Wurlitzer theater organ (page 40).

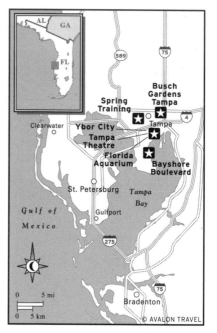

Tampa is a family-friendly town with plenty of upscale restaurants and shopping. The University of South Florida (USF), University of Tampa, and Hillsborough Community College lend a bit of youth and liveliness.

Tampa is centrally located on the Florida Gulf Coast, with an exceptional airport—an ideal city to fly into for trips to the region. It is home to Busch Gardens; a large cruise ship port; a great zoo and aquarium; professional football, baseball, and hockey teams; and affordable accommodations and restaurants.

Since Tampa isn't that old, it's not the best place for history lovers. It wasn't until Henry B. Plant extended his railroad into Tampa in 1884 and started a steamship line from Tampa to Key West and Havana, Cuba, that the city really began to grow. In 1891, Plant built the Tampa Bay Hotel, which launched the city as a winter resort for the northern elite. Around the same time, O. H. Platt created Tampa's first residential suburb, Hyde Park, which is still the residential area of choice for many wealthy citizens. The Old Hyde Park Village collection of boutiques and restaurants is one of the city's biggest draws.

Don Vicente Martinez Ybor, an influential cigar manufacturer and Cuban exile, moved his cigar business from Key West to land east of Tampa in 1885. His first cigar factory drew others, and the area's more than 200 cigar factories created a vivacious Latin community known as Ybor City. The area is now a mix of historic buildings, artisanal shops, restaurants, and nightclubs.

Another Tampa neighborhood, Davis Islands, developed during the Florida land boom. Two little islands off downtown Tampa, where the Hillsborough River empties into Hillsborough Bay, became booming real estate developments. Today the islands are home to an airport, Tampa General Hospital, and more than 100 of the original homes.

Rapid growth continued through the Roaring Twenties. Since then, Tampa hasn't been buoyed by the tourist dollar to the degree other Gulf Coast cities have, and so it has been less susceptible to the ups and downs of the Florida travel economy.

Previous: downtown Tampa; Plant Park in front of the Henry B. Plant Museum. **Above:** the iconic Tampa Theatre sign.

Tampa

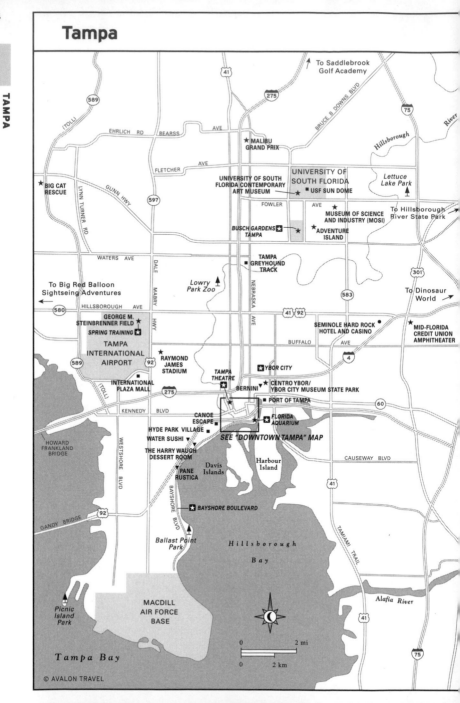

To Saddlebrook Golf Academy

★ MALIBU GRAND PRIX

EHRLICH RD   BEARSS   AVE

FLETCHER   AVE

★ BIG CAT RESCUE

UNIVERSITY OF SOUTH FLORIDA CONTEMPORARY ART MUSEUM

UNIVERSITY OF SOUTH FLORIDA

★ ■ USF SUN DOME

Lettuce Lake Park

FOWLER   AVE

To Hillsborough River State Park

MUSEUM OF SCIENCE AND INDUSTRY (MOSI)

BUSCH GARDENS ✪ TAMPA

★ ADVENTURE ISLAND

GUNN HWY

WATERS   AVE

TAMPA GREYHOUND TRACK

Lowry Park Zoo

To Big Red Balloon Sightseeing Adventures

HILLSBOROUGH   AVE

To Dinosaur World

GEORGE M. STEINBRENNER FIELD
SPRING TRAINING ✪

SEMINOLE HARD ROCK HOTEL AND CASINO

MID-FLORIDA CREDIT UNION AMPHITHEATER

TAMPA INTERNATIONAL AIRPORT

BUFFALO   AVE

★ RAYMOND JAMES STADIUM

✪ YBOR CITY

INTERNATIONAL PLAZA MALL

TAMPA THEATRE

BERNINI

★ CENTRO YBOR/ YBOR CITY MUSEUM STATE PARK

KENNEDY   BLVD

■ PORT OF TAMPA

CANOE ESCAPE

✪ FLORIDA AQUARIUM

HOWARD FRANKLAND BRIDGE

HYDE PARK VILLAGE
WATER SUSHI

SEE "DOWNTOWN TAMPA" MAP

THE HARRY WAUGH DESSERT ROOM

PANE RUSTICA

Davis Islands

Harbour Island

CAUSEWAY   BLVD

✪ BAYSHORE BOULEVARD

GANDY BRIDGE

Ballast Point Park

Hillsborough Bay

Alafia River

Picnic Island Park

MACDILL AIR FORCE BASE

Tampa Bay

0   2 mi

0   2 km

© AVALON TRAVEL

Unlike other urban centers along the Gulf, in Tampa there are no beaches to speak of. For beaches, you need to drive over the causeway to St. Pete or Clearwater, about 30 minutes from downtown Tampa.

PLANNING YOUR TIME

How long you spend vacationing in Tampa largely depends on whether you have kids in tow. Tampa is a paradise for children. Obviously, the big kahuna is Busch Gardens, but that's just Day One. There are four or five other attractions worthy of a day of family focus.

Many people choose to visit Orlando's Disney attractions and then tack on a day or two at Tampa's Busch Gardens. While this is a perfectly fine strategy (Orlando's only an hour away), it may be too much of a good thing. However, Busch Gardens is quite different from Disney, with more of a focus on thrill rides and wildlife excursions. If you love theme parks, visit Busch Gardens while you're in the area. If you are already spending a few days at Disney, consider coming to Tampa and renting a canoe, going to the zoo, visiting the science museum, and then heading over to Clearwater for a day of leisurely beach time.

As with much of the Gulf Coast, the fall and early spring are the most enjoyable weather-wise, with very dry days in the low 80s. The summer is unrelentingly hot and humid, right through each afternoon's huge thunderstorm. The best beaches are Clearwater Beach, Fort De Soto Park, Honeymoon Island and Caladesi Island, St. Pete Beach, Madeira Beach, Sand Key County Park, and Egmont Key State Wildlife Preserve.

The best way to see the greater Tampa area is with a car, especially if you want to explore some of the surrounding barrier islands. The area is served by **Tampa International Airport** (TPA, 4100 George J. Bean Parkway, 813/870-8700, www.tampaairport.com). If you just want to fly into Tampa and plan on staying downtown with occasional trips out to Clearwater and Busch Gardens, you can manage just fine with community transportation and taxis. I-75 runs down to Tampa from the north, I-4 brings visitors from Orlando, and I-275 and Gandy Boulevard North both lead to St. Pete, while West Courtney Campbell Causeway is the primary thoroughfare to Clearwater.

Sights

DOWNTOWN TAMPA
★ Florida Aquarium

The 152,000-square-foot **Florida Aquarium** (701 Channelside Dr., 813/273-4000, www.flaquarium.org, 9:30am-5pm daily, $25 adults, $23 seniors, $20 ages 3-11, parking $6) is smart, focusing on the waters of Florida. It doesn't contain an exhaustive catalog of the world's aquatic creatures, but it tells a compelling story about Florida's relationship to the Gulf, estuaries, rivers, and other waterways. There are some exotic exhibits (the otherworldly sea dragons, like sea horses mated with philodendrons), but the best parts are the open freshwater tanks of otters, spoonbills, gators, Florida softshell turtles, and snakes.

The aquarium manages to have a strong environmental message in its natives-versus-exotics exhibits, but it's all fun, never seeming heavy-handed. There's also a wonderful big shark tank, a colorful coral grotto, and a sea-urchin touch tank. It's a small enough aquarium that three hours is plenty of time, and it's not so crowded that kids can't do a little wandering on their own. Regularly scheduled shows involve native Florida birds and small mammals, as well as shark feeding (in fact, the aquarium offers "swim with the fishes" wetsuit dives into the shark tank for the stalwart). A cell phone audio tour may be the coolest thing yet.

After perusing the marinelife within the

Downtown Tampa

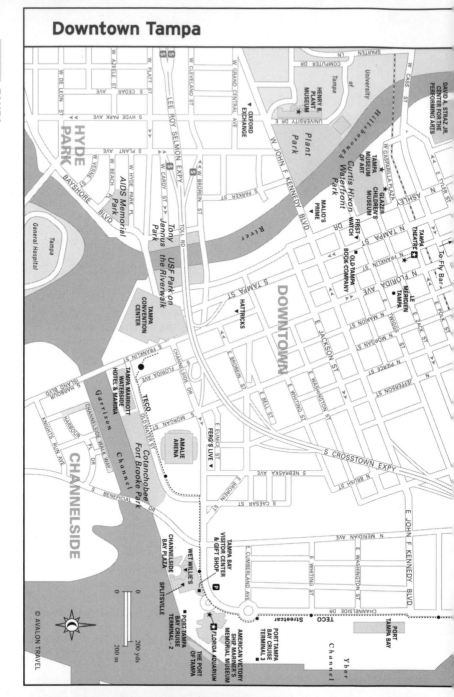

© AVALON TRAVEL

0   200 yds
0   200 m

eye-catching, shell-shaped building, you can take your newfound knowledge out on the bay on an aquarium-run **Wild Dolphin Cruise** (813/273-4000, passes are offered as a combo ticket that includes admission, $50 adults, $45 seniors, $41 ages 3-11, free under age 3). Tampa Bay is home to more than 400 bottlenose dolphins. Tickets are available at the aquarium box office the day of the tour only, when you'll head out in a 64-foot, 49-passenger Caribbean catamaran, watching for dolphins, manatees, and a huge number of migratory birds.

Tampa Museum of Art

The **Tampa Museum of Art** (120 W. Gasparilla Plaza, 813/274-8130, www.tampamuseum.org, 11am-7pm Mon.-Thurs., 11am-10pm Fri., 11am-5pm Sat.-Sun., $15 adults, $7.50 seniors, $5 students, under age 12 and college students free) moved to an impressive 60,000-square-foot facility in 2010. It hosts changing exhibitions ranging from contemporary to classical, and showcases its permanent collection of Greek and Roman antiquities as well as 20th- and 21st-century sculpture, paintings, photography, and works on paper.

Henry B. Plant Museum

The **Henry B. Plant Museum** (401 W. Kennedy Blvd., 813/254-1891, www.ut.edu/plantmuseum, 10am-5pm Tues.-Sat., noon-5pm Sun. Jan.-Nov., $10 adults, $7 students and seniors, $5 under age 12) is housed in the dramatic hotel that railroad magnate Henry B. Plant built in 1891 at a cost of $2.5 million, with an additional $500,000 for furnishings. Its 511 rooms were the first in Florida to be outfitted with electricity. It operated as a hotel until 1930 and is now part of the University of Tampa. The museum consists of opulent restored rooms with original furnishings that provide a window on America's Gilded Age, Tampa's history, and the life and work of Henry Plant. The best time to see it is at Christmastime, when the rooms are bedecked for the season with elaborately trimmed trees, lush greenery, antique toys, and Victorian-era ornaments.

Glazer Children's Museum

Very young children, up to age 10, will enjoy more an afternoon at the **Glazer Children's Museum** (110 W. Gasparilla Plaza, 813/443-3861, www.glazermuseum.org, 10am-5pm Mon.-Fri., 10am-6pm Sat., 1pm-6pm Sun., $15

the Florida Aquarium

adults, $12.50 seniors, teachers, and military, $9.50 ages 1-12, children under age 1 free). In a kind of miniature outdoor city, it has over 170 exhibits in 12 themed areas with hands-on exhibits about different kinds of work and play (a cruise ship, a mini theater, a giant telescope, a grocery store, etc.). Find out what you should be when you grow up.

★ YBOR CITY

Cigar makers Vicente Martinez Ybor and Ignacio Haya moved their cigar factories from Key West to Tampa in 1886, essentially settling 40 acres of uninviting scrubland northeast of the city. With a railroad, a port, and a climate that acted as a natural humidor, Tampa had all the ingredients for cigar success. Soon others joined them until there were 140 cigar factories in the area producing 250 million cigars a year. The new Cigar Capital of the World became home to Cuban, Spanish, and Italian immigrants who worked the factories. These men and women would hand-roll several kinds of tobacco into the signature shapes and sizes while listening to "lectors" read aloud great works of literature and the day's news. For a window into this world, read Nilo Cruz's Pulitzer Prize-winning drama, *Anna in the Tropics*, which depicts a Cuban American family of cigar makers in Ybor City in 1930.

The area flourished until the early 1960s, when embargoes against Cuban tobacco and declining cigar consumption (coincident with the ascendance of the cigarette as the smoke of choice) caused the market to dry up. Today Ybor City is one of only three National Historic Landmark Districts in Florida, with redbrick streets, wrought-iron balconies, and old-timey globe street lamps.

During the day visitors can still see cigars being hand-rolled and enjoy an authentic Cubano sandwich (invented here, some say), while at night Ybor is the city's nightlife district, drawing 40,000 visitors on weekends to dine at sidewalk cafés and drink and dance at nightclubs. Whether you explore during the day or at night, park your car in one of the many parking lots or garages (metered

the Henry B. Plant Museum

parking is strictly enforced 24 hours daily) and walk around or take the Ybor City trolley. You can still see little cigar shops and Latin social clubs mixed in with tattoo parlors and restaurants along La Setima (7th Ave.).

Centro Ybor (1600 E 8th Ave., 813/242-4660, www.centroybor.com, shops 10am-8pm Mon.-Wed., 10am-10pm Thurs.-Sat., 11am-7pm Sun., restaurant hours vary) is a shopping, dining, and entertainment complex right at the pulsing heart of the neighborhood. The trolley runs through the center, so it's easy to get here from almost anywhere in the Ybor area. Along with the shops, there is a comedy club, a large movie theater, an arcade, several bars, a salon, and plenty of great places to eat. The prices tend to be a bit higher than elsewhere in town.

The **Ybor City Museum State Park** (1818 E. 9th Ave., 813/247-6323, www.ybor-museum.org, 9am-5pm Wed.-Sun., $4 adults, free under age 6) contains photographs, cigar boxes, and other artifacts of the neighborhood's rich history.

Still, you may get a more three-dimensional look at Ybor just by walking around: Walk by the **La Union Marti-Maceo mural** (226 7th Ave.), pick up a copy of *La Gaceta* (the neighborhood's Spanish-language weekly for the past 75 years), and walk by the restored former cigar workers' casitas on your way to get a Cubano sandwich, or buy a cigar at **Metropolitan Cigars** (2014 E. 7th Ave., 813/248-3304, 10am-8pm Mon.-Fri., 10am-4pm Sat.-Sun.), a 1,700-square-foot walk-in humidor.

SOUTH TAMPA AND HYDE PARK
★ Bayshore Boulevard

Bayshore Boulevard may or may not be the world's longest continuous sidewalk, but it borders Tampa Bay for nearly five miles without a break in the gorgeousness. Joggers, walkers, skaters, and bikers dot its length, which goes from downtown through Hyde Park. Lined with the fanciest homes in Tampa, the boulevard was named one of AAA's Top Roads for its panoramic views. If you don't feel

Ybor City

like walking it, it's Tampa's signature drive. **Tampa Preservation** (813/248-5437, www.tampapreservation.org/heritage-education.) also has an excellent driving tour of Hyde Park and a walking tour of part of the neighborhood geared for young children.

BUSCH GARDENS AND NORTH TAMPA
★ Busch Gardens Tampa

How many people can say they rode on a Cheetah and a Congo River Rapid in one day? You can join the ranks of the thrill-seeking elite with a quick trip to **Busch Gardens Tampa** (10165 N. Malcolm McKinley Dr., 888/800-5447, www.buschgardens.com, generally 9:30am-6pm daily winter 9am-10pm daily summer, $83 adults Mon.-Fri., yearly pass $103, free under age 3). Busch Gardens is half high-energy amusement park and half first-class zoo. With something of a personality disorder, this is the only park I know where you can alternate between petting zoos and twisting, turning, high-speed roller coasters.

Rides for Little Kids: The amusement park has a huge section geared to children ages 2 to 7 in a Sesame Street-centric part of the park to the far left when you're looking at the map, near **Stanleyville,** as well as in sections near the **Congo** and in **Timbuktu.**

Rides for Big Kids: Major coasters are the biggest draw for those over 42 inches tall (48 inches for Cheetah Hunt and 54 inches for Montu, SheiKra, and Kumba). The rides at Busch Gardens are either little-kiddie or pee-your-pants huge. The roller coasters, in descending order of excellence: The **Cheetah Hunt** is the longest ride in the park and reaches 60 mph after climbing a nearly vertical 102-foot hill. The **SheiKra** has an incredible 90-degrees-straight-down thrill at the beginning, an underground tunnel, speeds of 70 mph, and water features late in the ride. The ride is a little short, but it's floorless, which adds another level of thrill. **Kumba** offers a full three seconds of weightlessness, an initial 135-foot drop, and cool 360-degree spirals. It offers good speed, a long ride, and one of the world's largest vertical loops. The **Cobra's Curse** opened in June 2016; it reaches a top speed of 40 mph after climbing a 70-foot hill and then plunging down for a bit of heart-in-your-throat fun. **Montu,** at the far right side of the park, is one of the tallest inverted roller coasters in the world. You are strapped in from above, so your feet dangle while you travel at 60 mph through 60-foot vertical loops.

Beyond the coasters, the **Stanley Falls** and **Congo River Rapids** boat ride are guaranteed to fully saturate you, so time them for the hottest part of the day.

Animal Attractions: Busch Gardens contains more than 2,700 animals. Colorful lorikeets will land on your shoulder in the aviary called **Lory Landing.** The fun-filled **Opening Night Critters** show features rescued dogs, cats, a horse, and even a kangaroo. The best animal attraction is the **Serengeti Plain,** which takes up the whole right half of the park—you can see it all by getting on the Serengeti Express Railway (or the Skyride or a Serengeti Safari). Ostriches may race the train, and there are big cats and huffing rhinos. It's thrilling as well as a wonderful opportunity to sit down and regroup. **Jungala,** set in the Congo area, is a four-acre attraction that has guests mingling with exotic creatures, exploring a village hidden deep in the jungle, and connecting with the inhabitants of the lush landscape through up-close animal interactions, multistory family play areas, rides, and live entertainment.

A Few Tips: To minimize walking, take the **Skyride** at the entrance (near the Cheetah Run exhibit) all the way to the back of the park (the Jungala area) and start there, making your way to the front again. For the best value on food, eat at the **Dragon Fire Grill and Pub** (Pantopia area in the middle of the park). They offer a large range of cuisines, including American, Chinese, Mexican, and Italian food. There's also a nice selection of salads, a full bar, and a Starbucks inside. There's a remarkable amount of seating, so it's usually easy to find a good seat.

The Details: Busch Gardens is expensive, so is it worth it? Definitely. It is a wonderful full-day extravaganza for people of any age (if you don't like rides, go to Beer School, where you can learn about the process of making beer, and then get what you really came for—free samples). Busch Gardens can entertain you for two full days, but if you do just one day, everyone will be clamoring for more. A 14-day, five-park **Orlando FlexTicket** ($355 adults, $335 kids) is a good deal if you have the stamina to hit SeaWorld Orlando, Universal Studios Florida, Islands of Adventure, and Wet 'n' Wild along with Busch Gardens.

The park hours change seasonally. If you visit in the summer, count on heavy rains in the afternoon. Restrooms are plentiful and clean, there are plenty of strollers to rent, the food is much better than it needs to be (Zambia Smokehouse also serves good ribs and chicken), and there's even a dog kennel to watch your pet while you enjoy the park. The park is eight miles northeast of downtown Tampa. Parking is an irritating additional $20, with a free shuttle that takes you from the 5,000-spot parking lot to the park's entrance.

Lowry Park Zoo

This zoo has recently made the overt decision to take it to the Big Time, going *mano a mano* with San Diego and the other big zoos. To this end, it imported four African elephants and created a huge habitat for them. The previous elephant program was curtailed years ago when a trainer was killed by a panicked pachyderm.

At the **Lowry Park Zoo** (1101 W. Sligh Ave., 813/935-8552, www.lowryparkzoo. com, 9:30am-5pm daily, $31 adults, $23 ages 3-11), habitats are naturalistic and nicely landscaped, but they are still designed for maximum viewing. All told there are around 2,000 native and exotic animals (white tiger cubs are a big draw), organized into reasonable housing developments, such as Wallaroo Station and Safari Africa. Lots of shade provided by big tropical plants seems to keep all the species comfortable, even in the substantial summer heat. One of the zoo's highlights is its Manatee and Aquatic Center, one of only three hospitals and rehabilitation facilities in Florida for sick sea cows.

Adventure Island

Adjacent to Busch Gardens but closed in winter is **Adventure Island** (10001 N. McKinley Dr., 888/800-5447, www.adventureisland.com, hours vary mid-Mar.-Oct., $44, free under age 3), a 30-acre water park with slides, corkscrews, waterfalls, a monstrous 17,000-square-foot wave pool, and a children's play area. There are 50 lifeguards on duty, but it's still only appropriate for the truly water-safe. There's also a championship white-sand volleyball complex. If you buy a ticket to Busch Gardens, you can combine it with a ticket here for a discount.

University of South Florida Contemporary Art Museum

University of South Florida is an enormous institution, casting its imposing shadow on the cultural scene of Tampa. Visitor have little reason to walk around the less-than-picturesque campus, but a visit to the **University of South Florida Contemporary Art Museum** (3821 USF Holly Dr., 813/974-4133, 10am-5pm Mon.-Fri., 1pm-4pm Sat., free) is a good excuse to drive around the university before parking at the small gallery. USFCAM maintains the university's art collection, comprising more than 5,000 artworks. There are exceptional holdings in graphics and sculpture multiples by internationally acclaimed artists such as Roy Lichtenstein, Robert Rauschenberg, and James Rosenquist, who have worked at USF's Graphicstudio. Contemporary photography and African art are also represented. The museum hosts USF student art shows and oversees public art projects on campus.

Museum of Science & Industry (MOSI)

You spent a day riding the rides at Busch Gardens, then a day with the fishes at the aquarium, what next? The third day is Tampa's **Museum of Science & Industry** (4801 E. Fowler Ave., 813/987-6000, www.mosi.org, 10am-5pm Mon.-Fri., 10am-6pm Sat.-Sun., $23 adults, $21 seniors, $19 ages 2-12), a wonderful resource for local schools, family vacationers, or local parents. It's a sprawling modern structure that contains 450 hands-on activities grouped into learning areas. There's some unique and fun stuff like the Gulf Coast Hurricane Chamber, which blows air at an incredible speed to simulate standing in the eye wall of a hurricane, and the High Wire Bicycle, the longest high-wire bike in a museum, which allows visitors to pedal while balanced on a one-inch steel cable suspended 30 feet above the ground. The Amazing You exhibit teaches all about the human body. The museum has an IMAX dome and—get this—the admission price to the museum includes one free viewing of an IMAX film. The museum hosts traveling exhibits as well. Through interactive exhibits, film, and immersion experiences, guests explore the principles of simple mechanics, optics, electromagnetism, math, and psychology.

If you time your visit to allow for some cooler temperatures, the free-flying butterfly garden is a treat, with microscope viewing, magnifying glasses, and chemistry stations.

Malibu Grand Prix

If they've been really, really good, take the kids to **Grand Prix** (14320 N. Nebraska Ave., 813/977-6272, www.grandprixtampa.com, noon-9pm Sun.-Thurs., noon-midnight Fri., 10am-midnight Sat., $3-50, depending on the activity). It has excellent miniature golf with lots of windmills, pagodas, and water play, Grand Prix-style go-kart racing, batting cages, and a frenetic game room with a wide variety of video games.

GREATER TAMPA
Big Cat Rescue

The world's largest accredited sanctuary for big cats, **Big Cat Rescue** (12802 Easy St., 813/920-4130, www.bigcatrescue.org), across from Citrus Park Town Center down a dirt road next to McDonald's, provides a permanent retirement home to over 200 animals. For the visitor, the center offers tours, outreach presentations, animal interaction, and the opportunity to spend an evening in the heart of the sanctuary. There are regular tours (ages 10 and over, 3pm Mon.-Wed. and Fri., 10am and 3pm Sat.-Sun., $36), a children's tour (noon Sat.-Sun., $36), and feeding tours (9am Fri.-Sun., $65). On the last Friday of each month, register for the Wild Eyes at Night tour (at dusk, $65), in which guests roam the grounds equipped with flashlights that illuminate the hundreds of shining eyes in the cat enclosures.

Dinosaur World

If you or your kids are dinosaur-obsessed, it is your duty to get in the car and drive about half an hour east of Tampa to an otherwise agricultural town called Plant City. It is known as the Winter Strawberry Capital of the World, but amid the strawberry fields lurks **Dinosaur World** (5145 Harvey Tew Rd., Plant City, 813/717-9865, www.dinosaurworld.com, 9am-5pm daily, $17 adults, $15 seniors, $12 ages 3-12, free under age 3). There are 150 huge models (well, maybe 149, because one disappeared a while back—now, there's a trophy) of prehistoric beasts arrayed in a huge subtropical garden. Having recently spent time in the dinosaur exhibit at the Museum of Natural History in New York, I have a sneaking suspicion that Dinosaur World isn't preoccupied with strict accuracy; for instance, we don't really know about dinosaur coloring, but these ones all sport the mottled green-brown made popular in movies. In addition to the dinosaurs, there are spooky fake caves to explore and an archaeological dig-sandbox area. This is best for kids under seven.

Big Red Balloon Sightseeing Adventures

Big Red Balloon Sightseeing Adventures (8710 W. Hillsborough Ave., 813/969-1518, www.bigredballoon.com, 8am-8pm daily year-round, weather permitting, by reservation only, $185 adults, $160 children) takes you up, up, and away in a beautiful hot-air balloon, and all you have to bring is a camera and your loved ones. Meet before dawn at a restaurant on the commercial strip of Dale Mabry at **Mimi's Café** (11702 N. Dale Mabry Hwy.), where you are whisked into the Red Balloon van and taken to your agreed-on launch site (there are more than 30 in the greater Tampa area from which to choose). Once inflated, the solid red balloon, the largest in the southeastern United States, is 8.5 stories tall and contains 210,000 cubic feet of air. The balloon, which comfortably accommodates eight passengers, takes a one-hour sunrise flight up to 1,000 feet, drifting over New Tampa, southeast Pasco County, Lutz, and Land O' Lakes. A champagne toast followed by a hearty breakfast back at Mimi's is included in the price.

After landing in a field, the pilot makes the champagne toast and recites a traditional balloonist prayer, "The winds have welcomed you with softness, the sun has left you with warm hands, you have flown so high, and so well, that God has joined you in your laughter, and set you gently back again into the loving arms of Mother Earth." Feel free to join in.

Pasco County Excursion

Naked people. That got your attention. The sleepy, mostly residential county to Tampa's north, Pasco County has at least a day's worth of a unique brand of fun that is definitely worth a side trip, a couple of meals, and maybe even an overnight at one of the area's upscale spa, golf, and tennis resorts.

Lake Como Family Nudist Resort in the town of Land O' Lakes is the area's original nudist community, started in 1947. Since then, Pasco County has become a hotbed of naturist activity, with six all-ages nudist communities and recreational activities. These days the biggest player is the 120-acre **Caliente Club and Resorts** (21240 Gran Via Blvd., Land O' Lakes, 813/996-3700).

Another Pasco original requiring a bit of courage is **Skydive City** (4241 Skydive Lane, off Chancey Rd., 813/783-9399, www.skydivecity.com, $199, plus $95 if you want a video documenting your experience) in Zephyrhills. The town has been a world-famous drop zone since the 1960s. Why here? According to owner T. K. Hayes, "It's in the middle of nowhere. It's really about the people—Zephyrhills is the largest skydiving place in the world." Tandem jumping, where a rookie jumps physically harnessed to an instructor, has opened skydiving up to people who never would have had the opportunity—the elderly, people with disabilities—really, anyone can do it.

If jumping out of an airplane sounds doable: It takes about an hour to prepare, with a 20-minute briefing. The whole experience is a three- to four-hour adventure, with free fall at 120 mph for about a minute from 13,500 feet, followed by up to six minutes of steering with the parachute open. Hayes says he's never had a student fatality or serious injury.

After that, take it down a notch and enjoy a walking tour of downtown **Dade City.** In the rolling hills of eastern Pasco County, the town has more than 50 antiques stores, gift shops, and boutiques. Stop into the historic 1909 Pasco County Courthouse and look at the sweet collection of artifacts from the turn of the 20th century. And then have a slice of pie at **Lunch on Limoges** (14139 7th St., 352/567-5685, www.lunchonlimoges.com, $12-18). It's a charming throwback to an era of structured and unhurried lunching, with a daily-changing menu served on Limoges china by waitresses in nurses' uniforms.

Not far from downtown and usually taking about an hour, the **Pioneer Florida Museum** (15602 Pioneer Museum Rd., 352/567-0328, www.pioneerfloridamuseum.org, 10am-5pm Tues.-Sat., $8 adults, $6 seniors, $4 students and ages 6-18, free under age 6 and active-duty military) consists of nine period buildings dating back to 1878. There's the John Overstreet House, the Lacoochee School, and the Enterprise Methodist Church, all displaying period furniture, clothing, toys, and tools.

If there's time, take a tour around **New Port Richey's Main Street** (walking tour maps at www.nprmainstreet.com) and then board a boat and ride the **Pithlachascottee River** to see historic homes once owned by Gloria Swanson, Thomas Meighan, and Babe Ruth. Then walk around **Centennial Park,** which contains the Pasco Fine Arts Council, the Centennial Library, and the 1882 Baker House, one of the oldest structures in Pasco County. If you're hungry, stop in at the waterside **Catches** (7811 Bayview St., 727/849-2121, 11:30am-9pm Sun.-Thurs., 11:30am-10pm Fri.-Sat., $15-30).

If you're thinking about bedtime now, **Saddlebrook Resort & Spa** (5700 Saddlebrook Way, 813/973-1111, $180-450) is Tampa's nicest four-star resort hotel, only it's in the sleepy Pasco town of Wesley Chapel. It has 800 guest rooms, all beautiful, as well as pools, tennis, the Palmer and the Saddlebrook golf courses and the Saddlebrook Golf Academy, and a variety of dining options (if you eat on the Tropics Terrace, you can see nesting wood storks).

For more information about Pasco County, visit www.visitpasco.net.

Sports and Recreation

LETTUCE LAKE PARK

If you're looking to get out in nature, head to **Lettuce Lake Park** (6920 E. Fletcher Ave., near the I-75 exit, 813/987-6204, 8am-8pm daily spring and summer, 8am-7pm daily fall, 8am-6pm daily winter, $2 per vehicle), just east of the University of South Florida. It's a stone's throw from urban sprawl, but don't hold that against it. The dense wilderness shelters a 3,500-foot-long raised boardwalk and a recently rebuilt tower overlooking the Hillsborough River, a perfect place from which to spy on tall wading birds, gators lurking among cypress knees in the swamp, or even delicate orchids and other epiphytes nestled in the trees' crooks. Rent a canoe for a closer look at the creatures that call this tannin-tinged water home, hike the fully accessible boardwalk or dirt trails (dogs are not allowed on the boardwalks), then settle in for a picnic at one of the waterfront shelters, equipped with barbecues. A kids' playground, restrooms, and water fountains make this wilderness park much more comfortable.

FISHING AND BOATING

The 400 square miles of Tampa Bay offer an abundance of excellent fishing and boating spots. You'll catch snook, spotted trout, redfish, flounder, and sheepshead, to name a few. May is the peak season for tarpon, an exciting fish to catch. They tend to congregate near the bridge and rock structures of the bay. For all types of fishing you will need a **Florida fishing license,** which is available at most bait shops, outdoor stores, and Walmarts throughout the state.

If you're looking to fish from the shore, one of the best spots is **Upper Tampa Bay Park** (8001 Double Branch Rd., 813/855-1765, 8am-6pm daily, $2 per vehicle, kayak rentals $25 for 4 hours). The park also has enjoyable nature trails that explore the mangrove forest and tidal ecosystems. Fish from the shoreline

or launch a canoe or kayak and cast a line in the creek for red drum and snook. In South Tampa, the pier and shoreline provide excellent fishing at **Ballast Point Park** (5314 Interbay Blvd., 813/831-2112, park sunrise-sunset daily, pier open 24 hours daily for fishing, free). Other good spots are the piers at **E.G. Simmons Park** (2401 19th Ave. NW, 813/671-7655, 7am-6pm daily, $2 per vehicle), and **Picnic Island Park** (7409 Picnic Island Blvd., 813/274-8615, 7am-6pm daily, $2 per vehicle).

If you'd like an expert to take you out on their boat, you can rent a charter with the best in the business by hiring **Tampa Fishing Charters** (401 Channelside Walk Way, 813/245-4738, www.tampafishingcharters.com, $425 half-day, $625 full-day), **Capt. Chet Jennings Fishing Charters** (611 Destiny Dr., 813/477-3576, www.fishintampa.com, $399 half-day for 2 people, $599 full-day), or **Tampa Flats and Bay Fishing Charters** (10913 N. Edison Ave., 813/727-8843, http://flatsandbay.com, $425 half-day for 2 people, $700 full-day for 2 people).

For more freedom to explore the bay and surrounding creeks on your own, rent a powered boat with **Tierra Verde Boat Rentals** (96 Pinellas Bayway, Tierra Verde, 727/867-0077, www.tvboatrentals.com, 22-foot center console $84 per hour, $339 full-day, 17-foot sundeck $65 per hour, $239 full-day, Jet Ski $75 per hour). Closer to downtown Tampa near the Convention Center, you can motor around the bay by renting a covered power boat that can hold up to 12 people from **eBoats Tampa** (333 S. Franklin St., 813/767-2245, www.eboatstampa.com, $90 per hour, $240 for 4 hours).

SAILING

Climb aboard the *S.V. Lionheart,* a 44-foot Caribbean Sailing Yacht, for a sailing sightseeing tour in Tampa Bay with **Olde World**

CANOEING

You want to see big gators? Great blue herons, river otters, turtles, and more fish than you can string on a lifetime of lines? Paddle down the gently flowing Hillsborough River in a 16,000-acre wildlife preserve called **Wilderness Park.** You can rent canoes or kayaks and head out on your own, choosing from six different self-guided day trips. All paddling adventures start at **Canoe Escape** (12702 U.S. 301, Thonotosassa, 4.5 miles east of I-75, 813/986-2067, www.canoeescape.com). Whether you go on a guided tour or on your own, call ahead. Staff will equip you, give you maps and paddling pointers, then take you over to your debarkation point (all paddles are downstream) and establish a pickup time.

The Sargeant Park to Morris Bridge Park trip is a 4.5-mile two-hour paddle, with 70 percent shade and alternating sun and shade. Morris Bridge Park to Trout Creek Park is a 4-mile two-hour paddle, with 80 percent shade and a little full sun at the end. From Trout Creek Park to Rotary Park it's 5 miles and two hours of full-sun paddling, and Sargeant Park to Trout Creek Park is a longer 8.5-mile paddle with the first 75 percent in the shade. Morris Bridge Park to Rotary Park is a long 9-mile route, and Sargeant Park to Rotary Park is for experienced paddlers only, with 14 miles of river to paddle.

Self-guided rentals are $49-69 pp for a tandem canoe or kayak depending on the trip (a child under 12 can usually fit as a center passenger). A solo kayak rents for $46-56. Prices include the shuttle fee, paddles, and life vests. If solo paddling seems daunting, Canoe Escape offers a 4.5-mile interpreted guided tour ($75 pp) for solo kayakers and $50 pp for tandem canoes. I'd recommend this for newcomers to the area, because the guides' vast knowledge of the local flora and fauna enrich the trip immeasurably.

GOLF

If you are thinking about picking up the sport, the **Saddlebrook Golf Academy** (5700 Saddlebrook Way, Wesley Chapel,

a boat in Tampa Bay

Sailing Line (97 Columbia Dr., 888/989-7245, www.oldeworldsailing.com, $89 half-day or sunset sail, $389 sunset dinner cruise for 2, $109 moonlight sail). Larger groups may enjoy a sail with **Tampa Bay Sailing Tours** (333 S Franklin St., 813/532 9530, www.tampabay-sailingtours.com, $79 pp half-day, $89 pp sunset sail, $119 pp full-day). Up to six people can cruise aboard the beautiful *Noshoz,* a wide and stable catamaran. All trips depart from the Riverwalk in downtown Tampa.

A less intimate but more affordable sunset cruise and sightseeing tour is found aboard the **Tampa Bay Fun Boat** (333 S. Franklin St., 727/204-9787, www.tampabayfunboat.com, $18 adults, $10 children under age 13, free under age 3). They operate a 35-passenger deck boat that takes one-hour fun cruises (noon, 2pm, 4pm, 6pm, and 7:30pm daily). Depart from the Convention Center downtown and take a slow ride around the bay, where you will probably see some dolphins and have a stunning view of downtown. It's a great way to spend a few hours with the family.

Tampa Golf

Tampa has several dozen public and semiprivate courses for visitors to try, many of them located in Tampa's swankier northeast residential developments. Here are a handful of the area's top public courses:

Babe Zaharias Golf Club
11412 Forest Hills Dr., 813/631-4375, www.babezahariasgolf.net
18 holes, 6,244 yards, par 70, course rating 68.9, slope 121
Greens fees: $9.35-20.56

Heritage Isles Golf & Country Club
10630 Plantation Bay Dr., 813/907-7447, www.heritageislegolf.com
18 holes, 6,976 yards, par 72, course rating 73.2, slope 132
Greens fees: $12-35

Rocky Point Golf Course
4151 Dana Shores Dr., 813/673-4316, www.rockypointgolf.net
18 holes, 6,444 yards, par 71, course rating 71.7, slope 122
Greens fees: $10-26

Rogers Park Golf Course
7910 N. 30th St., 813/356-1671, www.rogersparkgc.com
18 holes, 6,802 yards, par 71, course rating 72.3, slope 125
Greens fees: $10-32

TPC Tampa Bay
5300 W. Lutz Lake Fern Rd., Lutz, 813/949-0090, www.tpctampabay.com
18 holes, 6,898 yards, par 71, course rating 73.6, slope 135
Greens fees: $89-189, $20 juniors

University of South Florida Golf Course (also called "The Claw")
4202 E. Fowler Ave., 813/632-6893, www.theclawatusfgolf.com
18 holes, 6,863 yards, par 71, course rating 74.2, slope 132
Greens fees: $10-35

Westchase Golf Course
11602 Westchase Golf Dr., 813/854-2331, www.westchasegc.com
18 holes, par 72, 6,699 yards, course rating 72.0, slope 136
Greens fees: $29-59

813/973-1111, www.saddlebrook.com, $1,495) at the Saddlebrook Resort teaches golfers of all skill levels. Classes combine classroom and practice time with course play. The package includes accommodations for six nights, 18 holes of golf a day, instruction, meals, video analysis, and use of resort facilities. There are two 18-hole Arnold Palmer-designed championship courses on the property, as well as 45 tennis courts in the four Grand Slam surfaces. The resort is also home to the **Harry Hopman Tennis Academy.**

SPECTATOR SPORTS

Tampa Bay sports fans are fanatical about their professional sporting franchises. And why shouldn't they be? There are professional football, ice hockey, and baseball teams, not to mention spring training for the New York Yankees, Philadelphia Phillies, Toronto Blue Jays, and hometown Rays spread around the Tampa Bay Area, pro arena football, and the gamut of University of South Florida Bulls athletics.

Tampa Bay Buccaneers

Raymond James Stadium (4201 N. Dale Mabry Hwy.) is a wonderful venue in which to see Tampa's beloved **Buccaneers** (813/350-6500, www.buccaneers.com) play football. Completed in 1998, it holds more than 66,000 fans—52,000 in general seating—but tickets sometimes sell out for the season opener and other big games. Tickets for individual games are sold in person, by phone, and online at **TicketMaster** (800/745-3000, www.ticketmaster.com) outlets, or at the Raymond James Ticket Box three hours prior to kickoff on game days. Tickets for the 16 regular-season games from September to December are $55 for general admission; special seats range from $400. The stadium features Buccaneer Cove, a 20,000-square-foot replica of an early 1800s seaport village, complete with a 103-foot-long, 43-ton pirate ship that blasts its cannons (confetti and foam footballs) every time the Bucs score—six times for a touchdown, once for an extra point, twice for a safety or two-point conversion, and three times for a field goal.

Every New Year's Day, Raymond James also plays host to football's **Outback Bowl** (813/287 8844, kickoff 11am, $80). The game matches the third-pick team from the SEC and the third-pick team from the Big Ten Conference and is the culmination of a week-long festival in Tampa.

USF Bulls

The University of South Florida **Bulls football team** (800/462-8557, www.gousfbulls.com, game schedule varies, individual tickets $20-31), have gone from nonexistent to Division I-AA Independent to I-A to Conference USA, and into the Big East Conference in 2005. For the spectator, this means real college football is played during the fall at **Raymond James Stadium** (4201 N. Dale Mabry Hwy.).

Bulls basketball (813/974-3002, tickets $11-27) has also been notched up in recent years, resulting in the team moving to the Big

East Conference. Home games are played at the **USF Sun Dome** (4202 E. Fowler Ave.).

Tampa Bay Storm

The local arena football team, the **Tampa Bay Storm** (813/301-6500, www.tampabaystorm.com, upper-level tickets $10-35, lower level $35-150), five-time ArenaBowl champs, plays at the **Amalie Arena** (401 Channelside Dr.). Arena football is played on an indoor padded surface 85 feet wide and 50 yards long, with eight-yard end zones. There are eight players on the field at a time, and everyone plays both offense and defense, with the exception of the kicker, quarterback, offensive specialist, and two defensive specialists. It's a dynamic game in a more intimate space, and the Storm provides a good introduction, having made it to the playoffs for 16 consecutive seasons.

Tampa Bay Lightning

The 21,000-seat, $153 million **Amalie Arena** (401 Channelside Dr.) on Tampa's downtown waterfront is home to Tampa's professional ice hockey team, the **Tampa Bay Lightning** (800/559-2333, www.nhl.com/lightning, tickets $15-349), Stanley Cup champions in 2004. The season runs October to April.

Tampa Bay Rays

Since 1998 Tampa has also been home to Major League Baseball's **Tampa Bay Rays** (888/326-7297, www.tampabay.rays.mlb.com, game days vary, game times usually 2:15pm or 7:15pm, tickets $18-80), who play at **Tropicana Field** (1 Tropicana Dr., St. Petersburg). As a concession to summer temperatures and humidity in these parts, the ballpark has a dome roof (which is lit orange when the Rays win at home) and artificial turf.

There has been a great deal of dissatisfaction from Rays' fans with Tropicana Field over the years. The park is known for a heartbreakingly long list of lasts. It is the last park in Major League Baseball to have a retractable roof, the last of two parks to use artificial turf on their field instead of the fan-preferred

Lightning Strikes

Alligators are dangerous, but lightning is much more deadly in Florida. In fact, about 50 people are struck by lightning each year in the state. Most of them are hospitalized and recover, but there are about 10 fatalities annually. The Tampa area is the Lightning Capital of the United States (Rwanda is the lightning capital of the world), with around 25 cloud-to-ground lightning bolt blasts on each square mile annually. The temperature of a single bolt can reach 50,000°F, about three times as hot as the sun's surface.

The problem is the tropical afternoon thunderstorms each summer, about 90 of which are electrical storms. Short-lived but intense, the storms' clouds are charged like giant capacitors, the upper portion positively charged and the lower portion negatively charged. Current flows between the cloud bottom and the top, or in the case of cloud-to-ground lightning, the positively charged earth's surface. Bolts, sheets, ribbons, and, rarely, balls of lightning hit the ground.

There's not much you can do to ward off lightning except to avoid being in the wrong place at the wrong time. The summer months, June to September, have the highest number of lightning-related injuries and deaths. Usually lightning occurs during daylight hours, with the highest concentration between 3pm and 4pm, when the afternoon storms peak. Lightning strikes usually occur either at the beginning or end of a storm and can strike up to 10 miles away from the center of the storm.

Still, 9 out of 10 people survive being struck. As long as the electrical surge is not to your brain, you are likely to be treatable. A lightning strike will often singe and burn a person's skin or clothes, but even when the electrical surge stops a victim's heart, emergency rooms have a high success rate of restarting the ticker.

TIPS

- Stay vigilant and go inside as soon as clouds darken and thunderstorms develop.

- If the time between seeing the lightning flash and hearing the thunder is less than 30 seconds, take shelter.

- Stay away from the Gulf, pools, lakes, or other bodies of water.

- Avoid using a tree or other tall object as shelter. Lightning usually strikes the tallest object in a given area.

- Stay away from metal objects (bikes, golf carts, and fencing are bad, but a car's rubber tires render the automobile's interior a safe retreat).

- The safest place to be during an electrical storm is inside and away from windows and electrical appliances.

natural grass. Tropicana Field is also consistently ranked last in stadium rankings by *USA Today* and ESPN, and the Rays' games had the worst attendance record for the 2015 season (they have never made it above rank 22 since 2001). However, the low attendance record can't be blamed on the team's poor performance. Since 2008 the Rays have been to the playoffs four times, and made the trip to the World Series in 2008, but lost to the Phillies.

The problem for the Rays seems to be in the ball field, which is more than 20 miles from Tampa, where the majority of area residents live, and fans are separated from the park by often unbearable traffic over the bridge. The interior of the stadium is as aesthetically unpleasing as ballparks come, from the dumpy-looking artificial turf field to the distracting metal rafters of the dome that occasionally obstruct high fly balls. The difficulty of finding decent parking is also a common complaint. In 2014 the owner of the team, Stuart Sternberg, said he would sell the team if a new stadium wasn't built. In 2016 the St. Petersburg City Council voted to allow the Rays to search for a new stadium site in the Tampa, Hillsborough, and Pinellas County areas.

★ SPRING TRAINING

If you're in the area during spring training time, you can also catch the Rays at the **Charlotte Sports Park** (2300 El Jobean Rd., Port Charlotte, 941/206-4487, www.tampabay.rays.mlb.com, $10-29), their spring training home, with a 7,000-person capacity and a natural grass field that received a $27.2 million renovation to bring it up to modern standards for the Rays.

The Grapefruit League's spring training remains a serious draw for sports fans each March. Since 1988 the **New York Yankees** have based their minor-league operation, spring training, and year-round headquarters for player development in Tampa. Modeled after the original Yankee Stadium in New York City, **George M. Steinbrenner Field** (1 Steinbrenner Dr., off N. Dale Mabry Hwy., 813/875-7753, www.steinbrennerfield.com, $10-38) has been the Yankees' home since 1996. The complex houses a 10,000-seat stadium with 13 swanky luxury suites ($375-500), a community-use field, and a major league practice field. In 2016, the stadium underwent a $40 million renovation that included new seats, roof replacement, suite upgrades, a right-field bar, and a new outfield concourse. It's also the home of the five-time **Florida State League Champion's Tampa Yankees** (New York Yankees-Florida State League Single-A Affiliate) and the **Hillsborough Community College Hawks** baseball team.

George M. Steinbrenner Field

Entertainment and Events

MUSIC, THEATER, AND CINEMA
Straz Center for the Performing Arts

Tampa's heavy hitter for performing arts is the **Straz Center for the Performing Arts** (1010 N. W. C. MacInnes Place, 1 block off Ashley St., 813/229-7827, www.strazcenter. org), a huge arts complex housing four distinct theaters where audiences can see Opera Tampa (the resident company), the Florida Orchestra, comedies, dramas, cabaret, dance, music, alternative theater, children's theater, and an annual Broadway series. Many local arts series and events find a home at the performing arts center—Latin Nights, Patel Conservatory's Series—you name it, the curtain goes up here.

Tampa Improv

If music and drinking aren't your objective, stop into the **Tampa Improv** (1600 E. 8th Ave., 813/864-4000, www.improvtampa.com) for an evening of live stand-up with mostly local and regional acts.

Mid-Florida Credit Union Amphitheater

In 2004, Tampa welcomed the **Mid-Florida Credit Union Amphitheater** (formerly known as the Ford Amphitheater, then the 1-800-ASK-GARY Amphitheater, then the Live Nation Amphitheater, 4802 U.S. 301 N., 813/740-2446), a state-of-the-art venue for 30 to 40 big-league music concerts a year. The outdoor open-air theater was constructed with huge video screens, a 7,200-square-foot stage, 9,900 reserved seats, and room for 10,500 more on the lawn; shortly afterward, big space-age sound shields were erected, to the relief of the neighbors. It's gorgeous, like a huge circus tent mated with the *Millennium Falcon*. There are enough restrooms and lots of fairly tasty food options.

★ Tampa Theatre

Tampa has its share of movie multiplexes, but skip the 20-screeners in favor of two hours in the dark at the **Tampa Theatre** (711 N. Franklin St., 813/274-8981, www.tampa-theatre.org, $11 adults, $9 ages 2-11, seniors, and military, $9 before 5pm). Built in 1926, it's a beloved downtown landmark with an acclaimed film series, concerts, special events, and backstage tours. The motion picture palace's interior is vintage, with statues and gargoyles and intricately carved doors. Many believe that the theater is haunted by the ghost of Foster Finley, who spent 20 years as the theater's projectionist; if you feel a hand in your popcorn, it may not be your seatmate's. Some of the films shown are classics, complete with a Wurlitzer performance, and other times it's more indie; check the website for the schedule. Theater concessions include excellent popcorn, sophisticated candies, and beer and wine. Interesting fact: It was the first public building in Tampa to be equipped with air-conditioning.

FESTIVALS AND EVENTS
Gasparilla Pirate Fest

The biggest party in Tampa comes at the end of January or the beginning of February with the **Gasparilla Pirate Fest** (www.gasparillapiratefest.com), a fun celebration over 100 years old in honor of legendary pirate José Gaspar, "last of the buccaneers," who terrorized the coastal waters of western Florida during the late 18th and early 19th centuries. The weekend festivities start with 1,000 people in pirate costume sailing into downtown on a fully rigged pirate ship, a replica of an 18th-century craft that is 165 feet long by 35 feet across the beam, with three masts standing 100 feet tall. The ship is met by a flotilla of hundreds of pleasure craft intent on "defending the city." The upshot is that pirates

Cruising into Tampa

a cruise ship in the Port of Tampa

The Port of Tampa is said to be the fastest-growing cruise port in North America, with a passenger count rising from 200,000 in 1998 to nearly a million in recent years. Newer and larger vessels steam into the downtown Channelside port all the time. It started with Carnival and Holland America cruise lines back in 1994, but these days a number of lines head out of Tampa on four-, five-, and seven-day itineraries.

Tampa now homeports five vessels from four cruise lines:

- Carnival has one ship in Tampa. The *Paradise* has four- and five-day cruises to the western Caribbean.

- Royal Caribbean International has two ships here. *Brilliance of the Seas* offers four- and five-day cruises to the western Caribbean, and the *Rhapsody of the Seas* has seven-day cruises to Central America and the western Caribbean.

- Holland America Lines' *Oosterdam* offers passengers 7- and 14-day itineraries of the Caribbean and Mexico.

- Norwegian Cruise Lines' *Norwegian Jade* has seven-day cruises to Central America and the western Caribbean.

The port's cruise terminals include customer-friendly information areas, superior security, full passenger amenities, and a covered on-terminal parking garage (reservations recommended, $15 per day). Valet parking ($19 per day) is also available. The port is close to the interstate highway system. For directions to cruise terminals, call 866/938-7275.

take over Tampa for a while, like Mardi Gras, only with more "argh, me matey" and eye patches accompanying the beads and buried treasure. The length of Bayshore Boulevard is lined with bleachers for the occasion, musical acts sprout on stages all over town, and there's general merriment and carousing.

Guavaween

The second-biggest party is not unlike Gasparilla for its focus on wild costumes and wilder revelry. **Guavaween** (www. guavaweentampa.com) is the city's Cuban-style Halloween celebration, held at the end of October near Halloween. Riffing on the fact that Tampa was nicknamed the Big Guava, the celebration features the Mama Guava, who has sworn to take the "bore" out of Ybor City. Really, after the parade is over, it's just a big excuse to drink too much and wander the streets of Ybor City in preposterous attire.

Gasparilla International Film Festival

The **Gasparilla International Film Festival** (813/693-2367, www.gasparillafilmfestival.com) began in 2006 and takes place in early March at venues in and around Ybor City. Over five days, more than 40 films are screened in a variety of genres. It's spiced up with a handful of industry panel discussions, VIP parties, glamorous dinners, and celebrity sightings.

Florida State Fair

In mid-February is the **Florida State Fair** (813/740-2446, www.floridastatefair.com), a 12-day salute to the state's best in agriculture, industry, entertainment, and foods on a stick.

Florida Strawberry Festival

Also in February there's a county fair, the **Florida Strawberry Festival** (813/752-9194, www.flstrawberryfestival.com), with a huge midway and lots of strawberry cook-offs. Plant City is known as the Winter Strawberry Capital of the World, and these sweet babies are delicious.

Nightlife

DOWNTOWN TAMPA

Downtown mostly caters to tourists and sports fans. It's the place to be before or after the game.

Bars and Pubs

A top choice on game day is **Hattricks** (107 S. Franklin St., 813/225-4288, 11:15am-3am daily), which caters to the ice hockey crowd. If a Lightning game is on at the same time your favorite non-hockey sports team is playing, you may be out of luck, but this is a fun spot to be before and after any sports game that is taking place. Standing room only is the norm for the after-game parties. The menu for food and beverages is lengthy and delicious, the prices are reasonable, and the atmosphere is classic brick-and-wood-paneled sports bar.

    Fly Bar (1202 N. Franklin St., 813/275-5000, 4pm-3am Mon.-Fri., 5:30pm-3am Sat., 4pm-midnight Sun.) is trendier and mostly attracts the younger crowd. The taps carry smaller microbrews as well as the big names in beer. The hipster-inspired interior has colorful paintings crowding the walls and modern light fixtures, giving this artsy bar a Brooklyn vibe. The plush booths let you sink in for some tasty food on their surprisingly upscale and health-centric menu. The open-air rooftop bar is spectacular and offers some of the best sunsets downtown.

Live Music

For live music and drinks close to the Amelia Arena, go to **Ferg's Live** (490 Channelside Dr., 813/443-8403, 11am-midnight Mon.-Wed., 11am-1am Thurs., 11am-3am Fri.-Sat., 11am-11pm Sun.). This two-level bar is conveniently located near the arena. The first level has TVs lining the walls, so most big games can be tuned in. Tables fill a large outdoor seating area, and on the second floor you can hear live bands that tend to perform rock, alt-country, blues, and pop. The kitchen serves wings, sandwiches, burgers, and bar snacks to go with cold beers and cocktails.

YBOR CITY

Ybor City is where people come out to party in Tampa. It's quieter during the week, but it's the place to go if you're looking for fun on the weekends.

Bars and Pubs

Coyote Ugly (1722 E. 7th Ave., 813/241-8459, 5pm-3am Wed.-Sat., 7pm-3am Tues.) is often the biggest party in Ybor City, presided over by the most audacious women bartenders to ever wield a shot glass. If you have to ask what a body shot is, you're ripe for a hard life lesson. Just like in the eponymous movie, which was based on a bar in New York City, the bartenders drag the unsuspecting victim up on the bar for some raunchy drinking, dancing, and whatever. The bare-bones room is festooned with discarded brassieres from exuberant patrons.

The **Green Iguana** (4029 S. West Shore Blvd., 813/837-1234) is another bar for grown-ups: good drinks, perfectly acceptable food, and audible conversation.

James Joyce Irish Pub and Eatery (1724 E. 8th Ave., 813/247-1896, 11am-3am daily) can't decide if it's an Irish pub or a sports bar, but it does a perfect job as both. The wings, seafood, burgers, and traditional Irish food are excellent. The seven TVs make it easy to watch your game, and with more than 50 beers on tap, 30 Irish whiskeys, and a top shelf selection of scotch, they're certain to have your drink. The exquisite dark-wood interior is as classy and warm as their smooth Irish whisky.

Breweries

Confess your sins at **Coppertail Brewing Company** (2601 E 2nd Ave., 813/247-1500, noon-11pm Mon.-Thurs., noon-midnight Sat., noon-7pm Sun.) with a visit to the church confessional booth just steps from the bar. The beer is sinfully good, so sample as many as you can responsibly handle. The padded benches lining the walls make this a great space for groups small and large, and the high ceilings and glass viewing wall gives you a spectacular glimpse into the beer-brewing process as you sip the results. This is a drinking-only establishment.

Try the beer flights at **Tampa Bay Brewing Company** (1600 E 9th Ave., 813/247-1422, 11am-11pm Sun.-Thurs., 11am-midnight Fri.-Sat.), where the food is as good as the brews (try one of their huge calzones). The outdoor bar and seating area is a great spot to people-watch at Ybor Centro. The air conditioning inside is nice on hot Tampa days.

Clubs

Club Skye (1509 E. 8th Ave., 813/516-7593, 1pm-3am Mon.-Sat., cover varies, no cover before 11pm on Sat.) is a trendy spot for late-night partying that always draws a young crowd. The club mostly features hip-hop and DJs

Ferg's Live

spinning dance music. Whether you're here for College Ladies' Night, International Night, or DJ nights, Skye is the party to beat in Ybor.

Gay-Friendly

Liquid Tampa (1502 E 7th Ave., 813/248-6104, 2pm-3am Fri.-Sun., 3pm-3am Mon.-Thurs.) is one of the most hopping gay clubs in Tampa. There are themed nights, burlesque shows, and DJs and dancers on Saturdays. With two floors, three bars, and a usually lively crowd, you're bound to have a good time.

HYDE PARK

There's lots of good nightlife in this sophisticated South Tampa neighborhood, with some Irish zeal on and around Azeele.

Bars and Pubs

If you like your music—or your flirting—with a heavy brogue, head to everyone's favorite quaint Irish bar, **Dubliner Pub** (2307 W. Azeele St., 813/258-2257).

Four Green Fields (205 W. Platt St., 813/254-4444) is another legendary Irish pub, with lots of regulars and lively conversation. The french-fry basket is a bargain and could feed a small nation.

MacDinton's Irish Pub & Restaurant (405 S. Howard Ave., 813/251-8999, 4pm-3am Mon.-Fri., 10am-3am Sat., 11am-3pm Sun.) is another Irish entry, with a killer black and tan, a warming Irish coffee, and a fair representation of Irish staples, from rib-sticking, mashed-potatoey shepherd's pie to corned beef and cabbage. Sushi is also served if you want a departure from the traditional Irish fare. This is absolutely the biggest scene in Tampa, with lines down and around the block on weekend nights.

Irish 31 (1611 W. Swann Ave., 813/250-0031, 11am-midnight Mon.-Wed., 11am-1am Thurs., 11am-2am Fri.-Sat., 10am-midnight Sun.) opened their first pub in 2011, and quickly expanded to three locations in Tampa. The affordable drinks, traditional Irish fare, comfy pub atmosphere, nightly live music, and sports-centric theme have garnered rave reviews and loyal customers. They keep late hours and have dozens of TVs to cover a range of sporting events. Outside Hyde Park you can visit other Irish 31 locations in Westchase and at the Westshore Plaza.

Wine Lounges

In Old Hyde Park Village, **The Wine Exchange** (1609 W. Snow Ave., 813/254-9463, 11:30am-10pm Mon.-Thurs., 11:30am-11pm Fri.-Sat., 11:30am-9pm Sun.) focuses on the vine, and the extensive wine list doesn't disappoint. A favorite spot for business lunches, this gem also pulls in the brunch crowd on Sunday. The menu is eclectic with mostly American and Italian dishes. When the weather is nice, ask to be seated outdoors.

NORTH TAMPA

With the university nearby, the bars in this area tend to cater to the beer-swilling, late-night-partying college crowd. Several top-notch breweries provide plenty of options, whether you're looking to drink day or night.

Bars and Pubs

Near the university, you'll find over 500 beers at **World of Beer** (2815 E. Fowler Ave., 813/559-1530, 11:30am-midnight Mon.-Tues., 11:30am-1am Wed.-Thurs., 11:30am-2am Fri.-Sat., 11am-midnight Sun.). There is a tasty, beer-centric menu with burgers, bratwurst, and pretzels. The college crowd tends to frequent this place, but beer aficionados of any age will feel at home, and the TVs keep the place busy during game time. This reliable chain has four locations in Tampa.

Breweries

Tour the oldest brewery in the United States at the **Yuengling Brewing Company** (11111 N. 30th St., 813/972-8529, www.yuengling. com, tours 10am, 11:30am, and 1pm Mon.-Fri., 10:30am and noon Sat., free). The hour-long tour takes you through the brew house where they produce and bottle beer and offers two free nice-size samples of beer at the end. You must wear closed-toe shoes.

GREATER TAMPA
Bars and Pubs

Bahama Breeze (3045 N. Rocky Point Dr. E., 813/289-7922, roughly 11am-midnight Sun.-Thurs., 11am-2am Fri.-Sat.) is a tropical-themed singles hangout with a huge waterside deck from which you can view a great sunset.

In west Tampa, the **Brick House Tavern and Tap** (1102 N. Dale Mabry Hwy., 813/350-9108, 11am-1am Mon.-Thurs., 11am-2am Fri.-Sat., 11am-midnight Sun.) gets top nod from foodies, beer lovers, and dog lovers alike. This pet-friendly bar has games on the big screens indoors and a nice covered patio outdoors. The indoor fireplace gives the place a cozy feel. The menu has great sandwiches and delicious chicken and waffles. It's exceptionally popular for lunch and on weekends. If there's a home game on, you might find standing room only.

A memorable night on the town can only be complemented by a drink on the rooftop restaurant and bar at **Armani's** (2900 Bayport Dr., 813/207-6800, 6pm-9pm Mon.-Thurs., 6pm-10pm Fri., 5:30pm-10pm Sat.), located in the Grand Hyatt Tampa Bay. The glass panel-lined patio offers a breathtaking waterfront view, and sitting around a fire on a plush couch will turn any evening into a classy, romantic affair. The drinks are expensive, but the experience is worth it.

Breweries

The **Cigar City Brewing Company** (3924 W. Spruce St., 813/348-6363, 11am-11pm Sun.-Thurs., 11am-1am Fri.-Sat., tours $8) offers delicious craft beers at the bar. They also offer tours of the brewery, with exceptional guides and a generous tasting that make it well worth the money.

Wine Lounges

Cooper's Hawk Winery and Restaurant (4110 W. Boy Scout Blvd., 813/873-9463, 11:30am-9:30pm Mon.-Thurs., 11:30am-10pm Fri.-Sat., 11:30am-9pm Sun.) is a successful chain with a great wine list (glasses $6-13, bottles $20-32). The dining room is upscale casual, and the outdoor seating will make you feel comfortable if you're not as dressed up. You can also enjoy wine-tasting in the lobby or relax at the bar.

Shopping

DOWNTOWN AND CHANNELSIDE
Books and Music

Book lovers bound into **Old Tampa Book Company** (507 N. Tampa St., 813/209-2151, www.oldtampabookcompany.com, 10am-5pm Mon.-Fri., 11am-5pm Sat.), where the shelves are filled with collectible, current, and bargain novels and nonfiction. The prices are great, and the selection is diverse. It's located across from the Lykes Gaslight Park where you can browse through your new books.

Shopping Malls and Centers

Channelside Bay Plaza (615 Channelside Dr., 813/223-4250), the entertainment center on Tampa's downtown waterfront adjacent to the Florida Aquarium and the cruise terminal, has a few stores to investigate—a wine shop, Lit Premium Cigar Bar, Qachbal's Chocolatier, and a couple of galleries.

YBOR CITY

Shopping along **7th Avenue** in Ybor City, Tampa's Latin Quarter, will yield some interesting finds. It's a little grittier, with a few vintage clothing shops and a fair amount of racy lingerie.

Cigars

In addition to being a great café and bar, **King Corona Cigars Café and Bar** (1523 E. 7th Ave., 813/247-6738, www.kingcoronacigars. com, 8am-midnight Mon.-Wed., 8am-1am

Thurs., 8am-2am Fri., 10am-2am Sat., noon-midnight Sun.) sells excellent Cuban coffee, cigars, and many other things related to the smoking life.

SOUTH TAMPA AND HYDE PARK
Shopping Malls and Centers

Tampa's downtown doesn't really have a retail center. For that, you need to visit Hyde Park. It's not vast, but the outdoor shopping area along Hyde Park's West Swann Avenue, South Dakota Avenue, and Snow Avenue is the most appealing shopping destination in town, especially when the weather's nice. There's a large covered parking lot, free to shoppers, and a nicely landscaped plaza at the center. Pottery Barn and West Elm are among the bigger stores, with Lululemon, Brooks Brothers, Anthropologie, and Francesca's. Top restaurants include the Wine Exchange Bistro and Wine Bar, the indoor-outdoor Sinatra-addled Timpano Italian Chophouse, and a French-inspired gem called Piquant. In the summer, **Hyde Park Village** (744 S. Village Circle, 813/251-3500) hosts a free evening movie series, the classic films projected outside on a huge screen.

NORTH TAMPA
Shopping Malls and Centers

With anchor stores Neiman Marcus and Nordstrom, **International Plaza** (2223 N. Westshore Blvd., 813/342-3790, www.shopinternationalplaza.com, 10am-9pm Mon.-Sat., 11am-7pm Sun.), opened in 2001, gets the nod for fanciest shopping. A handful of usual mall stores (J.Crew, Banana Republic, Ann Taylor) are spiffed up by their proximity to 200 other specialty shops such as Tiffany & Co., Louis Vuitton, Montblanc, Gucci, Apple, and Coach. It's the most upscale assembly of stores in any shopping center on the Gulf Coast, served by an open-air village of restaurants called Bay Street, all in a location minutes from the airport and downtown. During the Christmas season, the Neiman Marcus store goes all out with decorations.

Located across the street from USF, **University Mall** (2200 E. Fowler Ave., 813/971-3465) is a typical indoor shopping center with mostly familiar mall stores, a 16-screen movie theater, and a standard food court.

In Wesley Chapel, **The Shops at Wiregrass** (28211 Paseo Dr., 813/994-2242, www.theshopsatwiregrass.com, 10am-9pm Mon.-Sat., noon-6pm Sun.) comprises over

Hyde Park Village

Cigar Basics

hand-rolled cigars

Want to try a cigar but don't know the first thing about them? Tampa's a good place to begin. Even before you light up, a cigar's visual specifications can give clues to its character. The outer wrapper's color indicates a great deal about a cigar's flavor. A *maduro* wrapper is a rich, deep brown, imparting a cigar with deep, strong flavors. A *claro* wrapper, on the other hand, is a light tan and lends little additional flavor to a cigar. There are essentially six color grades. Roughly from lightest to darkest, these are *candela* (pale green), *claro, natural* (light brown), *colorado* (reddish brown), *maduro,* and *oscuro* (almost black).

Shape is another central factor in cigar selection. Among *parejos,* or straight-sided cigars, there are three basic categories. A *corona* is classically six inches long, with an open foot (the end that is lighted) and a closed head (the end that is smoked). Within this category, *Churchills* are a bit longer and thicker, *robustos* are shorter and much thicker, and a *double corona* is significantly longer. *Panetelas,* the second category, are longer and much thinner than *coronas,* and the third category, *lonsdales,* are thicker than *panetelas* and thinner and longer than *coronas.*

Figurados are the other class of cigar, which spans all of the irregularly shaped types. This includes torpedo shapes, braided *culebras,* and pyramid shapes that have a closed, pointed head and an open foot.

A cigar band is generally wrapped around the closed head of a cigar. Its original function was to minimize finger staining, not to identify brands. Nonetheless, on the band you will find the name a manufacturer has designated for a particular line of cigars—names like Partagas, Macanudo, Punch, and Montecristo. Keep in mind that after 1959, many cigar manufacturers fled Cuba to open shop elsewhere, taking their brand names with them. Thus, a brand name does not always betray a cigar's country of origin.

For neophytes lighting up for the first time, a milder cigar may ease you in. The Macanudo Hyde Park is a mild smoke, as is the Don Diego Playboy Robusto or Lonsdale. For a fuller-bodied cigar, the Punch Diademas and the Partagas Number 10 are both popular. If you're looking for a robust, ultra-full-bodied taste, you might try the Hoyo de Monterrey Double Corona. The best way to discover your own personal tastes is to stop into a tobacconist or cigar-friendly restaurant and have a chat.

Market to Market

Spend a few hours at the **Ybor City Saturday Market** (Centennial Park, 1901 N. 19th St., at 8th Ave., www.ybormarket.com, 9am-3pm Sat., free), where vendors typically sell produce, arts and crafts, sweets, cigars, and souvenirs. The prices are much lower than you'll find in the shops around Ybor, but you'll have more variety with cigars in the more popular cigar stores. Use the free parking in the city lot across from the market. Well-behaved pets are welcome.

In Thonotosassa, near Busch Gardens, the **Big Top Flea Market** (9250 E. Fowler Ave., 813/986-4004, www.bigtopfleamarket.com, 9am-4pm Sat.-Sun.) has more than 1,200 booths in four large buildings. Pretty much anything and everything can be found at this large flea market. You can buy tools, eat fair-style food, or even get a tattoo. It's a good way to spend a few hours on a rainy day if you love shopping and don't mind sorting through junk for a great deal.

Bearss Groves (14316 Lake Magdalene Blvd., 813/963-5125, www.bearssgroves.com, 9am-7pm daily) is the place for fresh, local produce. From oranges and watermelons to corn and collards, you'll find low prices, excellent quality, and superb customer service. They also sell fresh-squeezed juices that hit the spot on a hot Florida summer day. The fruit pies are winners as well. Food trucks are on-site if you want to pick up lunch or dinner during your visit.

50 stores in a fairly upscale outdoor and indoor shopping center. The mall is anchored by JCPenney, Macy's, Dillard's, and a Barnes & Noble. You'll find plenty of other chain shops and restaurants.

For sales from leading retailers, head to **Tampa Premium Outlets** (2300 Grand Cypress Dr., Lutz, 813/909-8716, www.premiumoutlets.com, 10am-9pm Mon.-Sat., 10am-7pm Sun.), where you'll find the usual outlet mall suspects, including Gap, Under Armour, and Tommy Hilfiger. The shopping center has excellent outdoor space and several chain restaurants to keep you fueled for a full day of credit card-swiping. Several upscale chains, such as Saks Fifth Avenue, Polo Ralph Lauren, and Michael Kors have outlet stores here with exceptional bargains.

About a minute from International Plaza, **Westshore Plaza** (250 Westshore Plaza,

International Plaza

813/286-0790) features more than 100 similarly fancy specialty shops and four major department stores, including a Macy's. It contains a 14-screen AMC Theater and restaurants like Maggiano's Little Italy, P. F. Chang's, and Mitchell's Fish Market.

GREATER TAMPA
Shopping Malls and Centers

Fairly far from where most visitors stay, **Westfield Brandon** (459 Brandon Town Center Dr., 813/661-6255) and **Westfield Citrus Park** (8021 Citrus Park Town Center

Blvd., 813/926-4644) are both enjoyable malls with the full gamut of small shops and anchors, mostly serving the local community. Citrus Park is a little nicer, with a 20-screen Regal Cinema.

And if you want to get some great deals on name brands, you need to drive south on I-75 for 40 minutes until you reach the **Ellenton Premium Outlets** (5461 Factory Shops Blvd., 941/723-1150). There you'll find Perry Ellis, Ann Taylor, Nautica, Under Armour, Nike, and Polo Ralph Lauren—all offering deep discounts.

Food

Maybe it's Tampa residents' deep streak of loyalty, maybe their plodding constancy, but marketing geniuses have determined that Tampa is the perfect test market for new chain restaurant concepts. They are trotted out here, and if they fly, launched upon the rest of the country. For this reason, Tampa is the home base of numerous national and regional chains—Hooters, Durango Steakhouse, Beef O' Brady's, Checkers, Hops Restaurant Bar and Brewery, Shells' Seafood Restaurant, Carrabba's, and Outback Steakhouse. Outback is also the mastermind behind chains Lee Roy Selmon's, Fleming's Prime Steakhouse, Bonefish Grill, and Roy's.

You will find more Chili's, Macaroni Grills, TGI Fridays, and Bennigan's restaurants than you could possibly patronize. For this reason, only the unique, discrete, more-or-less independently owned restaurants that are the exception to the rule in Tampa are covered here.

DOWNTOWN AND CHANNELSIDE

Channelside is located dockside at the Port of Tampa, where all the cruise ships come in. The shopping, dining, and entertainment complex has a big movie theater with IMAX; a fun, upscale bowling alley; small, mostly

independently owned shops; and about a dozen restaurants.

American

Head first to the bowling alley-restaurant **Splitsville** (615 Channelside Dr., 813/514-2695, 4pm-1am Tues.-Fri., noon-2am Sat.-Sun., $7-18). Spares, strikes, whatever: It's good food, a whimsical environment, and the coolest bowling shoes ever. The decor sets you straight with oversized "bowling pin" columns, red velvet ropes, and 12 faultless lanes, and the food is excellent bar snacks.

Wet Willie's (615 Channelside Dr., 813/221-5650, 11am-midnight Sun.-Thurs., 11am-2pm Fri.-Sat., $7-12) is a fun place for daiquiris and live music. The restaurant serves tasty bar food; the wings, nachos, and piña colada shrimp are favorites.

Breakfast

Enjoy breakfast, lunch, or brunch near the University of Tampa in a stunning setting at **Oxford Exchange** (420 W. Kennedy Blvd., 813/253-0222, www.oxfordexchange.com, 7:30am-5:30pm Mon.-Fri., 9am-5:30pm Sat.-Sun., $10-20). Eat indoors surrounded by stylish wood-paneled walls or enjoy a meal in the glass-roofed conservatory. The exquisite architecture of this building, once a stable for the Tampa Bay Hotel, was painstakingly renovated to preserve its brick walls and wood-beamed ceilings. For breakfast, the eggs benedict is an excellent choice, and for lunch, the grilled chicken sandwich with garlic aioli on a ciabatta is a favorite.

Steakhouse

For a great steak, head to **Malio's Prime** (400 N. Ashley Dr., 813/223-7746, 11:30am-9:30pm Mon.-Thurs., 11:30am-10:30pm Fri., 5pm-10:30pm Sat., $21-37). It opened downtown in Rivergate Tower, only in name similar to a historic restaurant that Malio Iavarone ran on Dale Mabry. It has prime steaks served in a soaring-ceilinged dining room with banks of riverside windows.

YBOR CITY

The neighborhood's restaurants are spread along many blocks on **7th Avenue,** closed to cars on weekends. It gets packed on the weekend with younger partiers, but the area is calmer during the week.

American

Tampa Bay Brewing Company (plaza level under Muvico, 813/247-1422, www.tampabaybrewingcompany.com, 11am-11pm Sun.-Thurs., 11am-midnight Fri.-Sat., $7-12) anchors Centro. There's good live music, excellent proprietary brews (try the Redeye Ale), and a fresh American bistro menu.

Asian

Samurai Blue Sushi and Sake Bar (813/242-6688, 11:30am-11pm Mon.-Tues., 11:30am-midnight Wed.-Thurs., 11:30am-1am Fri., 5pm-1am Sat., 5pm-11pm Sun., $10-30) is another big lively joint, but this one serves sake bombers, "spontaneous combustion rolls," and other unique spins on Japanese bar staples.

Cuban/Spanish

Nearly at the end of the strip of commerce you'll find the **Columbia Restaurant** (2025 E. 7th Ave., 813/248-4961, 11am-10pm

The Cubano

In Tampa, the Cubano is the king of sandwiches, or should I say the earl of sandwiches? It starts with the bread. If you've eaten anywhere in Ybor City, you've probably eaten Cuban bread. But why not go to the source? Rumor has it that **La Segunda Central Bakery** (2512 N. 15th St., 813/248-1531, www.lesugundabakery.com, 6:30am-5pm Mon.-Fri., 7am-3pm Sat.-Sun.) churns out up to 12,000 Cuban loaves daily.

You only need one loaf, in the form of the archetypal Cubano sandwich. The loaves themselves are about 36 inches long with a zipper-like seam down the top. The third-generation owners of La Segunda have reason to be proud of their bread's thin, flaky crust and soft, pillowy interior, even more so when piled high with roast pork and Genoa salami (a strictly Tampa twist), Swiss cheese (some say emmentaler), sour pickles, and spicy mustard—the whole thing warmed and flattened in a special hot press. The outside is crisp, and the inside warm and a little gooey. It's perfection.

Mon.-Thurs., 11am-11pm Fri.-Sat., noon-9pm Sun., $21-30), which bears the distinction of being the oldest restaurant in Florida (started in 1905) and the nation's largest Spanish-Cuban restaurant (13 rooms extending one city block). The food is authentic, and the experience is worth it. Some of these waiters have been here a lifetime, the many rooms manage to stay packed, and there are stirring flamenco shows Monday-Saturday nights.

Italian

Grab a slice of Italian heaven at **La Terrazza Restaurant** (1727 E 7th Ave., 813/248-1326, www.laterrazzayborcity.com, 11:30am-2pm and 5:30pm-10pm Tues.-Fri., 5pm-10:30pm Sat., $15-25). The menu features traditional Northern Italian favorites and an extensive wine list. Owner Chef Andrea Fenu created an unpretentious atmosphere that makes you feel as if you're dining in Italy at a quaint café.

People-watching is a popular pastime in Ybor City. For the best sidewalk seat in town, pull up a chair at ★ **Bernini** (1702 E. 7th Ave., 813/248-0099, 11:30am-10pm Mon.-Thurs., 11:30am-11pm Fri.-Sat., 4pm-9pm Sun., $10-24). It's set in the historic Bank of Ybor City building and serves Cal-Ital cuisine—beef carpaccio and filet mignon with sweet corn puree. It generally attracts an older crowd than the bars and clubs around it.

Mexican

Centro Cantina (813/241-8588, 11am-9pm Mon., 11am-11pm Tues., 11am-1am Wed.-Sat., noon-1am Sun., $7-15) is more a drinking establishment. They have good margaritas and the usual Mexican dishes, so the draw is the rustic indoor-outdoor space and abounding colorful atmosphere. After this, regroup at the Centro Ybor movie theater across the plaza.

HYDE PARK

This is the upscale part of town. It's a historical residential district, serviced by the Old Hyde Park Village of high-end shops and the long stretch of South Howard Avenue, or SoHo, where some great restaurants are located.

American

Not among the 35 or so restaurants along South Howard, but still considered to be in Hyde Park, **Mise en Place** (442 W. Grand Central Ave., 813/254-5373, 11:30am-2:30pm and 5:30pm-10pm Tues.-Thurs., 11:30am-2:30pm and 5:30pm-11pm Fri., 5pm-11pm Sat., $15-32) is a romantic, intimate spot near the University of Tampa. The weekly changing menu ranges from pizza with chorizo, roast corn, chilies, and manchego to mole spice-rubbed seared tuna with purple potatoes, vanilla bean pineapple salad, and a prickly pear habanero vinaigrette. They also take great care to accommodate folks with special diets.

Asian

Picking out just a handful along Restaurant

Row is difficult. For casual dining, ★ **Water Sushi** (1015 S. Howard Ave., 813/251-8406, 11:30am-9:30pm Mon., 11:30am-10pm Tues.-Wed., 11:30am-11pm Fri., 11am-11pm Sat., 11pm-9:30pm Sun., $8-12) is a Japanese-inspired seafood joint and a late-night hang-out for the neighborhood that has live music almost nightly. Water specializes in rice paper-rolled sushi (no nori) paired with punchy sauces and dynamic side dishes. A minimalist design aesthetic and a no-reservations policy cannot douse the enthusiasm for vibrant combos like *unagi,* banana, and avocado.

TC Choy's Asian Bistro (301 S. Howard Ave., 813/251-1191, 11:30am-2:30pm and 5:30pm-10pm Mon.-Fri., 11am-3pm and 5:30pm-10:30pm Sat.-Sun., $10-20) serves authentic Cantonese cuisine and noonday dim sum as well as an assortment of other pan-Asian dishes in a stylish open space with big tables perfect for large parties.

European Fusion

Haven (2208 W. Morrison Ave., 813/258-2233, 5pm-10pm Mon.-Thurs., 5pm-11pm Fri.-Sat., $18-32), affiliated with the famous Bern's, offers a more contemporary approach than the formal steakhouse. The kitchen turns out great world-beat small plates and charcuterie with European, Asian, and Mediterranean influences. The daily-changing selection of breads is absolutely knockout (curry sesame flatbread, kalamata and fig loaf).

French/Vietnamese

After 15 years of being at the forefront of Tampa's restaurant scene, B. T. Nguyen may have reached her pinnacle in **Restaurant BT** (2507 S. MacDill Ave., 813/258-1916, 11:30am-2:30pm and 5:30pm-9:30pm Tues.-Sat., $10-30), located at the dead center of Old Hyde Park Village. Classic Vietnamese and French dishes are innovatively presented in the stylish indoor-outdoor dining room. Trained as a sommelier, Nguyen has created an exceptional wine list and a short list of cocktails, which explains the locale's popularity as an evening gathering place.

Italian

A thin-crust pizza hotshot by day, ★ **Pane Rustica** (3225 S. MacDill Ave., 813/902-8828, 8am-5pm Tues., 8am-10pm Wed.-Sat., 8am-3pm Sun., $8-25) hosts some of the fanciest Cal-Ital dinners around Wednesday to Saturday, with full table service and a well-selected short wine list. You can still opt for one of those delicious thin-crust pizzas (maybe one with gorgonzola and sweet caramelized shallot, or perhaps ricotta salata with olive tapenade and sun-dried tomatoes), or even a laid-back burger with brie and roasted red peppers. Don't miss Kevin and Karyn Kruszewski's awesome cookies, cakes, and other house-made desserts.

Mexican

From the same company who owns Water Sushi, **Green Lemon** (915 S. Howard Ave., 813/868-5463, 11:30am-11pm Mon.-Fri., 11am-midnight Sat.-Sun., $6-12) is a super lively hangout for fresh Mexican fare and good margaritas.

Green Lemon

Spanish

Not on the row, but on the more upscale waterside Bayshore, the late-night **Ceviche Tapas Bar & Restaurant** (2500 W. Azeele St., 813/250-0203, 5pm-10pm Sun.-Mon., 5pm-11pm Tues.-Wed., 5pm-1am Fri.-Sat., $14-28) serves its namesake citrus-cured fish, sea scallops with manchego, and a variety of compact dishes with olives and almonds, all in a sleek nightclub atmosphere.

Steakhouse

The biggest gorilla on the Tampa dining scene is located on what is now a somewhat run-down stretch of South Howard, but fans of **Bern's Steak House** (1208 S. Howard Ave., 813/251-2421, reservations recommended, 5pm-10pm Sun.-Thurs. 5pm-11pm Fri.-Sat., $18-100) are undeterred. This world-famous decades-old landmark has a wine list that could break a toe and a menu that so thoroughly explains dishes that it can sometimes seem a bit exaggerated. Waiters go through a grueling years-long apprenticeship, resulting in a staff that could, and does, quote verbatim from the offerings. What's offered is prime beef, aged and nurtured in Bern's own meat lockers. You, the customer, dictate the size, cut, cooking temperature, and many other details. After dinner, take the tour of the kitchen and wine cellar.

Then head upstairs to ★ **The Harry Waugh Dessert Room at Bern's Steak House** (1208 S. Howard Ave., 813/251-2421, 6pm-10:30pm Sun.-Thurs., 6pm-11:30pm Fri.-Sat., $10-20). Nothing prepares you for it. People tell you, "You dine in individual hollowed-out wine casks." Someone says, "There are individual wall-mounted radios to set the mood at your table." You hear a rumor about an accordionist, maybe something about flambéing waiters. The romantic date-night possibilities of this dessert-only upstairs at Bern's (named after a wine-writing crony of Bern himself) are endless. If that's not enough, there's Chocolate-Chocolate-Chocolate. That's actually the name of the chocolate-shellacked cylinder packing chocolate cheese pie, chocolate mousse, and chocolate cheesecake into one deadly package.

DAVIS ISLANDS
American

Nestled in the charming business district of Davis Islands, opinions on the best tables at **220 East** (220 E. Davis Blvd., 813/259-1220, 11am-10pm Mon.-Thurs., 11am-11pm Fri.-Sat., $15-20) are divided—out front at one of the handful on the patio, or inside at one of the deep green booths. The restaurant stays pretty busy. The waitstaff is exceptionally friendly, serving fairly priced, casual meals that range through American, Asian, or even Cajun dishes.

NORTH TAMPA
Asian

One of the innovative Hawaiian-fusion restaurants founded by acclaimed chef Roy Yamaguchi, **Roy's** (4342 W. Boy Scout Blvd., 813/873-7697, 11am-10pm Mon.-Thurs., 11am-11pm Fri., 5pm-11pm Sat., 5pm-9pm Sun., $20-40) is an expense-account favorite in Tampa. An exceptionally good deal can be had with the three-course dinner for $35. It may start with grilled Hawaiian satay skewers, then segue to Thai lemongrass chicken with bok choy, finishing up with Roy's signature melting hot chocolate soufflé.

European

In the upscale neighborhood of Carrollwood near northwest Tampa, Andrea and Michael Reilly's little **Michael's Grill** (11720 N. Dale Mabry Hwy., 813/964-8334, 11am-9pm Mon.-Thurs., 11am-10pm Fri., 9am-10pm Sat., 9am-3pm Sun., $15-27) is an institution, as much for the warm and neighborly service as for the friendly patio and spare, brasserie-style dining room. You can eat your French onion soup or penne Bolognese at the bar and take in all the drama of the bustling open kitchen, but the patrons out on the patio always seems to be having more fun. The daily breakfast

and Sunday brunch are a treat with items like Belgium waffles and Sicilian omelets.

New American

Also in Carrollwood, **Grille One Sixteen** (612 N. Dale Mabry Hwy., 813/265-0216, 11am-10pm Sun.-Thurs., 11am-11pm Fri.-Sat., $20-40) has become a favorite with its hip-like-Miami design. Chef James Maita has a strong New American approach with a world beat-inspired menu.

Peruvian

Look for **Happy Fish** (4046 N. Armenia Ave., 813/871-6953, www.happyfishtampa. com, 11:30am-8pm Mon.-Thurs., 11:30am-9pm Fri.-Sat., noon-8pm Sun., $8-15) tucked in the corner of Fiesta Plaza, a strip mall just south of St. Joseph's Children Hospital. It's a casual Peruvian food spot that has garnered high praise for its unique fusion of South American flavors. Try the delicious ceviche or Jalea con yuca, a platter of fried fish, shrimp, and calamari topped with yuca, onions, and lemon juice. For desert, the Peruvian doughnuts drizzled with sweet syrup are the perfect complement.

Seafood

Eddie V's Prime Seafood (4400 W Boy Scout Blvd., 813/877-7290, 5pm-10pm Sun.-Wed., 5pm-11pm Thurs.-Sat., $20-40) is a formal white-tablecloth restaurant that specializes in steaks and seafood. The food, service, and atmosphere are exceptional. Try the lobster bisque or lobster tacos to start and the steak or the red snapper for dinner. The wine list is expertly selected, and the cocktails are mixed to strong perfection. For your sweet course, don't miss the bananas foster. Live music from the baby grand piano is always tasteful, soft, and usually jazzy. This is the perfect place for a special occasion or if you want some of the best food in Tampa.

NEW TAMPA
American

New Tampa, as the name indicates, is all new.

The upside is that things are clean, pristine, and hygienic; the downside is that there's no sense of history, no gritty timeworn ambience. If you are jonesing for something that seems older than a decade or so, ★ **Skipper's Smokehouse** (910 Skipper Rd., 813/971-0666, 11am-10:30pm Tues.-Fri., noon-11pm Sat., 1pm-9:30pm Sun., $7-15) has the ambience of a place 10 times its age. It's Tampa's best live music venue (blues, alt-rock, Tuvan throat singers—the gamut), with concerts held outdoors under the canopy of a huge moss-festooned live oak. It has a lively 30s-and-up bar scene (and a mighty fine mojito). A ramshackle restaurant serves a wonderful blackened grouper sandwich, gator nuggets, and black beans.

Fusion

A favorite restaurant in New Tampa—the mostly residential area northeast of downtown—is **Ciccio Cali** (17004 Palm Pointe Dr., 813/975-1222, 11am-9:30pm Mon.-Thurs., 11am-10pm Fri., 10am-10pm Sat., 10am-9pm Sun., $9-12). Most nights it teems with families devoted to this health-conscious neighborhood favorite. Ciccio Cali serves thin, crunchy New York-style pizzas topped with interesting picks like caramelized eggplant and goat cheese, as well as a wide variety of sushi, sandwiches, and Asian-inspired entrées at lunch. Ciccio Cali is owned by the same company that owns Water Sushi and Green Lemon in Hyde Park.

Greek

The **Acropolis Greek Tavern** (14947 Bruce B. Downs Blvd., 813/971-1787, 11am-midnight Sun.-Thurs., 11am-1am Fri.-Sat., $6-15) offers late hours, lively fun, and people yelling "opa" regularly.

GREATER TAMPA
Asian

About three miles south of the Hard Rock Casino, you'll discover something entirely different at the **Wat Mongkolratanaram Thai Temple** (5306 Palm River Rd., 813/621-1669, www.wattampainenglish.com, 8:30am-2:30pm Sun., $4-10). On Sunday, the authentic and extremely ornate Buddhist Temple opens its doors to the public for a market and brunch. You'll find a wide variety of traditional Thai foods, including spring rolls, curries, *pad thai, som dow* (Thai papaya salad), and fried bananas. The food is very reasonably priced, with most entrées costing around $5. Grab one of the fresh fruit juices ($1) as well. Be sure to explore the temple while you're here—the inside is even more impressive than the exterior. There is excellent outdoor seating with a view of the river. Parking is limited, so it is recommended to arrive early, as this is a very popular Sunday event in the area.

Deli

Wright's Gourmet House (1200 S. Dale Mabry Hwy., 813/253-3838, www.wrights-gourmet.com, 7am-6pm Mon.-Fri., 8am-4pm Sat., $5-12) is near the Palma Ceia Golf and Country Club in Southwest Tampa, dishing out fresh breakfast, lunch, and baked goods from the café and deli. The servings are generous and the ingredients high-quality. The Cuban, Reuben, or turkey sandwiches are excellent, and any of the cakes will make you a regular.

Brocato's Sandwich Shop (5021 E Columbus Dr., 813/248-9977, www.broca-tossandwich.com, 7:30am-5:30pm Mon.-Fri., 7:30am-4pm Sat., $6-15) is a popular lunch and breakfast spot. It gets very crowded, so make sure you have an hour or so for lunch if you're arriving at noon, or get there during less popular hours for a quick bite. The sandwiches are piled high with meat, and the Cubano here is one of the best. The deviled crab and stuffed potatoes are also legendary.

International Plaza

Tampa's fanciest mall (there's a Louis Vuitton store next to a Gucci store), **International Plaza** (2223 N. Westshore Blvd., 813/490-5288), is also home to good restaurants. It contains **The Cheesecake Factory** (813/353-4200, 11am-11pm Mon.-Thurs.,

11am-12:30am Fri.-Sat., 10am-11pm Sun., $12-20), **California Pizza Kitchen** (813/353-8155, 11am-9:30pm Mon.-Sat., 11am-7pm Sun., $8-15), **Earl of Sandwich** (813/879-1762, 9am-9pm Mon.-Sat., 11am-6pm Sun., $6-12), and **The Capital Grille** (813/830-9433, 11:30am-10pm Mon.-Thurs., 11:30am-11pm Fri.-Sat., 5pm-9pm Sun., $30-60), for when you want to splurge on a $40 dry-aged steak. The mall's Bay Street is a Caribbean-themed pedestrian promenade lined with several good restaurants.

Best bets for a drink: **Bar Louie** (813/874-1919, 11am-2am daily, $12-20) has 40 beers on tap, cooks up excellent burgers, and offers a large variety of small plates from pan-seared pork pot-stickers to hand-battered calamari. **Blue Martini** (813/873-2583, 4pm-3am Mon.-Thurs., 1pm-3am Fri.-Sun., $10-20) is for when you aim to go the martini route, with a menu that leans to small plates (seared tuna, hummus and pita chips). There's also an elevated stage behind the bar to see live rock.

Fine Dining

When you want to get a sense of Tampa's scale, distance, and scope, you have to dig deep into your wallet and head to **Armani's** (2900 Bayport Dr., 813/207-6800, 6pm-10pm Mon.-Sat., $25-40) atop the Grand Hyatt Tampa Bay. It's the undisputed top special-occasion restaurant in town, partly for the view, partly for the solicitous service, and partly for the scaloppine Armani (thin-pounded veal sautéed with wild mushrooms and cognac in a truffle sauce) or the grilled duck breast stuffed with liver pâté and dried cherries in a vanilla sauce. The wine list is extensive, with an emphasis on California and French wines.

Fusion

Named after a young Native American Princess, **Ulele** (1810 N. Highland Ave., 813/999-4952, www.ulele.com, 11 am-10pm Sun.-Thurs., 11am-11pm Fri.-Sat., $20-40) blends traditional Native American food with American, Floridian, and European cuisine. This adventurous restaurant and brewery

in Tampa Heights has excellent dishes like Native Chili, a delicious combination of alligator, wild boar, venison, duck, and ground beef with beans and spices. Or try the oven-roasted chicken crusted with citrus-herb garlic and served with a cheddar jalapeño grit cake. If you'd like something more familiar, they have wonderful steak and seafood choices. Located on the Riverwalk, you have your pick between indoor and outdoor seating with excellent water views.

Italian

Another great restaurant is **Pelagia Trattoria** (4200 Jim Walter Blvd., 813/313-3235, 6:30am-10pm daily, $15-25), located on the main level in the Renaissance Tampa Hotel, Bay Street. Chef Brett Gardiner serves Mediterranean-inspired dishes: Breakfast brings special items like Godiva chocolate pancakes with a white chocolate mousse; at lunch, ricotta and asparagus ravioli served in a hot truffle butter sauce; and for dinner, lamb T-bone with juniper berry sauce. It's the most beautiful hotel restaurant in all of Tampa that also has an express lunch menu that gets people in and out lickety-split.

Seafood

Oystercatchers (2900 Bayport Dr., 813/207-6815, 11:30am-10pm daily, $18-35) is a top pick for seafood. It offers exceptionally fresh seafood in a beautiful and upscale but still comfortably casual waterfront setting. The outdoor dining area features romantic fire pits right on the water that can be reserved. For dinner, choose between dishes like wood-grilled Gulf snapper served with tuxedo orzo and baby vegetables, or seared tuna drizzled with key lime and caper butter. The incredible water views and superb brunch make this a Tampa favorite.

In east Tampa, **Council Oak** (5223 N. Orient Rd., 813/627-7600, 5pm-10pm Sun.-Thurs., 5pm-midnight Fri.-Sat., $24-40) opened with much fanfare as part of the Seminole Hard Rock Hotel and Casino. Smack in the center of the gaming excitement, it mainly serves seafood and steaks, all well prepared and offered by an extremely knowledgeable waitstaff.

Charley's Steakhouse and Market Fresh Fish (4444 W. Cypress St., 813/353-9706, 5pm-10pm Sun.-Thurs., 5pm-11pm Fri.-Sat., $30-44) has fat grilled steaks and California wines. Some of the selections include five-pepper-encrusted filet mignon with pesto, roast garlic mashed potatoes, and oak-grilled vegetables, or shrimp and scallop scampi with a side of grilled asparagus and a baked potato.

Steakhouse

Some of the old guard are fairly far-flung: **Shula's Steak House** (Westshore Grand Hotel, 4860 W. Kennedy Blvd., 813/286-4366, 6:30am-10pm daily, $20-40), is in Beach Park inside the Westshore, which used to be the Intercontinental. Not surprisingly, given coach Don Shula's hand in it, the white-tablecloth chop house features decor in tribute to the Miami Dolphins. It's the most elegant experience with football you are ever likely to have. Everything at Shula's is huge, and the steaks are well-seasoned and perfectly prepared, available up to 48 ounces. Even the salads are wonderfully oversize. The waitstaff is exceptional, and Shula's serves exemplary mixed drinks. Some prefer Bern's or Ruth's Chris, but football fans will root for Shula's and want season tickets.

Accommodations

Tampa's hotel scene is stymied by one thing: Tampa has no beaches. Although it's on the water—with the active Port of Tampa and waterside residential communities like Davis and Harbour Island—there is no possibility for a luxury resort hotel or charming bed-and-breakfast just steps from the waters of Hillsborough Bay. For that kind of experience, you must head over the bay to St. Pete or Clearwater.

Still, Tampa has a preponderance of pleasant, fairly priced accommodations spread around the greater Bay Area, including the Latin Quarter of Ybor City, the Westshore business district, the Tampa Convention Center, and near Busch Gardens and the University of South Florida.

DOWNTOWN AND CHANNELSIDE
$200-300

Le Meridien Tampa (601 N. Florida Ave., 813/221-9555, www.lemeridientampa.com, $230-450) is the only four-diamond hotel in downtown Tampa. Formerly a federal courthouse, the building had a $27 million renovation in 2014, which gave the classical building a sleek, modern uplift. The desk in the lobby was once the judge's bench, and the granite columns and marble walls date to 1905. On-site is Bizzou Brasserie, which serves impeccable international cuisine, as well as an ultramodern cocktail lounge, a fitness center, and a beautiful outdoor pool.

Over $300

Enjoy excellent views of Hillsborough Bay, Downtown Tampa, and Davis Islands at the **Tampa Marriott Waterside Hotel & Marina** (700 S. Florida Ave., 813/221-4900, www.marriott.com, $310-400). This is a great location if you'll be cruising from Tampa, or if you want to explore downtown. There is a rooftop pool, a full-service spa, a fitness center, and several restaurants and bars on-site. The rooms are elegantly appointed, and suites include a balcony with excellent views. The pool area is surrounded by palm trees and includes a hot tub where you can soak your feet after shopping downtown all day. Note that if you're not Marriott Rewards member, Internet access will cost you $13 per day.

YBOR CITY
$100-200

The **Bonita Casitas de Ybor** (1813 and 1815 E. 5th Ave., 813/334-1857, $100-200) offers two charming private guest cottages with full kitchens and two bedrooms each.

SOUTH TAMPA, HYDE PARK, AND DAVIS ISLANDS
$100-200

The **Tahitian Inn** (601 S. Dale Mabry Hwy., 813/877-6721, www.tahitianinn.com, $95-169) is a lovely two-story family-run motel yielding 60 Tahitian-themed (dark wood, tropical accessories) moderately priced rooms and 20 executive suites, a lovely pool with tiki huts and hammocks, and the Serenity Spa with massage and Tahitian hot stone treatments. There's also a lovely little on-site café with patio seating near a koi pond. The location is close to I-275 and lots of commerce.

Over $300

★ **The Epicurean Hotel, Autograph Collection** (1207 S Howard Ave., 813/999-8700, www.marriott.com, $350-600) is a boutique hotel across the street from Bern's Steakhouse. The hotel has a modern style that highlights its focus on fine food and wine; there are even butcher-block countertops and wine crate-lined walls in the lobby. The excellent on-site restaurant Elevage is open for breakfast, lunch, and dinner and serves elevated American classics. Or treat yourself at Chocolate Pi, the hotel's bakery, specializing in handmade chocolates, gourmet cakes, and exceptional teas and coffees. The hotel also offers cooking classes at their culinary theater. There is an outdoor heated pool, and Bayshore Boulevard is nearby.

NORTH TAMPA
Under $100

If you want to stay near USF or Busch Gardens and MOSI, there are a handful of reasonably priced chains. **La Quinta Inn Tampa Near Busch Gardens** (9202 N. 30th St., 813/930-6900, $70-120) is adjacent to Busch Gardens' entrance, with 144 nicely appointed rooms with roomy baths, good lighting, large desks, and Wi-Fi. There's also a good-size pool.

$100-200

Holiday Inn Express New Tampa (8310 Galbraith Rd., 877/859-5095, www.ihg.com, $170-240) is a pet-friendly hotel about three miles from Busch Gardens and the

the beautiful lobby of The Epicurean Hotel, Autograph Collection

University of South Florida. Conveniently located off I-75 at exit 270, this is the perfect home base for families traveling between Orlando and Tampa or a wonderful place to stay before a cruise. A full, free breakfast is included, and the outdoor heated pool is a plus. There are many shops and restaurants in the area, so dining out will not be a chore. In the evening, they offer free ice cream. Try to say no to that!

Six miles from Busch Gardens, you'll find a wonderful bargain at the **Hampton Inn & Suites Tampa North** (8210 Hidden River Pkwy., 855/605-0317, www.hamptoninn.com, $120-200). Budget-minded travelers will enjoy the free breakfast and free Internet access. Located in the Hidden River Corporate Park, this hotel is also favored by business travelers. There is a large pool in the cozy courtyard and a fitness center on-site. The rooms are simple but elegantly furnished. Suites offer a full kitchen with a fridge, stove, dishwasher, sink, and microwave, which can be a real money-saver when traveling with a family.

$200-300

The USF hotel of choice is **Embassy Suites USF Near Busch Gardens** (3705 Spectrum Blvd., 813/977-7066, $150-300), across the road from the university. It's a tall suites-only hotel with a soaring atrium. Rooms are nice, with spacious living rooms, private bedrooms with either a king or two double beds, and two TVs in every room. Although the rooms cost a little more, included in the price is a nice daily cooked-to-order breakfast buffet and the manager's reception, where you get a free cocktail and some chips in the early evening.

Emerald Greens Condo Resort (13941 Clubhouse Dr., 813/961-9400, www.emeraldgreensresort.com, $200-300) is perfect for families or couples looking for an extended-stay option. The fifty units are each 1,200 square feet, have two bedrooms, and feature a full kitchen, separate living and dining areas, and a private balcony. The resort is on the Carrollwood Country Club property, and

you will have access to the golf course, tennis courts, and pool. Daily housekeeping service and free Internet are included.

GREATER TAMPA
Under $100

For a wild experience at a tame price, **Gram's Place** (3109 N. Ola Ave., 813/221-0596, www.grams-inn-tampa.com, dorm $25, private room $50-60) in Ybor City fits the bill. It's eccentric, with a different music theme (jazz, blues, rock) in each of the private suites and youth hostel-style bunks. All rooms come with a music menu of CDs. The hostel part looks like a railroad car fashioned around a 100-year-old train depot. The rooms are set in two circa-1945 cottages and share an oversize in-ground whirlpool tub, a BYOB bar in the courtyard, and a multitrack recording studio. The "Gram" in question is the late musician Gram Parsons, once a member of the Byrds and the Flying Burrito Brothers, responsible for that great song "Grievous Angel," made famous by Emmylou Harris.

$100-200

Hilton Garden Inn Tampa Airport Westshore (5312 Avion Park Dr., 855/618-4697, www.hilton.com, $150-230) is an excellent choice if you want to stay close to the airport (sometimes you will hear jets taking off). The bright color scheme and updated furnishings make the rooms feel modern and cheerful. Breakfast costs extra, but it's highly recommended. The hotel is reliable, has great customer service, and is a top choice for business travelers.

The ★ **Grand Hyatt Tampa Bay** (2900 Bayport Dr., 813/874-1234, www. tampabay. grand.hyatt.com, $150-350) is a big hotel near the airport that caters mainly to corporate travelers. There are 445 deluxe guest rooms and suites, including 38 Spanish-style casita rooms and 7 casita suites in a secluded area at the south end of the property, which is set in a 35-acre wildlife preserve on the shores of Tampa Bay. The Hyatt contains two of

the Seminole Hard Rock Hotel and Casino

For a more independent approach in the same location, try **Sailport Waterfront Suites** (2506 N. Rocky Point Dr., 813/281-9599, $110-230), a four-story all-suites hotel (all rooms have a queen-size sleeper sofa in the living room, convenient for families) with full-size kitchens, barbecue grills, an outdoor heated pool, a lighted tennis court, and a fishing pier.

$200-300

The **Seminole Hard Rock Hotel and Casino** (5223 Orient Rd., 866/388-4263, www.seminolehardrocktampa.com, $249-359) is the huge tower that rises in the middle of nowhere off I-75. With an illuminated 12-story tower that shifts colors, the signature huge guitar at the entrance, a 90,000-square-foot casino, and popular restaurants like Kuro and Council Oak, it's like a little piece of Vegas right here in Tampa. The complex opened in 2004 and has been swamped with casino and overnight guests ever since. The 250 guest rooms and suites have a hip art deco design. The most luxurious part is the pool area, with cascading fountains and private cabanas with TVs and refrigerators. In 2012 the Seminole Tribe completed a $75 million expansion for the Hard Rock, which made it the sixth-largest casino in the world and larger than any casino in Las Vegas.

Hilton Garden Inn Tampa East/ Brandon (10309 Highland Manor Dr., 855/618-4697, www.hilton.com, $220-350) is an excellent alternative to staying at the Hard Rock. They offer shuttles to and from the action at the Hard Rock Casino, while offering a quiet retreat from the action at the gaming center. The rooms are quiet and spacious, and there is a beautiful courtyard outside with plenty of places to sit and relax. Shoot a game of pool in the billiard room, relax at the outdoor pool, or dine in one of the two restaurants that serve a variety of American favorites at breakfast, lunch, and dinner.

the best restaurants in town, Armani's and Oystercatchers. Armani's underwent an impressive renovation in 2012. The rooftop fire pit offers one of the best views of Tampa Bay in the city and is an excellent spot to watch the sunset.

Numerous hotels cluster along Rocky Point Drive and Cypress Street, just a couple of minutes from the airport, Westshore business district, and Tampa Convention Center. These hotels have lots of business amenities and often offer significantly cheaper rates on the weekend. Of the chains, there's **DoubleTree Hotel Tampa Airport Westshore** (4500 W. Cypress St., 813/879-4800, www.doubletreetampawestshore.com, $100-300), **Courtyard by Marriott Tampa Westshore** (3805 W. Cypress St., 813/874-0555, $100-250), and the **Holiday Inn Express and Suites Rocky Point** (3025 N. Rocky Point Dr., 813/287-8585, $150-250), among many others, all with water views of the bay and pools and other amenities.

Over $300

One of Tampa's nicest luxury hotels is the ★ **Renaissance Tampa International Plaza Hotel** (4200 Jim Walter Blvd., 813/877-9200, $339-389), near the Westshore business district at the International Plaza mall. The lavish decor is reminiscent of a Mediterranean villa. The hotel is not small, with 293 guest rooms on eight floors, but the service is personal and attentive, and it seems especially geared to repeat-business, high-end business travelers.

Information and Services

Tampa is located in the **eastern time zone.** All telephone listings are within the **813 area code** unless otherwise indicated. If you're trying to call the other side of the bay (Clearwater, Dunedin, St. Petersburg), the area code is **727.**

VISITOR INFORMATION

Tampa Bay and Company's **Visitor Information Center** is in the waterfront Channelside entertainment complex (401 E. Jackson St., 813/223-1111, www.visittampabay. com, 9:30am-5:30pm Mon.-Sat., 11am-5pm Sun.) at the Port of Tampa. It provides lots of brochures and information on attractions, events, and accommodations.

Tampa's daily newspaper is the **Tampa Bay Times** (727/893-8111, www.tampabay. com) which covers the greater Tampa Bay area. **Creative Loafing** (813/739-4800, www.cltampa.com), the city's free alternative weekly, has great entertainment schedules, restaurant reviews, and a view into local politics. For quick and easy info on events, attractions, and restaurants, visit www.tampabay.citysearch.com. There are also numerous magazines: **Tampa Bay Magazine** covers the city of Tampa, **Tampa Style** covers only the northern suburbs of the city, and there are many glossy freebies in Hyde Park.

POLICE AND EMERGENCIES

In any emergency, dial 911 for immediate assistance. If you need police assistance in a nonemergency, visit or call the **Tampa Police Department** (411 N. Franklin St., 813/276-3200). The police department operates three districts that serve the greater Tampa Bay area—they will assign your problem to the proper district. Tampa has several hospitals equipped with emergency rooms: If you have a medical emergency in the Hyde Park area, go to **Memorial Hospital of Tampa** (2901 Swann Ave., 813/873-6400). In Carrollwood, visit the **Florida Hospital Carrollwood** (7171 N. Dale Mabry Hwy., 813/932-2222). In the Westshore area, go to **University Community Health** (5101 E. Busch Blvd., 813/830-6236). In the downtown area, make your way to **Tampa General Hospital** (1 Tampa General Circle, 813/844-7000), near the causeway to Davis Islands.

RADIO AND TV

Of the local radio stations, my favorite is **WMNF 88.5 FM,** which has a huge following for its independent and eclectic programming—tune in and you'll hear salsa, or maybe Hawaiian slack-key guitar, or maybe a little alt-country. It has a snuggly relationship with Skipper's Smokehouse, and together they sponsor many of the city's best concerts. For a nonthreatening mix of pop, turn to **WMTX 100.7 FM;** for hits of the 1970s, turn to **107.3 FM The Eagle;** and for sports talk, turn to **WDAE 1250 AM.**

On the TV, if you're looking for the Fox affiliate, turn to **Channel 13,** for NBC **WFLA Channel 8,** for ABC **WFTS Channel 28,** and for CBS **WTSP Channel 10.**

LAUNDRY SERVICES

If you find yourself in need of coin-op laundry, head to **Busch Laundromat** (4810 E. Busch Blvd., 813/987-9847) near Busch Gardens, **Gator Wash** (3316 Henderson Blvd., 813/874-7050) near Tampa University, **Ybor City Coin Laundry** (1410 E. 17th Ave.) in Ybor City, **Hillsborough Coin Laundry** (3016 W Hillsborough Ave., 813/874-9274) north of Tampa near the Lowry Park Zoo, or **Laundromat of Tampa** (8215 N Florida Ave., 813/932-2900) across from River Tower Park in North Tampa.

Transportation

AIR

Tampa International Airport (TPA, 4100 George J. Bean Pkwy., 813/870-8700, www.tampaairport.com) is perhaps the best mid-size airport in the country—clean, easily traversed, with good signage and efficient staff. With one of the best on-time records around, it's Florida's fourth-busiest airport, located just seven miles southwest of downtown Tampa. It's served by Air Canada, Alaska, American, British Airways, Cayman Airways, Copa, Delta, Edelweiss, Frontier, JetBlue, Lufthansa, Silver, Southwest, Spirit, Sun Country, United, WestJet, and World Atlantic.

Located on the airport premises, **Avis** (800/831-2847), **Budget** (800/527-0700), **Dollar** (800/800-4000 domestic, 800/800-6000 international), **Enterprise** (800/736-8222), **Hertz** (800/654-3131), and **Thrifty** (800/847-4389) provide rental-car service. Tampa has unbelievably good deals on rental cars from the airport—celebrate by upgrading to something stylish.

CAR

Both I-75 and I-275 travel north-south, but I-75 skirts the edge of Tampa while I-275 travels through the city and over the bay. Both connect to I-4, which travels east-west, connecting Tampa Bay to Orlando and the east coast of Florida.

Once in town, from north to south, Bearrs, Fletcher, Fowler, and Busch Boulevards are the big east-west roads. Dale Mabry and Bruce B. Downs are the biggest north-south roads. This all sounds fairly simple, but once you get downtown in Tampa, you need a map to find your way out. There are lots of one-way streets, and the highway on-ramps are difficult to find. The Busch Gardens area and University of South Florida lie between I-75 and I-275 northeast of downtown. The airport is just southwest of downtown.

BUS AND TRAIN

Taxi service from the airport to downtown is about $18. Taxis must be called rather than flagged down. Most hotels offer shuttle service to the airport and major attractions.

Amtrak and **Greyhound** (813/229-2174) both serve Tampa with stations downtown. **Amtrak** (800/872-7245) operates out of historic Tampa Union Station (601 N. Nebraska Ave.), offering north-south connections as well as links to nationwide rail travel.

Within the city, **Hillsborough Area Regional Transit Authority** (813/623-5835, www.gohart.org, $4 unlimited rides all day) provides city bus service, with nearly 200 buses on 26 routes, nine trolleys, and eight electric streetcars. The In Town Trolley runs north-south through downtown and connects to the TECO Line Streetcar System, which runs from downtown to the Channel District and Port as well as Ybor City. Still, Tampa is so spread out that it's not easy to be without a car.

St. Petersburg and Pinellas County

I n some ways, Henry Ford's affordable $400 Model T foreshadowed the real estate boom in St. Petersburg in the early 1920s. It was the beginning of road-tripping—folks hopping in the car in search of sun, sand, and fun. They found the

peninsula that hangs down Florida's west side like a thumb, the east side of it nestled against the placid Old Tampa Bay, its west side flanked by sandy beaches and the Gulf of Mexico. People liked what they saw. They bought up land, building big resort hotels, affordable motels, and homes.

Before the hordes of sun worshippers came, what is now Pinellas County had a diverse set of visitors-turned-residents. As was so common along the Gulf Coast, Spanish conquistadores ran off the original pre-Columbian Native Americans in the 1500s. Long after that, there came an intrepid Frenchman, Odet Philippe, who established a large orange grove near Safety Harbor in 1842; just after that came the Scottish merchants who settled Dunedin, the Russian immigrants who worked the Orange Belt Railroad and named St. Petersburg after their old-world hometown, and finally the Greeks, who came to harvest the area's rich sponge beds around 1900.

Today, St. Petersburg is Florida's fourth-largest city, the anchor of Pinellas County. Combined with neighboring Tampa, it's the largest market in the state. It has had another boom period in recent years, an influx of tech businesses drawing younger families and driving down the median age. The city's downtown—on the bay, not the Gulf—has seen lots of growth, from pricey condos to the $40 million BayWalk shopping complex.

St. Pete Beach is not just the shortened name for St. Petersburg Beach. St. Petersburg is the big city adjacent to Old Tampa Bay, which looks out across at the big city of Tampa. St. Pete Beach, on the other hand, is an autonomous barrier-island town to the south and west of St. Petersburg. St. Pete Beach stretches seven miles from Pass-A-Grille on the south to Blind Pass on the north, before Treasure Island. Also, the city of Clearwater is on the mainland, but Clearwater Beach is

Previous: downtown St. Petersburg; St. Pete Beach. **Above:** Sunshine Skyway Bridge.

Look for ★ to find recommended
sights, activities, and dining, and lodging.

Highlights

★ **Salvador Dalí Museum:** The famous Spanish surrealist is honored in a sleek museum of his work and the work of those inspired by him (page 67).

★ **St. Pete Beach:** Watch the sunset or search for shells along this white, sandy shore lined with hotels and restaurants (page 74).

★ **Clearwater Beach:** The whole family will enjoy the evening fairs that take place at this beautiful beach (page 74).

★ **Fort De Soto Park:** Beyond the site of a fort built during the Spanish-American War, this park features over seven miles and 1,136 acres of pristine coastal environment to explore (page 75).

★ **Honeymoon Island and Caladesi Island Beaches:** Why settle for just one beach when you can opt for a pair of white-sand barrier islands (page 75)?

★ **Sunken Gardens:** It puttered along as a kitschy Old Florida attraction for years, until the city of St. Petersburg restored the four-acre tropical garden to its former glory (page 77).

★ **Sunshine Skyway Fishing Piers:** A local bridge has been repurposed as the world's longest fishing pier, taking advantage of a tremendous concentration of sport fish lurking in the deep waters below (page 80).

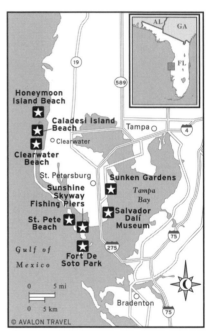

St. Petersburg and Pinellas County

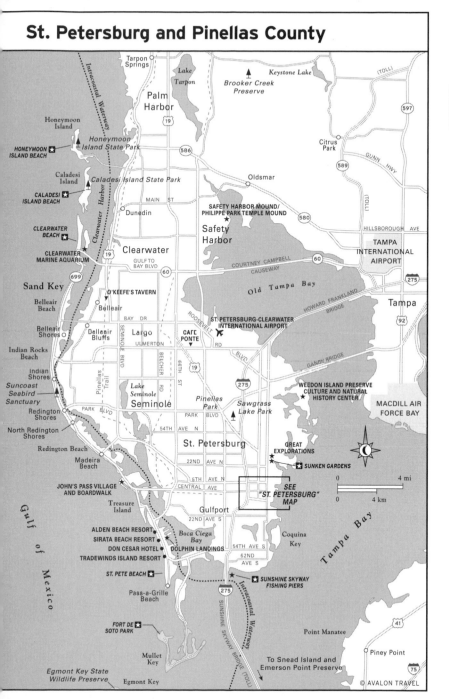

on a barrier island connected by Memorial Causeway.

The Gulf beaches are 20 minutes from downtown St. Petersburg across the peninsula. More than 20 little towns dot the coastline in Pinellas County, St. Pete Beach and Clearwater Beach being perhaps the favorites for family vacations. Clearwater Beach offers a wide, inviting shore, serious beach volleyball, and lots of nightlife and casual seafood restaurants. The Jolley Trolley whisks visitors from their hotel through town and right to the beachside Pier 60, something like the center of town.

Clearwater and St. Pete Beaches aren't the only strands that draw accolades. Caladesi Island State Park, accessible only by boat to the north of Clearwater Beach, is often rated one of the top 10 beaches in the country, as is Honeymoon Island.

PLANNING YOUR TIME

Pinellas County is a peninsula, with Tampa Bay to the east and the Gulf of Mexico to the west. Its location, adjacent to Tampa, but with the benefit of long and wonderful beaches, makes it an ideal home base for a lengthy Gulf Coast stay, especially for families. Even Disney World is a fairly convenient 90 minutes to the east. The sights and attractions are more compelling on the Tampa side of the bay (Busch Gardens, lots of professional sports), and these are easily accessed by either the Howard Frankland Bridge (I-275) or the Courtney Campbell Causeway (Hwy. 60). In high-season traffic, the drive can be 45 minutes. The best way to explore the area is by car, especially if you want to drive the length of the barrier islands. The area is served by **Tampa International Airport** (TPA, 4100 George J. Bean Pkwy., 813/870-8700) and **St. Petersburg-Clearwater International Airport** (PIE, 14700 Terminal Blvd., Clearwater, 727/453-7800).

Where you stay depends on your priorities: The city of St. Petersburg lies on the bay side of the peninsula. It has more history, more of a sense of place and sophistication than the beach towns along the Gulf side. There are romantic bed-and-breakfasts, fine restaurants, and cultural attractions. Clearwater Beach and St. Pete Beach on the Gulf side have the densest concentrations of beachside accommodations—in Clearwater this often means tall resort hotels and condos right on the beach; in St. Pete Beach it's low-rise motels that date back a few decades. The communities in between these two—Belleair and Belleair Beach; Indian Rocks Beach and Indian Shores; Redington Shores, North Redington Beach, and Redington Beach; Madeira Beach; and Treasure Island—are fairly residential, but with pockets of beachside hotels, motels, and rentals. The whole Gulf side is really composed of a series of tiny barrier islands connected to the mainland by causeways—it may not be totally clear to you when driving, but spend a little time with the map so you know whether you're looking at boats bobbing on the Intracoastal Waterway, Boca Ciega Bay, Clearwater Harbor, or the Gulf.

The peak season typically runs November to May. It's a little more spread out than elsewhere among the Gulf Coast's beach spots, partly because American families on spring break come in March and April, and lots of European travelers fill in the time around that. In the summer the waters here are so warm as to be slightly off-putting. September and October are great times to visit. In October, added enticements include the beloved annual **Clearwater Jazz Holiday** (727/461-5200, www.clearwaterjazz.com) during the third week of the month, with four days of free world-class jazz in Coachman Park. There's also the local **Stone Crab Festival** (www.stonecrabfestival.org) at the same time.

The best camping is at Fort De Soto Park, and the best beaches in the area are at Clearwater Beach, Fort De Soto Park, Honeymoon Island and Caladesi Island, St. Pete Beach, Madeira Beach, Sand Key County Park, and Egmont Key State Wildlife Preserve.

Sights

DOWNTOWN ST. PETERSBURG
★ Salvador Dalí Museum

Perhaps the most popular art museum in Pinellas County is the **Salvador Dalí Museum** (1 Dali Blvd., St. Petersburg, 727/823-3767, www.thedali.org, 10am-5:30pm Fri.-Wed., 10am-8pm Thurs., $24 adults, $22 seniors, military, police, firefighters, and educators with ID, $17 students, $10 ages 6-12, free under age 6), the world's most comprehensive collection of permanent works by the famous Spanish surrealist master, with other exhibits relating to Dalí. Opened in 2011 to worldwide acclaim, the architect Yann Weymouth designed an awe-inspiring building described as a "building that combines the rational with the fantastical: a simple rectangle with 18-inch thick hurricane-proof walls out of which erupts a large free-form geodesic glass bubble known as the enigma." The impressive helical staircase inside the building recalls Dalí's own obsession with spirals and the double helix shape of the DNA molecule.

The new Avante Garden outside the building extends this theme and provides a calming space to explore the relationship between math and nature. The new museum has quickly become nearly as popular as the collection housed inside. AOL Travel News listed the museum as one of the top 20 buildings to see in your lifetime, and the Florida Association of the American Institute of Architects named it as the top museum design in the state.

Dalí himself is as recognizable as his "paranoiac-critical" paintings. Maybe only Van Gogh in his post-ear incident self-portrait is more reliably identified than Dalí, with his long waxed mustache and extreme arched eyebrows. Upon moving to the United States in the 1940s, Dalí made himself the lovable eccentric who introduced the average American to surrealism—and the average American really liked it.

The Salvador Dalí Museum is a dense concentration of his surrealist works, what he described as a "spontaneous method of irrational knowledge based on the critical and

the Salvador Dalí Museum

St. Petersburg

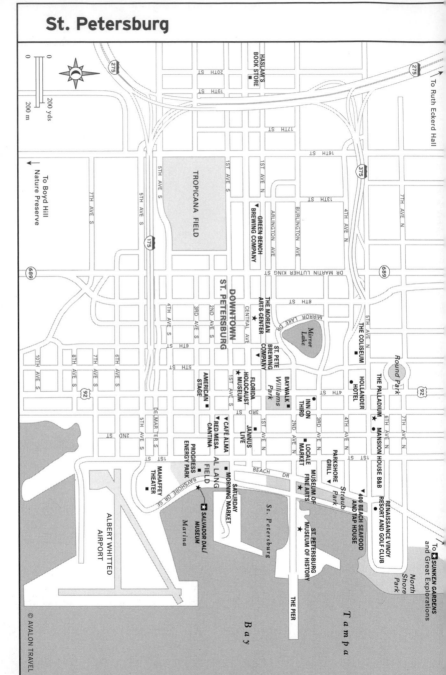

0
0
200 yds
200 m

To Ruth Eckerd Hall

To Boyd Hill
Nature Preserve

275
275
375
689
689
92
175

TROPICANA FIELD

HASLAM'S BOOK STORE

GREEN BENCH BREWING COMPANY

DOWNTOWN ST. PETERSBURG

THE MOREAN ARTS CENTER

ST. PETE BREWING COMPANY

Mirror Lake

THE COLISEUM

THE PALLADIUM

Round Park

North Shore Park

HOLLANDER HOTEL

MANSION HOUSE B&B

RENAISSANCE VINOY RESORT AND GOLF CLUB

To SUNKEN GARDENS and Great Explorations

BAYWALK

Williams Park

FLORIDA HOLOCAUST MUSEUM

AMERICAN STAGE

INN ON THIRD

JANNUS LIVE

LOCALE MARKET

400 BEACH SEAFOOD AND TAP HOUSE

PARKSHORE GRILL

Straub Park

CAFE ALMA
RED MESA CANTINA

MUSEUM OF FINE ARTS

ST. PETERSBURG MUSEUM OF HISTORY

MAHAFFEY THEATER

PROGRESS ENERGY PARK

AL LANG FIELD

BEACH DR

SATURDAY MORNING MARKET

St. Petersburg

SALVADOR DALI MUSEUM

BAYSHORE DR SE

Marina

ALBERT WHITTED AIRPORT

THE PIER

T a m p a
B a y

© AVALON TRAVEL

5TH AVE N
7TH AVE N
5TH AVE N
6TH AVE N
7TH AVE N
4TH AVE N
4TH AVE N
1ST AVE N

20TH ST
19TH ST
17TH ST
16TH ST
15TH ST
13TH ST
11TH ST
8TH ST
4TH ST
3RD AVE N
2ND AVE N
1ST AVE N

DR MARTIN LUTHER KING ST
BURLINGTON AVE
ARLINGTON AVE
CENTRAL AVE

5TH AVE S
7TH AVE S
4TH AVE S
3RD AVE S
2ND AVE S
5TH AVE S
6TH AVE S
7TH AVE S
8TH AVE S
10TH AVE S

1ST ST
3RD ST
5TH ST
8TH ST

1ST AVE S
5TH ST S
DEL MAR TER S
2ND ST
5TH ST S
1ST ST

systematic objectivation of delirious associations and interpretations."

The museum is wonderful—a great space where the work is described and presented well. Even if you don't care for what you have seen of his work in books and prints, it is an incredible experience to view the original works in their larger-than-life sizes. And if you have never experienced his works at all, the museum is almost sure to make you a fan.

Museum of Fine Arts

In 2008, the **Museum of Fine Arts** (255 Beach Dr. NE, St. Petersburg, 727/896-2667, www.mfastpete.org, 10am-5pm Mon.-Sat., noon-5pm Sun., $17 adults, $15 seniors and military, $10 students and ages 7-18, free under age 7) unveiled its much-anticipated Hazel Hough Wing. It started with a gangbuster exhibition of works that have been rarely on view, or in some cases never before displayed at the MFA. Featuring works by such noted artists as Renoir, Léger, Pissarro, Matisse, Fabergé, Chuck Close, and James Rosenquist, it showcased just how marvelous the museum's collection is. Right on the waterfront adjacent to Straub Park, the museum contains a full range of art from antiquity to the present day. The collection of 4,000 objects includes significant works by Cézanne, Monet, Gauguin, Renoir, Rodin, and O'Keeffe. Its permanent collection's strength is 17th- and 18th-century European art, and the museum has a lovely garden as well.

St. Petersburg Museum of History

St. Petersburg Museum of History (335 2nd Ave. NE, St. Petersburg, 727/894-1052, www.spmoh.org, 10am-5pm Mon.-Sat., noon-5pm Sun., $15 adults, $12 seniors, $9 military, veterans, students, and ages 6-17) is one of the oldest historical museums in the state, with family-friendly displays and exhibits depicting St. Petersburg's past. It was remodeled and enlarged in 2005, with a local history exhibit that contains a Native American dugout canoe, an exact replica of the world's first

scheduled commercial airliner (it flew out of St. Petersburg), and lots of other interesting exhibits.

Florida Holocaust Museum

The **Florida Holocaust Museum** (55 5th St. S., St. Petersburg, 727/820-0100, www.flholocaustmuseum.org, 10am-5pm daily, $16 adults, $14 seniors, $10 college students, $8 under age 18) is the third largest of its kind in the United States. Part of the museum is devoted to the memory of the millions of victims of the Holocaust, and it also showcases loosely linked exhibits, such as the work of Czech artist Charles Pachner (who lost his whole family during the war) or the mixed-media paintings, sculptures, and installations of contemporary French artist Marc Ash.

The Morean Arts Center

The arts are booming in St. Petersburg, especially visual arts. Opened in 2010, the 5,000 square feet of gallery space at the **Chihuly Collection at the Morean Arts Center** (719 Central Ave., 727/822 7872, 10am-5pm Mon.-Sat., noon-5pm Sun., $20) is a beautiful showcase for the Seattle glassblower's eccentric work. The center is divided into six small galleries, plus classroom space for ceramics, painting, drawing, digital imaging, photography, printmaking, jewelry making, metalworking, and sculpture classes.

Great Explorations

After spending time at Sunken Gardens, give the kids their due next door at **Great Explorations** (1925 4th St. N., St. Petersburg, 727/821-8992, www.greatex.org, 10am-4:30pm Mon.-Sat., noon-4:30pm Sun., $10, $9 seniors, free under age 2). The hands-on science center has lots of slick educational exhibits on things like the hydrologic cycle or ecosystem of the estuary. Many of the exhibits are best appreciated by kids up to about age 11, but exhibits such as Gears and the Laser Harp have appeal even to older kids. If your family enjoys hands-on science museums, head over to Tampa's MOSI for a bigger dose.

The St. Petersburg Pier

As of 2017, **The Pier** (800 2nd Ave. NE, St. Petersburg, 727/895-7437) is undergoing a massive renovation that will bring more waterfront commerce space and extend the park along the shoreline. When it's finished, you'll be able to rent bikes, grab a rental rod and reel and fish off the end, visit the little aquarium, dine in the family-friendly food court, or browse the complex's many shops. During renovation, you can still depart from the marina on a sightseeing boat charter, or see a flick at the 20-screen movie theater nearby.

ST. PETE BEACH AND GULFPORT
Dolphin Landings

Farther south, **Dolphin Landings** (4737 Gulf Blvd., behind the Dolphin Village Shopping Center, St. Pete Beach, 727/360-7411, www.dolphinlandings.com, sailing times vary, $25-35) conducts two-hour dolphin-watch cruises and longer three- to four-hour trips to Shell Key, an undeveloped barrier island. The scheduled trips and private charters are conducted on one of 40 locally owned sailboats, pontoon boats, and deep-sea fishing yachts.

CLEARWATER, CLEARWATER BEACH, AND DUNEDIN
Clearwater Marine Aquarium

Just over the bay in Tampa, the Florida Aquarium usually gets most of the visitors. **Clearwater Marine Aquarium** (249 Windward Passage, Clearwater, 727/441-1790, www.seewinter.com, 10am-6pm daily, $22 adults, $20 seniors, $17 ages 3-12) is a smaller, more modest facility. Reopened in 2008 after some major renovations, it's a working research facility and home to rescued and recuperating dolphins, whales, and otters, among other marine mammals, including Winter, the dolphin that lost her tail and was made famous in the Disney movie *Dolphin Tales*. For the visitor, the thrust is

education, with hourly animal care and training presentations and exhibits on animal rescue, rehabilitation, and release—and how the public can help to protect and conserve endangered marinelife. The aquarium offers on-site feeding and care programs for interested visitors and operates a daily 90-minute **Sea Life Safari** (25 Causeway Blvd., Slip 58, Clearwater Beach, 727/462-2628, $26 adults, $23 seniors, $17 children) that takes visitors around the Clearwater estuary and Intracoastal Waterway with commentary by a marine biologist.

Captain Memo's Original Pirate Cruise

Bilgewater Bill, Mad Dog Mike, Gangplank Gary, and the other pirates will greet you with an "argh, me matey" on the deck of **Captain Memo's Original Pirate Cruise** (25 Causeway Blvd., Dock 3, Clearwater Beach, 727/446-2587, www.captainmemo.com, 10am, 2pm, and sunset daily, $36 adults, $33 seniors, $28 ages 3-12, $11 under age 3), a two-hour pirate cruise on a fancy bright-red pirate ship.

Celebration Station

If you're looking for something a little more exciting, **Celebration Station** (24546 U.S. 19 N., Clearwater, 727/791-1799, www.celebrationstation.com, 11am-9pm Sun.-Thurs., 11am-11pm Fri., 10am-11pm Sat., prices vary by activity) brings you go-karts, bumper boats, games, miniature golf, batting cages, laser tag, and pizza.

GREATER PINELLAS COUNTY
Beach Art Center

Beach Art Center (1515 Bay Palm Blvd., Indian Rocks Beach, 727/596-4331, 9am-5pm Mon.-Thurs., 10am-4 Fri., class and exhibit fees vary) is another sweet nonprofit arts center with classes for locals in fine arts and crafts. It also has two small galleries set up in the old American Legion Hall.

Dunedin Fine Art Center & Children's Art Museum

The **Dunedin Fine Art Center & Children's Art Museum** (1143 Michigan Blvd., Dunedin, 727/298-3322, www.dfac.org, 10am-5pm Mon.-Fri., 10am-2pm Sat., 1pm-4pm Sun., class and exhibit fees vary) has four galleries, studio classrooms, a children's museum, the Palm Cafe, and a gallery gift shop. The exhibits are often the work of students.

Heritage Village

Beyond these, the history buff can visit the restored homes and buildings of the **Heritage Village** (11909 125th St. N., Largo, 727/582-2123, www.pinellascounty.org, 10am-4pm Wed.-Sat., 1pm-4pm Sun., free). It's a living history museum with people in period costume, spinning, weaving, and acting out other period activities. Most of the 25 structures date back to the late 19th century.

Florida Botanical Gardens

If you go to Heritage Village, make a day of it and visit the **Florida Botanical Gardens** (12520 Ulmerton Rd., Largo, 727/582-2100, www.flbg.org, 7am-sunset daily, garden entry free, tours $20 pp), where you can take a tour through gardens led by a local master gardener. You walk 1.5 miles, it takes 1.5 hours, and you learn all about Florida gardening. The approaches can be vastly different—there's a rose garden, a beach garden, a tropical courtyard, a topiary garden, a bromeliad garden, and more. On a nice day, it's a wonderful spot. Call ahead for tour times and reservations, which are required.

Tarpon Springs Aquarium

Smaller, more like a really big pet store, the **Tarpon Springs Aquarium** (850 Dodecanese Blvd., Tarpon Springs, 727/938-5378, www.tarponspringsaquarium.com, 10am-5pm Mon.-Sat., noon-5pm Sun., $7.75 adults, $7 seniors, $5.75 children, free under age 4) has a 120,000-gallon main tank aquarium with more than 30 species of fish, including nurse sharks, bonnet head sharks, snook, tarpon, and protected goliath grouper. The best time to visit is shark or alligator feeding times: alligators at 12:30pm and 3:30pm daily; sharks at 11:30am, 1pm, 2:30pm, and 4pm daily.

Safety Harbor Mound

Pinellas County's rich Native American heritage is not very noticeable today—but there are a couple of sites that command quite a bit

Captain Memo's Original Pirate Cruise ship heads out of the marina.

Soaking Up Greek Culture

Tarpon Springs, a coastal town 15 miles north of Clearwater, has a storied past. John Corcoris, a sponge diver from Greece, brought his capabilities along with his sponge-diving equipment (a rubber suit and a heavy copper helmet) to Tarpon Springs around 1900. Soon he persuaded friends and family, sponge divers all, to relocate from Hydra and Aegena, Greece, to this little Florida backwater.

sponges for sale in Tarpon Springs

A booming town of Greek restaurants, Greek Orthodox churches, and Greek festivals was born, centering on the sponge industry. Tarpon Springs was the largest U.S. sponge-diving port in the 1930s. The town is still more than one-third Greek, with a nice Old Florida charm and several fine restaurants. Sponges are still everywhere, but most of them are now imported from more sponge-rich lands.

Take an afternoon to see **Spongeorama** (510 Dodecanese Blvd., 727/943-2164, 10am-6pm Mon.-Sat., 11:30am-6pm Sun., free), an attraction that has displays of sponge divers and shows an interesting movie called *Men and the Sea*. Visit the sponge docks, shop a little, and have dinner.

If you're still angling for more sponge action, the **St. Nicholas Boat Line** (693 Dodecanese Blvd., 727/942-6425, $6 adults, $2 ages 6-12, free under age 6) offers a fun 30-minute narrated boat cruise through the sponge docks, with its own sponge-diving demonstration.

Out on the main drag, Dodecanese Boulevard, there are seven blocks of shops and restaurants. Before you settle on a place to eat, stop into nearby **St. Nicholas Church** (36 N. Pinellas Ave., 727/937-3540), made of 60 tons of Greek marble. The church is a copy of the Byzantine Revival St. Sophia in Constantinople, with beautiful Czech chandeliers and stained glass.

If the weather's nice, stroll along one of the paths in nearby **Anclote River Park** (1119 Baileys Bluff Rd., Holiday, 727/938-2598, dawn-dusk daily, free). The park boasts an easy two-mile round-trip trail, as well as fishing access, a boat ramp, a playground for the kids, a swimming beach, and picnic facilities. It's also a notable destination for birders—favored for its resident reddish egrets and osprey nests. Actually, it's part of a cluster of parks on the Great Florida Birding Trail, along with the nearby **Key Vista Nature Park** (2700 Baileys Bluff Rd., Holiday, 727/938-2598, dawn-dusk daily, $2 parking), which has even more diverse natural habitats, from fresh- and saltwater marshes to pine uplands and tidal flats, all the better for observing species like loons and migratory warblers.

So now you're hungry. Everyone has a different favorite Greek restaurant here. One favorite is **Hellas Restaurant and Bakery** (785 Dodecanese Blvd., 727/943-2400, 11am-10pm daily, $10-20), a lively spot with a full bar and a wonderful Greek bakery attached to it. The best entrée is its slowly braised tomatoey lamb shanks. There are addictive garlic shrimp, gyros in warm Greek pita, and a delicious Greek salad. Others swear by **Mykonos** (628 Dodecanese Blvd., 727/934-4306, 11am-10pm daily, $10-20) for the lamb chops, Greek meatloaf, and the slightly more upscale atmosphere. Still, **Mama's** (735 Dodecanese Blvd., 727/944-2888, 11am-10pm daily, $7-14) often gets the nod for casual family-friendly booths and delicious but messy chicken souvlaki sandwiches.

For more information about Tarpon Springs, contact the **Tarpon Springs Cultural Center** (101 Pinellas Ave., 727/942-5605, www.tarponarts.com) or the **Chamber of Commerce** (111 E. Tarpon Ave., 727/937-6109, www.tarponspringschamber.com).

of enthusiasm among history buffs. One is a platform mound in a beautiful country park called both the **Safety Harbor Mound** and the **Philippe Park Temple Mound** (2525 Philippe Pkwy., Safety Harbor, 727/669-1947, 7am-sunset daily, free). The mound is behind shelter number 2 and is described with interpretive markers. The large mound complex is believed to be the village of Tocobaga, for which the Tocobaga people are named. It is said that in 1567 Pedro Menéndez de Avilés, the founder of St. Augustine, visited this Tocobaga village. For a little more insight, two miles south of Philippe Park is the **Safety Harbor Museum of Regional History** (329 S. Bayshore Dr., 727/724-1562, 11am-4pm Tues.-Fri., 10am-2pm Sat., free), which contains artifacts from the Weedon Island, Safety Harbor, and Mississippian periods.

Pinellas Point Temple Mound

Seeing more Tocobaga handiwork requires only a short drive to the **Pinellas Point Temple Mound** (7am-sunset daily, free). The large flat mound, topped by a comfy bench, is all that remains of a sizable village. To get here, head east on 62nd Avenue South and turn south onto 20th Street, which ends at the mound.

John's Pass Village & Boardwalk

In a similar vein, **John's Pass Village & Boardwalk** (12901 Gulf Blvd. E., between Madeira Beach and Treasure Island, 727/423-7824, www.boattoursjohnspass.com) offers a **Pirate Ship at John's Pass cruise** (11am, 2pm, and sunset daily, $35 adults, $30 seniors, $25 ages 2-20, $10 under age 2) on a fully outfitted pirate ship. You'll engage in water pistol battles and treasure hunts and listen to pirate stories.

John's Pass Village is home to a large commercial and charter fishing fleet, as well as art galleries, restaurants, and boutiques along a waterfront boardwalk. Families also enjoy the dolphin tours out of John's Pass and into scenic Boca Ciega Bay. A couple of companies offer these; **Hubbard's Sea Adventures dolphin tours** (departs from John's Pass boardwalk, 727/398-6577, www.hubbardsmarina.com, 1pm, 3pm, and 5pm daily spring-summer, 1pm and 3pm daily fall, $20 adults, $10 ages 2-11, free under age 2) brings you face-to-face with the bay's abundance of wildlife.

David L. Mason Children's Art Museum

Artistically inclined kids might enjoy visiting Dunedin Fine Art Center, which contains the **David L. Mason Children's Art Museum** (1143 Michigan Blvd., Dunedin, 727/298-3322, www.dfac.org, 10am-5pm Mon.-Fri., 10am-2pm Sat., 1pm-4pm Sun., $4, $3 seniors, free under age 3), a gallery space for children. This smaller part of the museum provides hands-on activities that assist families in understanding and appreciating the work of Florida artists exhibited in the galleries. Even if you spend your time in the art center and not the children's museum, the scale is such that it's not intimidating or boring for kids.

Beaches

The beaches of Clearwater and St. Pete are textbook stretches of white sand and clear, warm Gulf water, with lots of comfy beachside hotels and waterside amenities for families. The area is home to a couple of world-class beach destinations, the kinds of places that often make Dr. Stephen Leatherman's (Dr. Beach has been ranking the nation's beaches for 12 years) annual top 10 list.

★ St. Pete Beach

St. Pete Beach has a lot of low-rise pastel motels and its fair share of high-rise hotel towers. For some reason you'll run into a lot of European travelers here; it has a livelier vibe than many Gulf Coast beaches, but not quite the spring break magnitude of Panama City Beach and other popular party spots. It is also a popular destination for families, and the resorts and hotels in the area commonly provide great children's amenities and entertainment to keep them occupied and having a good time.

The beach itself is long and wide, mostly as a result of sand restoration projects, with plenty of room to spread out and find a private patch of sand on the Gulf. There are concessions, picnic tables, lots of parking, showers, and restrooms.

★ Clearwater Beach

A fairly urban city beach, **Clearwater Beach** (west on Hwy. 60), the only Pinellas County beach with year-round lifeguards (9:30am-4:30pm daily) is a long, wide stretch offering showers, restrooms, concessions, cabanas, umbrella rentals, volleyball, and metered parking. **Pier 60,** where the beach meets the causeway, is the locus of lots of local revelry and activity—during the day it's a heavily trafficked fishing pier, while at night the focus is **Sunsets at Pier 60,** a festival that runs every evening two hours before sunset to two hours past sunset, with crafts, magicians, and musicians vying for your attention with the showy sunset display over the Gulf of Mexico. Pier 60 contains a covered playground for the little ones, who will also like catching the bright-red **Jolley Trolley** (727/445-1200, www.clearwaterjolleytrolley.

Clearwater Beach

com, $2.25 per ride, $5 unlimited daily pass, free under age 6) from Clearwater Beach back to your hotel, downtown, or Sand Key.

Clearwater Beach has a few rules to follow: No alcohol on the beach. Swim within the "safe bathing limit" area, extending 300 feet west of the high water line and clearly marked by buoys or pilings. Personal watercraft and boats are not allowed within this area.

★ Fort De Soto Park

South of St. Petersburg, **Fort De Soto Park** (3500 Pinellas Bayway S., Tierra Verde, 727/582-2267, www.pinellascounty.org, sunrise-sunset daily, parking $5 per vehicle, free for pedestrians and bicyclists) is 1,136 unspoiled acres with seven miles of beaches, two fishing piers, picnic and camping areas, a small history museum, and a 2,000-foot barrier-free nature trail for guests with disabilities set on five little interconnected islands. The fort itself is in the southwest corner of Mullet Key, and there's a toll ($0.85) on the bridges leading into the park. The islands were once inhabited by the Tocobaga people and visited by Spanish explorers. It was surveyed by Robert E. Lee before the Civil War, and during the war Union troops had a detachment on both Egmont and Mullet Keys. The fort was built in 1898 to protect Tampa Bay during the Spanish-American War and is listed on the National Register of Historic Places. And during World War II, the island was used for bombing practice by the pilot who dropped the bomb on Hiroshima. But you thought we were talking about beaches, right?

Well, exploring the old fort is part of what makes this experience special, drawing more than 2.7 million visitors annually. After checking out the four 12-inch seacoast rifled mortars (the only ones of their kind in the United States), head over to one of the two swim centers, the better of which is the North Beach Swim Center (it has concessions). At the beach you're likely to see laughing gulls, ibis, and ospreys, as well as beach sunflowers and beach morning glories peeking out from the sea oats. Fishing enthusiasts can choose between the 500-foot-long pier on the Tampa Bay side or the 1,000-foot-long pier on the Gulf side. Each has a food and bait concession.

Once in the park, take a right at the stop sign, go one mile, and on the right look for **United Park Services** (3500 Pinellas Bayway S., Tierra Verde, 727/864-1376, 10am-5pm daily, last rental 3:30pm). It issues maps of the area and rents out single kayaks ($23 for 1 hour, $29 for 2 hours) and canoes ($30 for 1 hour, $40 for 2 hours). Bicycle rentals ($8 per hour) are available inside the park. Numbered signs along the shore mark a 2.25-mile kayak trail through Mullet Key Bayou.

Fort De Soto Park has the best **camping** ($33-40 tent sites, $40-46 RV sites) in the area, with campsites right on the Gulf. The problem for visitors is that most of the 236 campsites require reservations, which must be made *in person* far in advance. I figure it's a way to give locals the benefit of first pick. There are a handful of walk-in campsites available, but they are in high demand. All sites have water and electrical hookups, and there are modern restrooms, dump stations, a camp store, washers and dryers, and grills. Primitive campsites are available at the Shell Key Preserve area of the park. Permits to camp at this primitive area are free and must be obtained from the park office in person. Pets are allowed in Area 2, and some of the spots are directly on the water. Be advised that the resident raccoons are more skillful than most, able to pick cooler locks and unwrap lunch meat with ease.

★ Honeymoon Island and Caladesi Island Beaches

Honeymoon Island and Caladesi Island are a double whammy, perfectly suited to visiting back-to-back. In fact, the two islands were once part of a single larger barrier island, split in half during a savage hurricane in 1921. Together, they offer nearly 1,000 acres of mostly undeveloped land, not too changed from how it looked when Spanish explorers surveyed the coast in the mid-1500s.

The Tocobaga people were the first known

residents of Honeymoon Island, with settlements in more recent centuries having been quashed by deadly hurricanes. First known as Sand Island, then more inelegantly as Hog Island, it got its current name in the 1940s when marketers tried to pitch it as a retreat for newlyweds, with little palm-thatched bungalows and cottages. It didn't quite take, foiled also by World War II, and the island went through several owners before becoming a state park.

After a huge beach replenishment project in 2007, **Honeymoon Island** (1 Causeway Blvd., west end of Hwy. 586, Dunedin, 727/469-5942, 8am-sunset daily, $8 per car for up to 8 people, $4 per car with a single driver, $2 pedestrians and bicyclists) offers visitors all kinds of fun activities, but especially good is the fishing—you're likely to catch flounder, snook, trout, redfish, snapper, whiting, sheepshead, and, occasionally, tarpon. The island is home to 208 species of plants and a wealth of shore and wading birds, including a few endangered bird species. There is also a popular pet beach worth visiting if you're traveling with your pet.

Directly to the south of Honeymoon and accessible only by boat, **Caladesi** (727/469-5918, hourly ferry service 8am-sunset daily from Honeymoon, $14 adults, $7 children) is the wilder of the two islands. There's the state park marina and swim beach near where the ferry drops you, but the rest of the island remains undeveloped. The Gulf side of the island has three miles of white-sand beach, which always makes the top rankings for beaches; the Tampa Bay side has a mangrove shoreline and sea grass flats. So, the Gulf side is for swimming and beach lolling, and the bay side is for birding and wildlife-watching.

If you're a strong kayaker or sailor, you might take advantage of the kayak and sailboat rentals on the causeway near Honeymoon Island. Once on Caladesi, there's a 3.5-mile canoe trail starting and ending at the south end of the marina that leads paddlers through mangrove canals and tunnels and along sea grass flats on the bay side of the island.

Two cautions about Caladesi: Don't miss the last ferry, or you'll be stuck. And if you brought a dog over to the dog beach at Honeymoon, Caladesi doesn't allow pets on the ferry. If you go by private boat, pets are allowed on a leash.

OTHER BEACHES

There are several good beaches along **Sand Key,** which contains eight communities between John's Pass and Clearwater Pass. **John's Pass Beach,** at the southern end of Sand Key, and north for a couple of miles in **Madeira Beach** have beautiful sand and good fishing. Going north, the beaches in **Redington Beach** have limited public access but are pretty. Still farther north, **Indian Rocks Beach** has good public access and a party vibe, with lively beach bars. Bypass the beaches in **Belleair,** as access and amenities are limited, in favor of an afternoon at **Sand Key County Park** (north end of Gulf Blvd. at Clearwater Pass, 727/588-4852, parking $5 per vehicle), which has lifeguards, playgrounds, cabana rentals, and lots of wide white-sand beach.

Sports and Recreation

GARDENS AND PARKS
★ Sunken Gardens

The four-acre, 100-year-old **Sunken Gardens** (1825 4th St. N., St. Petersburg, 727/551-3102, www.sunkengardens.org, 10am-4:30pm Mon.-Sat., noon-4:30pm Sun., $10 adults, $8 seniors, $4 ages 2-11) was snatched from the jaws of death in 1999 and nursed back to health with $3 million from the city of St. Petersburg. There are 50,000 tropical plants and flowers, demonstration gardens, a 200-year-old oak tree, cascading waterfalls, and flamingos.

It's more than a garden—it's St. Petersburg's most beloved Old Florida attraction. In 1903, a plumber named George Turner Sr. bought the property, which contained a large sinkhole and a shallow lake. By dint of effort and a huge maze of clay tile, he drained the lake and prepared the soil for gardening. He sold the tropical fruit he grew here at a roadside stand, but folks liked walking through the tranquil greenery so much that he started charging admission. By 1935 the garden was officially opened as Turner's Sunken Gardens (because of the former lake and sinkhole, the whole thing sits low in a basin), attracting approximately 300,000 visitors per year. It was followed by some other attractions: the World's Largest Gift Shop and the King of Kings Wax Museum.

But, as is common for these kinds of Florida attractions, business fell off as more upscale attractions became popular in the area. It poked along until the city felt compelled to help, also restoring the gift shop and wax museum space to its former glory; the children's museum **Great Explorations** (1925 4th St. N., 727/821-8992, www.greatex.org, 10am-4:30pm Mon.-Sat., noon-4:30pm Sun., $10, $9 seniors, free under age 2) is housed here. If you're only able to visit one attraction here, make it Sunken Gardens. It is beautiful and a slice of local history—a must if you can tear yourself away from the beach.

Brooker Creek Preserve

For an outdoors experience, drive up to **Brooker Creek Preserve** (3940 Keystone Rd., Tarpon Springs, 727/453-6800, www.brookercreekpreserve.org, trail sunrise-sunset daily). It's an 8,700-acre wilderness in the northern section of the county near Tarpon Springs. Currently, its environmental education center offers four miles of self-guided hiking trails at the southern end of Lora Lane off Keystone Road, about 0.5 miles east of East Lake Road. The preserve also offers guided hikes every Saturday (reservation required, by phone or online) and hosts the annual **Music Jamboree** in October, a multi-genre acoustic jam session where musicians are encouraged to bring their instruments and join the fun.

Weedon Island Preserve Cultural and Natural History Center

Extending along the west side of Tampa Bay in Pinellas County, **Weedon Island Preserve Cultural and Natural History Center** (1800 Weedon Island Dr., St. Petersburg, 727/453-6500, www.weedonislandpreserve.org, preserve 7am-sunset daily, cultural center 9am-4pm Thurs.-Sat., 11am-4pm Sun., free) is hard to classify. The group of low-lying islands in north St. Petersburg was home to Timucua and Manasota people as long as 10,000 years ago. The largest estuarine preserve in the county, it is also home to a large shell midden and burial mound complex. Visitors to the cultural center can see artifacts excavated from the site by the Smithsonian in the 1920s in exhibits designed collaboratively by anthropologists, historians, and Native Americans.

But you can't spend all your time at the cultural center watching videos about the art and history of the early peoples of Weedon Island—the park has a four-mile canoe trail loop, a boardwalk and observation tower, three gentle miles of hiking trails, a fishing pier (snook, redfish, spotted trout), and waterfront picnic facilities. Weedon Island Preserve Center offers guided nature hikes every Saturday and regularly scheduled guided canoe excursions (registration 727/453-6506).

Egmont Key State Park

Accessible only by ferry or private boat, at the mouth of Tampa Bay, **Egmont Key State Park** (4905 34th St., St. Petersburg, 727/893-2627, www.floridastateparks.org, 8am-sunset daily, free) makes a great day trip. There aren't a lot of facilities on the island, which is wilderness except for the ruins of historic **Fort Dade** and brick paths that remain from when it was an active community with 300 residents. You'll see the 150-year-old working lighthouse, constructed in 1858 to "withstand any storm" after a first one was ravaged by hurricanes in 1848 and 1852, as well as gun batteries built in 1898, a pretty stretch of beach, and lots of gopher tortoises and hummingbirds. There is no camping on Egmont Key.

Snead Island

Owned by the state of Florida and maintained by the Manatee County Conservation Lands Management team, **Snead Island** (941/776-2295, 8am-sunset daily, free) is just east of Egmont Key, and another good opportunity to get out into the wilderness of this area—15 miles of it bordering shoreline along the Gulf and the lovely Manatee River. The park is favored by hikers because of its variety of trails and loops, with occasional boardwalks hugging the waterways. To get there, take Highway 41 to Palmetto, turn right onto 10th Street West, and follow signs to the island.

Emerson Point Preserve

The west end of Snead Island is home to **Emerson Point Preserve** (5801 17th St. W., Palmetto, 941/721-6885, 8am-sunset daily, free), worth tacking on to your adventure—the park's 195 acres of salt marshes, beaches, mangrove swamp, lagoons, grass flats, hardwood hammocks, and semi-upland wooded areas are viewable from a well-maintained eight-foot-wide shell path, as well as more rustic walking and biking paths. Manatee County has poured money into this park in recent years such that master gardeners convene here regularly for guided walking tours of the varied plant and animal life. Call for the tour schedule.

Of special note to Native American history buffs, Emerson Point Park is home to the **Portavant Temple Mound** (east end of 17th St. W., Snead Island), an impressive mound complex. Walkways and boardwalks take you over and around a huge 150-foot flat-top temple mound and several horseshoe-shaped shell middens. Interpretive markers describe the site.

Anclote Key Preserve State Park

Anclote Key Preserve State Park (1 Causeway Blvd., Dunedin, 727/469-5943, 8am-sunset daily, free) is a similar island preserve accessible by boat, but Anclote Key offers primitive camping and is pet-friendly. During nesting season, rangers ask pet owners to keep their pets on the southeast end, as protected nesting birds take up residence in the north.

BIKING AND RUNNING

The best way to get oriented in the greater Tampa Bay area is to take a bike ride. **Northeast Cycles** (1114 4th St., St. Petersburg, 727/898-2453, $20 per day, nice road bikes $50 per day) will rent you bikes and a rack for an additional $10 so you can load them up and take them wherever you like, as will **Chainwheel Drive,** with two locations (1770 Drew St., Clearwater, 727/441-2444; Palm Lake Plaza, 32796 U.S. 19 N., Palm Harbor, 727/786-3883; 10am-7pm Mon.-Fri., 10am-5pm Sat., 11am-5pm Sun., hybrid $30 full-day, road bike $40 full-day).

an egret on St. Pete Beach

Now that you've got the bikes, you may want to visit one of the most popular bike trails, the 34-mile-long **Pinellas Trail** (727/464-8400), one of the longest linear parks in the southeastern United States, running essentially from St. Petersburg up to the sponge docks of Tarpon Springs. A rails-to-trails kind of deal, the original rail track was home to the first Orange Belt Railroad train in 1888 and is now a well-maintained, 15-foot-wide trail through parks and coastal areas for cyclists, in-line skaters, and joggers. There is a free guide to the Pinellas Trail available at the trail office, area libraries, and the Pinellas County Courthouse information desk; it can also be downloaded at www.pinellascounty. org—click on Overview Map of the Trail under Mileage Maps. It lists rest stops, service stations, restaurants, pay phones, bike shops, and park areas along the trail.

Note that it is not recommended to visit this trail after dark, especially along the section that travels through the southern part of St. Petersburg where there has been a significant uptick in robberies and crime in the past two years. Officials have increased their patrols of the trail, and the city even installed cameras along certain sections of the trail where crime has been an issue.

BIRDING

Every October, Pinellas County hosts the annual **Florida Birding and Nature Festival** (www.floridabirdingandnaturefestival.com), to which more than 3,000 avid birders flock every year. They come to hear a dynamic array of speakers and attend seminars, but mostly they come to tramp around on field trips to some of the region's top birding and wildlife areas. They come to look for some of the state's rarer bird species, like the reddish egret, little burrowing owls, and the Florida scrub jay, the only bird species unique to Florida.

If you're an avid birder or would like to learn more about birds, go to the **Great Florida Birding Trail** website (www.floridabirdingtrail.com) and print out the West Section guide to the birding trail, which lists 117 sites in 21 counties. Many important birding sites are in Pinellas County.

Brooker Creek Preserve and **East Beach** at Fort De Soto Park are both wonderful for birding. Beyond these, **Shell Key** (southern end of Pass-A-Grille channel, just west of Tierra Verde), an undeveloped 180-acre barrier island only accessible by shuttle or charter boat, is an important place for wintering and nesting seabirds and shorebirds, with more than 100 species sighted. **Boyd Hill Nature Preserve** (1101 Country Club Way S., St. Petersburg, 727/893-7326, 9am-7pm Tues.-Fri., 7am-7pm Sat., 9am-6pm Sun., $3 adults, $1.50 ages 3-16, free under age 3) is 245 acres of pristine Florida wilderness with five distinct ecosystems—hardwood hammocks, sand pine scrub, pine flatwoods, willow marsh, and the Lake Maggiore shoreline. This may be my favorite, as it is incredibly convenient, just minutes from downtown, but nonetheless it feels far from the crowds. Precious green space in an urban landscape, it is an important stopover on the Atlantic Flyway—165

Smokin'

Here's a tricky scenario. You're on a great Gulf Coast vacation, the weather's perfect, you're feeling relaxed, so you decide to do a little charter fishing. You're out on the boat, you feel a yank, and there's a 40-pound greater amberjack on your line. You work for a while and haul in a couple more of those and a whole mess of 20-inch Spanish mackerel. What a great day. My question: Now what? Are you going to take that fish cooler back to the Radisson and stink up the joint?

Here's what to do: Go to **Ted Peters Famous Smoked Fish** (1350 Pasadena Ave., South Pasadena, 727/381-7931, www.tedpetersfish.com, 11:30am-7:30pm Wed.-Mon., $10-23, cash only) and they'll smoke them for you for $1.50 per pound. They can even make kingfish taste good, and that's saying something. They fillet them, throw them over a smoldering red oak fire in the smokehouse, then package them up for you to take. The smoked fish keeps 4-5 days in the fridge.

If you don't have fish to smoke, still go to Ted Peters. An institution for more than 50 years and prized for its laid-back style and inviting picnic tables, the main attraction is smoked fish—try the smoked fish spread with saltines, and the salmon and mullet. Ted Peters also produces some legendary cheeseburgers and potato salad (no fries here). This beer-drinking establishment gets busy in high season and closes early.

bird species have been observed here. You can camp at Boyd, and there's a small educational center with exhibits on the five ecosystems.

Another spot on the Great Florida Birding Trail, also lauded by the National Audubon Society, is **Sawgrass Lake Park** (7400 25th St. N., Pinellas Park, 727/582-2100, 7am-sunset daily, free), immediately west of I-275. Thousands of birds migrate through the park during the fall and spring. A one-mile elevated boardwalk winds through a maple swamp and oak hammock. There's an observation tower with views of the park's swamps, canals, and lake, where you're likely to see wood storks, herons, egrets, and ibis in addition to gators and turtles. The park has naturalist-led nature tours and field trips, and its Anderson Environmental Center contains a large freshwater aquarium and exhibits on the area. My only caution is that during the wet months, the park can get flooded.

If you find an injured bird in your wandering, call **Suncoast Seabird Sanctuary** (18328 Gulf Blvd., Indian Shores, 727/391-6211), one of the country's largest nonprofit wild bird hospitals. With a new hospital facility, the sanctuary rescues and releases hundreds of birds each year into the wild. The

sanctuary offers a free tour at 2pm Wednesday and Sunday, meeting at the beachfront deck.

FISHING
★ Sunshine Skyway Fishing Piers

It must have been a sight to see. In 1980, Hardaway Constructors of Tampa and a demolition team from Baltimore joined forces to perform the largest bridge demolition in Florida history. They were doing away with the 1954 Sunshine Skyway Bridge, a 15-mile crossing from St. Petersburg to Bradenton. From a long causeway on both sides, the steel bridge had a steep cantilever truss, 750 feet wide and with 150 feet of clearance above the water.

It wasn't enough clearance: At least five freighters or barges were roughed up by this bridge, most of them with minor damage, but during a violent storm on May 9, 1980, at 7:38am, when Captain John Lerro's visibility was nil, the empty phosphate freighter *Summit Venture* slammed into the No. 2 south pier of the southbound span. It knocked 1,261 feet out of the center span, the cantilever, and part of the roadway into Tampa Bay. Thirty-five people on the bridge at the time died, most of them in a Greyhound bus headed for

Miami. The only survivor had his truck land by chance on the deck of the *Summit Venture.*

One of the worst bridge disasters in history, it prompted the design, funding, and building of a new **Sunshine Skyway Bridge.** At a cost of $245 million, it's the world's longest cable-stayed bridge, with a main span of 1,200 feet and a vertical clearance of 193 feet. The four-mile bridge opened for business in April 1987, equipped with a bridge protection system involving 36 large concrete bumpers (oddly called dolphins) built to withstand impact from rogue freighters and tankers up to 87,000 tons traveling at 10 knots.

So, you probably think I'm leading up to saying, "It's a gorgeous bridge, a real local landmark, you must drive over this thing." It's all true, but it's only part of the story. During the demolition of the old bridge spans, portions of it were preserved as fishing piers and the rubble piled alongside to form fish-friendly artificial reefs.

Since the original bridge span was built, fisherfolk have been bragging about the variety of game they catch: shark, tarpon, goliath grouper, kingfish, Spanish mackerel, grouper, sea bass. Usually you have to be in a boat to find water deep enough for many of these species. Anglers have caught 1,000-pound tiger sharks from the bridge, traffic honking behind them. And now, with the artificial reefs adding extra enticement to the fish, the Sunshine Skyway Fishing Piers are killer fishing spots.

There's a 0.75-mile-long **North Pier** (727/865-0668) and a 1.5-mile-long **South Pier** (941/729-0117)—together said to be the world's longest fishing pier. You can drive your car onto the pier and park it right next to your fishing spot, parallel parking on the left lane, with room for cars to drive and walkways on either side of the span. There are restrooms on both piers, and bait shops sell live and frozen bait, tackle, drinks, and snacks. They also rent rods. The North Pier has a large picnic area next to the bait shop.

To get here, head south on I-275 toward Bradenton. The North Pier ($4 per vehicle, $4 pp, $2 ages 6-11, free under age 6) is about one mile past the toll gate ($1). To reach the South Pier, continue over the bridge and follow the signs. You don't need a fishing license to fish off the piers.

So drive over the new bridge, but, more importantly, wet a line on the remnants of the old one.

SAILING

For sailing charters, head to St. Pete Beach or Clearwater Beach for the most variety and availability.

Families won't want to miss the opportunity to board the **Pirate Ship at John's Pass** (140 Boardwalk Place W., 727/423-7824, www.boattoursjohnspass.com, $30 over age 64, $35 ages 21-64, $25 ages 3-20, $10 under age 3). It's a recreated pirate ship that departs from the John's Pass Village and Boardwalk on Madeira Beach. The crew dresses up as pirates and will fill your ear with all the "aye, mateys" and "batten down the hatches" you can handle.

The same company also offers 1.5-hour dolphin tours aboard the **Dolphin Quest** (727/392-7090, noon, 2pm, 4pm, and 6pm daily, $19.50 adults, $17.50 seniors, $15 ages 3-20, free under age 3), which departs at the same dock as the Pirate Ship. You're guaranteed to see dolphins, and the onboard narrators will teach you all about Boca Ciega Bay. There are restrooms onboard and the seats are cushioned. Snacks and drinks are available throughout the cruise.

Adults will also enjoy boarding a sailboat for a sightseeing cruise with **Dolphin Landings Charter Boat Center** (4737 Gulf Blvd., 727/367-7411, St. Pete Beach, www.dolphinlandings.com, $35 adults, $25 children, free under age 2). They offer two-hour sailing trips that look for dolphins. The sunset sail is particularly enjoyable. You can bring your own alcoholic drinks, and free soda and bottled water are provided. It's hard to come up with a better way to spend a few hours on St. Pete Beach.

SPECTATOR SPORTS
Baseball

Tropicana Field (1 Tropicana Dr., St. Petersburg, 727/825-3250) is currently home to the Tampa Bay Rays professional baseball team (game days vary, times usually 2:15pm or 7:15pm, tickets $5-32). As a concession to summer temperatures and humidity in these parts, the ballpark has a domed roof (which is lit orange when the Rays win at home) and artificial turf. Out of season, Tropicana Field hosts other athletic events, conventions, trade shows, concerts, and other entertainment, with a seating capacity of 43,773.

For spring training, until 2008 the Rays played locally at Progress Energy Park, home of Al Lang Field. Now the Rays relocate each spring to the **Charlotte County Sports Park,** a grass-surface park with a 7,000 seats located a couple of hours south in Port Charlotte. Don't fret, though, because there's other spring training action nearby. Spring training games run all month in March, and tickets usually go on sale January 15. The **Philadelphia Phillies** have been training at **Bright House Field** (601 Old Coachman Rd., 727/712-4300, game days vary, times usually 1:05pm or 7:05pm, tickets $15-32) in Clearwater since 1948. It's a great venue, with a tiki-hut pavilion in left field, a kids play area, group picnic areas, party suites, and club seats. The **Toronto Blue Jays** also have spring training in the area, playing at **Florida Auto Exchange Stadium** (373 Douglas Ave., Dunedin, 727/733-9302, game days vary, times usually 1:05pm, tickets $13-24), formerly Dunedin Stadium. Built in 1990, it's a smaller ballpark in a fairly residential area; you end up paying almost as much for parking as for your ticket. There are upper and lower sections, the upper section having a slight overhang, which can be cooling during warm day games.

Florida Auto Exchange Stadium

Entertainment and Events

MUSIC

A couple of big venues host a range of performances. **Ruth Eckerd Hall** (1111 McMullen Booth Rd. N., Clearwater, 727/791-7400, www.rutheckerdhall.com) is the locus for much of the area's lively arts activity. The 2,200-seat space was designed by the Frank Lloyd Wright Foundation 25 years ago, and the space still looks fresh, the sound still full and lush; acoustically, it had a fairly recent overhaul. It's home to the **Florida Orchestra** (727/892-3331, www.floridaorchestra.org), the top regional orchestra, performing more than 130 concerts annually here, at the Mahaffey Theater, and elsewhere. Beyond symphonic music, Ruth Eckerd hosts pop acts, visiting theater, and other performing arts. Its educational wing, the **Marcia P. Hoffman School of the Arts,** features the 182-seat Murray Studio Theatre, three studio classrooms, four private teaching studios, a dance studio and rehearsal space, and an arts resource library.

The **Mahaffey Theater at the Duke Energy Center for the Performing Arts** (400 1st St. S., St. Petersburg, 727/892-5798, www.themahaffey.com) changed entirely in 2004 when it was determined that its Bayfront Center Arena was no longer viable in the marketplace. The arena was demolished at the end of that year, opening up space for the current Mahaffey Theater renovation. The $20 million project more than doubled the lobby size and expanded capacity and versatility. The signature component of the renovated theater is a three-story glass-curtain wall and glass-enclosed atrium that overlooks the city's beautiful downtown waterfront. A lovely theater, it hosts the Broadway Across America series, many performances of the Florida Orchestra, jazz, ballet, opera, the circus, and contemporary performers. The Mahaffey is directly on the waterfront, within walking distance of shopping, some of the area's finest restaurants, and many of the downtown museums.

A smaller venue for rock and contemporary acts, **Jannus Live** (200 1st Ave. N., St. Petersburg, 727/565 0550, www.jannuslive.com) is supposedly the oldest outdoor concert venue in Florida. From jam bands like the Allman Brothers to Grizfolk to Lucinda

the historic Coliseum

Williams, it all sounds great from a spot in the outdoor courtyard. It's bigger than a nightclub, with bigger acts, but there's still a cool club vibe and usually a 30s-and-up crowd.

The historic **Coliseum** (535 4th Ave. N., 727/892-5202, $5 parking on the left) was built in 1924 and purchased by the city of St. Petersburg in 1989. It has updated the beautiful space and reopened it as a multiuse facility, hosting a variety of events such as Florida Orchestra pops concerts, the Toronto All Star Big Band, and an exotic bird show.

THEATER

At the top of the dramatic arts heap in Pinellas County, **American Stage Theatre Company at the Raymond James Theatre** (163 3rd St. N., St. Petersburg, 727/823-7529, www.americanstage.org, curtain usually 7:30pm Tues.-Thurs., 8pm Fri.-Sat., 3pm Sat.-Sun., tickets $22-35) is Tampa Bay's oldest professional theater, with a six-play season on the main stage plus children's theater, educational outreach, and the annual Shakespeare in the Park festival.

In its 39th year in 2017, American Stage entered into a partnership with St. Petersburg College and built a brand-new state-of-the-art building in the heart of downtown St. Petersburg, facing Williams Park only four blocks from the original location. The theater has expanded its audience capacity to 182 and added two large lobbies. There is free parking at the nearby Synovis Bank during performances.

For local community theater, several companies are worth checking out, all with reasonable ticket prices. Throughout its 83 years as Florida's oldest continuously operating community theater, **St. Petersburg City Theatre** (4025 31st St. S., St. Petersburg, 727/866-1973, www.spcitytheatre.org, curtain 8pm, 2pm Sun., $15-22) has presented up to six community productions per season, split among musicals, comedies, and dramas, usually crowd-pleasers like *Noises Off* or Neil Simon's *Brighton Beach Memoirs*.

Francis Wilson Playhouse (302 Seminole St., Clearwater, 727/446-1360, www.franciswilsonplayhouse.org, curtain 8pm and 2pm Sun., $26 adults, $15 children and students) is another venerable community playhouse, having opened in 1930. The intimate 182-seat theater showcases eight comedies and musicals per season and a family-oriented program in December.

In the little town of Gulfport on Boca Ciega Bay, the **Catherine Hickman Theater** (5501 27th Ave. S., 727/893-1070) hosts Gulfport Community Players community theater productions and Pinellas Park Civic Orchestra concerts.

FESTIVALS AND EVENTS

In late April, the **Mainsail Art Festival** (www.mainsailart.org) draws over 100,000 visitors to Vinoy Park. More than 250 fine artists display their work and compete for cash prizes, and visitors can peruse or purchase some of the best contemporary art in the country. *Sunshine Artist Magazine* ranked the festival in the top 100 fine art festivals in the country.

In mid-October, music lovers can shake a tail feather at the **Clearwater Jazz Holiday** (www.clearwaterjazz.com). While the festival focuses on jazz artists new and old, the lineup regularly contains plenty of pop and dance groups. In recent years, the Jazz Holiday has hosted acts such as UB40, Kool and the Gang, the beautiful Grace Potter, Sheryl Crow, and the Preservation Hall Jazz Band, straight out of New Orleans. A wide variety of food and drink vendors also congregate downtown at the waterfront Coachman Park.

In April, a bit north of Clearwater, you can visit Scotland in spirit at the **Dunedin Highland Games and Festival** (www.dunedinhighlandgames.com). You can watch Scottish athletes compete in traditional Highland games, such as tipping the caber and shot put, or listen to traditional Scottish musicians compete for prizes.

Nightlife

DOWNTOWN ST. PETERSBURG
Bars and Pubs

For something fun and memorable, hop aboard the **PedalPub St Pete** (1975 3rd Ave. S., 727/581-3388, www.pedalpubstpete.com, $30 pp), a 2-hour tour through the city on a 16-person bicycle. The party bike pedals to three local breweries. Patrons can choose from a list of routes and stops that include Pinellas Ale Works, Green Bench, and Ferg's. It's a rollicking good time, and you'll get some light exercise while you wheel around with brews and cocktails in hand.

Two blocks north of Tropicana Field, you can buy a locally crafted beer before or after the baseball game at **Green Bench Brewing Company** (1133 Baum Ave. N., 727/800-7836, www.greenbenchbrewing.com, noon-10pm Tues.-Thurs., noon-midnight Fri.-Sat., noon-10pm Sun., $5-10). The brewery makes IPAs,

St. Pete Brewing Company

ales, stouts, and a good wheat beer, Skyway Wheat. The most popular is the Green Bench IPA with a citrus flavor and a dry, bitter finish. They show movies once a month and have live music regularly. Check their website for event dates.

Four blocks east of Green Bench Brewery, the **St. Pete Brewing Company** (544 1st Ave N., 727/623-4837, www.stpetebrewingcompany.com, 2pm-10pm Mon.-Thurs., noon-midnight Fri.-Sat., noon-10pm Sun., $5-10) has nearly a dozen brews to choose from and serves a variety of bar snacks, salads, and pizzas. Well-behaved dogs are welcome in the bar, but you may find it hard to keep your pooch from begging for food if you order the pint of bacon ($7). They offer beer flights to taste a sampling of the excellent suds prepared by their brewmaster, John McCracken.

Live Music

For a night of live music, put on your dancing shoes and head to **Jannus Live** (200 1st Ave N. St., 727/565-0550, www.jannuslive.com). The outdoor venue is nestled in a courtyard near the corner of 1st Avenue and 2nd Street North near Williams Park. Focusing on rock, blues, and reggae, the venue has hosted acts like the Red Hot Chili Peppers, Pearl Jam, Cheap Trick, and Ted Nugent. All shows are all-ages and will take place rain or shine. There are several full-service bars that surround the venue, and you can satisfy your munchies with pizza from Joey Brooklyn's Pizza. There are only a few benches for sitting, so be prepared to stand and walk around.

ST. PETE BEACH
Bars and Pubs

One of the most fun and casual beachside bars is **Bongo's Beach Bar and Grill** (5250 Gulf Blvd., 727/360-1811, www.grandplazaflorida.com, 11am-2am daily). Put your toes in the sand and enjoy the waterfront view as you sip tropical drinks at this tiki-style paradise. It's an excellent spot to watch the sunset, and there is live music nearly every night. There is also a menu of hearty burgers, sandwiches, tacos, and seafood, and there are multiple TVs playing sports games. Located at the Grand Plaza Hotel, the place is open to everyone and is a local favorite.

Also in the Grand Plaza Resort, the **Level 11 Rooftop** (5250 Gulf Blvd., 727/360-1811, www.grandplazaflorida.com, 3pm-11pm daily) has 360-degree views of beautiful St. Pete Beach and is located just steps away. After spending the day in the sun, enjoy the sunset with a cocktail and some light bites on the outdoor deck. The cheese board is excellent and the seating is exceptionally comfortable.

In the "dive bar" category, **The Drunken Clam** (46 46th Ave., 727/360-1800, www. drunkenclambar.com, 11am-2am daily) is a small no-frills sports bar. It's a wonderfully kitschy spot to watch a game on the beach or hang out until the wee morning hours with a lively mix of locals and tourists. They have live music many nights a week, and their affordably priced menu features wings, nachos, steamed shrimp, and good burgers. Domestic pitchers are $8.50 and well drinks are $3,

which makes it one of the cheapest spots to drink on this stretch of coast.

Jimmy B's Beach Bar (6200 Gulf Blvd., 727/367-1902, www.beachcomberflorida. com) is a casual bar just steps from the beach at the Beachcomber Beach Resort. The low-rise bar is nestled between two pools at the resort and has spectacular waterfront views. There is live music day and night featuring beach music like reggae, yacht rock, and Jimmy Buffett-style songs. To continue the Key West vibe, you can order coconut shrimp or a slice of key lime pie from their extensive menu with American, Mexican, and Caribbean choices.

CLEARWATER BEACH
Bars and Pubs

Hooters (381 Mandalay Ave., 727/443-7263, www.originalhooters.com, 11am-10pm Sun.-Thurs., 11am-11pm Fri.-Sat.) is exactly what you would expect: cold beer, hot wings, and waitresses wearing short orange shorts. They call it a family restaurant, but use your own judgment. The bar is mostly open-air and located near the end of the main pier, giving it great ocean views. It's an incredibly popular place with a lively scene most nights. Wings are king on this menu, but you'll also

Bongo's Beach Bar and Grill

Market to Market

ST. PETE BEACH

The **Corey Avenue Sunday Market** (Corey Ave. between Boca Ciega Ave. and Gulf Blvd., www.coreyave.com, 10am-2pm Sun. Oct.-May) is a favorite open-air farmers market, featuring local vendors selling fresh produce, plants, home-baked goods, crafts, art, and a variety of ready-to-eat food. During the market hours, the surrounding shops, galleries, and restaurants are also open for business. This is a great stop to pick up a lunch and more on your way to the beach on Sunday morning.

CLEARWATER

The **Pierce Street Market** (2 Drew St., 10am-3pm 2nd and 4th Sat. Oct.-May) happens every 2nd and 4th Saturday near the Clearwater Bridge and Coachman Park. Vendors sell produce, food, jewelry, soaps, clothes, vintage items, flowers, and more in a relaxing, open-air setting near the waterfront. From the market you can take the Clearwater Ferry to Clearwater Beach or the Clearwater Marine Aquarium and save money on parking for the day. If you're having trouble finding it, put Clearwater Harbor Marina in your GPS, and you'll be directed right to it.

DOWNTOWN ST. PETERSBURG

The **Locale Market** (179 2nd Ave. N., 727/523-6300, www.localegourmetmarket.com, $6-17) is a gourmet market and café that sells a wide variety of high-end cheeses, meats, coffees, wine, beer, and raw foods. In the café, you can choose from a huge menu, with burgers, pizza, sushi, and a variety of sweets. All of the ingredients are high-quality and hand selected by the resident chefs and owners. It's a foodie's paradise. I suggest wrapping your hands around a thick burger that has local dry-aged beef, double smoked bacon, grilled mushrooms and onions, and gooey gouda. There's also a large selection of organic, vegetarian, and generally healthy options.

If you love fresh food, visit the **Saturday Morning Market** (101 1st St SE, 727/455-4921, www.saturdaymorningmarket.com, 9am-2pm Sat.) located downtown in the Al Lang Field parking lot. The delightful open-air market has delicious fresh fruits and vegetables as well as food trucks and stands serving a wide variety of food from around the globe. The market includes craft booths, artists, and live music. It's a fun, family atmosphere, and a great way to spend a few hours on Saturday morning.

find burgers, salads, and other American bar regulars. They have daily drink specials, and you can get buckets of five Coronas ($15) every day.

At the south end of Mandalay Park, **Frenchy's Rockaway Grill** (7 Rockaway St., 727/446-4844, www.frenchysonline.com, 11am-midnight Sun.-Thurs., 11am-1am Fri.-Sat.) is a beachfront bar with a sprawling deck and excellent sunset views. The drinks are tropical and fruity and the menu leans toward seafood. Try the she crab soup and the grouper Santorini for lunch or dinner. The margarita and rum runners are good drink choices. There's live music nightly, and inside you'll find pool tables and indoor seating.

The drinks are pricier at the **Pier House 60 Rooftop Bar** (101 Coronado Dr., 855/859-2952, www.pierhouse60.com, noon-midnight daily), but the incredible views make them worth the price. It's a small, intimate place that feels equally suitable for a break from the beach or a romantic glass of wine. It gets quite packed in the evening on weekends and can become standing room only, so be prepared for a crowd if you visit at these times.

Shopping

DOWNTOWN ST. PETERSBURG

Art

The Morean Art Center (719 Central Ave., 727/822-7872, www.moreanartscenter.org, 10am-5pm Mon.-Sat., noon-5pm Sun., $20 adults, $18 seniors, $13 students, free under age 6) houses the incredible glass art collection by the world renowned artist Dale Chihuly. If you don't recognize his name, you'd still most likely recognize his work. His signature pieces are large chandelier-like sculptures with twisted strands of glass that resemble something close to a colorful mass of jellyfish tentacles. A whimsical 20-foot sculpture was produced by Chihuly specifically for the entrance to the gallery. Along with your admission fee you'll have access to a separate glass art gallery and shop that features the work of over 40 local artists, as well as access to live glassblowing demonstrations at the glass art studio.

For more glass art, visit the gallery and shop at **The Duncan McClellan Gallery** (2342 Emerson Ave. S., www.dmglass.com, 855/436-4527, 10am-5pm Tues.-Sat.), west of downtown St. Petersburg in the Art Warehouse district. The 7,800-square-foot warehouse has been transformed from a former fish-packing plant into an impressively beautiful gallery housing the works of over 60 artists, a glass art workshop, and an on-site shop that gives you the opportunity to purchase one of their glass creations. Make sure to check the calendar and visit while there is a glass blowing demonstration happening in the workshop.

Books and Music

Florida's largest new and used bookstore merits a couple of hours of browsing, especially if the weather is inclement (a rarity). The independent **Haslam's Book Store** (2025 Central Ave., St. Petersburg, 727/822-8616, www.haslams.com, 10am-6:30pm Mon.-Sat., noon-5pm Sun.) is now owned by the third generation of the same family and has more than 300,000 volumes. The store has a large number of rare books, and they seem to be really into science fiction.

Shopping Malls and Centers

Sundial St. Pete (153 2nd Ave. N., 727/800-3201, www.sundialstpete.com) is a shopping center near South Straub Park. It features a gourmet market, a movie theater, a day spa, and a variety of retail and health-and-wellness stores.

Tyrone Square Mall (6901 22nd Ave. N., 727/347-3889, 10am-9pm Mon.-Sat., 11am-7pm Sun.), in West St. Petersburg near Azalea park, is a typical indoor mall experience with more than 170 restaurants and shops, including Macy's, Dillard's, JCPenney, and Sears.

Sundial St. Pete shopping center

ST. PETE BEACH
Shopping Malls and Centers

North of St. Pete Beach on Madeira Beach, **John's Pass Village** features more than 100 retailers, restaurants, and attractions. Most of the shops sell beachy souvenirs, clothes and accessories, and surf gear.

Food

Pinellas County is awash in restaurants, most of them fun and casual, many of them worthy of recommendation. Because the area is densely populated and traffic can get congested during high season, you're more likely to grab a bite near where you're staying or near the beach from which you're departing. There are, however, places that are worth a drive in traffic—what restaurateurs call "destination restaurants."

DOWNTOWN ST. PETERSBURG

Remember that downtown St. Petersburg is on the east side of the peninsula, not on the Gulf but on Old Tampa Bay. There are several wonderful picks here—definitely the densest concentration of fine dining in Pinellas County.

American

For a simple burger, go to **El Cap** (3500 4th St. N., 727/521-1314, 11am-11pm Mon.-Sat., 11am-10pm Sun.).

Italian

Mazzaro's Italian Market (2909 22nd Ave. N., 727/321-2400, 9am-6pm Mon.-Fri., 9am-2:30pm Sat., $8-16) comprises a store and a deli-market housed in two separate buildings. The store sells a variety of housewares and Italian themed decor, and the deli serves hot or cold Italian sandwiches on the outdoor patio. Indoors you'll find a large market that sells fresh-roasted coffees, meats, cheeses, handmade pastas, pastries, gelato, gourmet imports, seafood, wine, and beer, most of which are sourced from Italy. It's a wonderfully authentic Mediterranean environment.

Mazzaro's Italian Market

If you love Italian food and culture, this is a must-stop.

Mexican

For some excellen
t Mexican food, try **Red Mesa Cantina** (128 3rd St. S., 727/896-8226, 11am-10pm Sun.-Wed., 11am-11pm Thurs.-Sat., bar until midnight Sun.-Wed., 2am Thurs.-Sat.), which offers a hip menu of regional Mexican and ceviche.

Seafood

Near the pier, you can sit outside on the patio and enjoy the waterfront views beyond North Straub park at **400 Beach Seafood and Tap House** (400 Beach Dr. NE., 727/896-2400, www.400beachseafood.com, 11am-10pm Mon.-Thurs., 11am-11pm Fri.-Sat., 10am-10pm Sun., $17-28). The fare is casual American with great steak and seafood options, and the beer and wine menu are extensive. There is nice outdoor seating and a beautiful dining room indoors with large floor-to-ceiling arched windows. The brunch buffet (10am-3pm Sun., $25) is very popular, offering a wide range of pastries, breakfast items, seafood, and meat.

The **Parkshore Grill** (300 Beach Dr. NE, 727/896-3463, 11am-10pm Mon.-Thurs., 11am-11pm Fri.-Sat., 10am-10pm Sun.), has a wonderful outside patio within sight of the Museum of Fine Arts. The menu leans to smart spins on contemporary American cuisine, with spice-seared tuna and roasted organic salmon fillet. The restaurant has received numerous accolades in recent years, the most remarkable being two Golden Spoon Awards in 2012 and 2013.

ST. PETE BEACH
Breakfast

On the other hand, if you go only to The Hurricane, you'll miss out on the orange-pecan French toast or the creamed chipped beef on toast for breakfast at **Skyway Jack's Restaurant** (2795 34th St. S., 727/867-1907, 5am-3pm daily, $5-10). It's a local classic that once moved because it was on the approach to the Sunshine Skyway Bridge and got pushed out to make room for more lanes. Stick with regular breakfast food or the smoked mullet and you won't be disappointed.

Italian

Located in the Tradewinds Island Grand Resort, the **Palm Court Italian Grill** (5500 Gulf Blvd., 727/367-6461, www.tradewindsresort.com, 11:30am-2pm and 5pm-10pm Mon.-Sat., 11am-2pm Sun., $20-35) serves traditional Italian fare in a beautiful Mediterranean environment. The outdoor courtyard is better for more casual dining, while indoors you'll find an environment more suited to special occasions. The menu is traditional Italian with a variety of seafood, beef, chicken, pasta, and vegetarian options. Try the linguini with Cedar Key clams or the lobster tortellini for the main course. On Sunday, there's an excellent brunch with eggs benedict, fresh shrimp, salad, fruits, desserts, and complimentary Bellinis and mimosas.

Seafood

If you can go to just one place in St. Pete Beach, get the blackened grouper sandwich at ★ **The Hurricane** (really on Pass-A-Grille Beach, 809 Gulf Way, 727/360-9558, 7am-10pm Sun.-Thurs., 7am-11pm Fri.-Sat., $8-24). I don't care if the place seems a little touristy; give me a grouper fillet, add some tomato and lettuce on a bread roll, and that's as good as it gets in Pinellas County. There's a nice bar adjacent to the restaurant and a rooftop sundeck up top for watching the sunset.

The Grand Plaza Hotel has several excellent dining choices, including **Level 11** (5250 Gulf Blvd., www.grandplazaflorida.com, 727/360-1811, 3pm-2am daily, $8-15) on the rooftop of the hotel. Enjoy excellent views of the beach from plush love seats and chairs. This place is great for getting drinks and sharing small plates with a group. The menu is very diverse, with options like seared sea scallops, kebabs, crab-stuffed shrimp, and glazed pork shanks. Try the fig and filet plate, which has pieces of seared filet mignon, prosciutto, and figs. For dessert, the key lime pie or chocolate cake with keokee coffee (brandy, Kahlua, and dark crème de cacao) are always good bets.

Also in the Grand Plaza Hotel, **Spinners Rooftop Revolving Bistro and Lounge** (5250 Gulf Blvd., www.grandplazaflorida. com, 727/360-1811, 11am-11pm daily, $25-40) is a fine-dining restaurant with floor-to-ceiling windows looking out onto the beautiful coastline. The entire restaurant rotates so that diners can see the view from all sides. It takes about an hour and a half to complete a full rotation, so take this into consideration when you're choosing your table. The lunch menu offers salads, wraps, tacos, burgers, sandwiches and a small number of entrées like grilled salmon and bowtie chicken pasta. The dinner menu features a wide selection of mostly steak and seafood entrées with a few chicken dishes as well. Try the steak and shrimp or the coconut crusted mahimahi. The prices are a bit high, but the food is excellent, and the views and experience are worth it.

GULFPORT
American

Like the sound of candied bacon? If so, you might want to try **Little Tommie's Tiki** (5519 Shore Blvd. S., 727/498-8826, 11am-midnight daily, $7-12). The tiki bar has water views and indoor and outdoor seating. It's a great place to go for an ultracasual experience where you can get a drink and watch the sunset. The menu features bar staples like fish tacos, wings, and nachos; the fried pickles and salmon burger are good choices, too. There is a nice selection of brews on tap, several of them local crafts. If you're traveling by boat, you can dock at the marina near the Gulfport Casino.

French and Vietnamese

Gulfport has exploded on the dining scene in the past few years, with worthwhile restaurants lining several blocks. A local favorite is **Alesia Restaurant** (7204 Central Ave., 727/345-9701, 11:30am-2:30pm and 5:30pm-9pm Tues.-Fri., 10am-2:30pm and 5:30pm-9pm Sat., $16-24), which serves up an interesting mix of French and Vietnamese cuisine. It's definitely strange to see ratatouille and Vietnamese pho on the same menu, but the food is so good that the bizarre concept works like a charm.

Italian

A local favorite for Italian food is **Pia's Trattoria** (3054 Beach Blvd. S., 727/327-2190, 4pm-10pm Mon.-Thurs., 4pm-11pm Fri., 11am-11pm Sat., 11am-10pm Sun., $8-20). Try the chicken piccata cooked in a wonderful caper and butter sauce. The lasagna is a lunch specialty and is highly recommended. If the weather is nice, don't miss the charming outdoor patio area.

Southern

One block northeast of Little Tommie's Tiki, **Stella's** (3119 Beach Blvd. S., 727/498-8950, www.stellasingulfport.com, 7am-2pm daily, $6-10) serves a fantastic breakfast, lunch, and brunch any time it's open. It has a casual diner-style setting with nostalgic pictures from around Gulfport on the walls. The outdoor seating area is shaded and a nice spot for people watching and enjoying the Beach Boulevard scenery. The breakfast fare is classic Southern, like shrimp and grits, with a few European options like quiche. The fried green tomato benedict is delicious. For lunch, it's exceptional for sandwiches and burgers. Stella's is dog-friendly—so much so that they give a free dog treat to every pooch that visits, and there is even a dog menu. Like Tommie's, Stella's is within walking distance if you are traveling by boat and would like to dock at the marina near the Casino.

Vegetarian

For a healthy breakfast or lunch, look no further than **Mangia Gourmet** (2930 Beach Blvd. S., 727/321-6264, www.mangiagourmet.com, 8am-3pm Tues., 9am-10pm Wed.-Sat., 10am-8pm Sun., breakfast $6-10, lunch $7-20). It serves healthy breakfast options, wraps, smoothies, bean burgers, salads, soups, and a variety of entrées such as meat lasagna, Mediterranean chicken, and spinach-stuffed Portobello mushroom. Many of the menu items are vegetarian, organic, gluten-free, or vegan. The fresh-squeezed juices are delicious. There are daily specials that are exceptional deals, and the outdoor seating is shaded and comfortable. Look for the little bright-orange building two blocks south of the Gulfport Public Library.

CLEARWATER
American

The **Beach Shanty Café** (397 Mandalay Ave., 727/443-1616, 7am-4pm daily, $4-8) serves remarkably cheap and tasty breakfast featuring classic American staples. They offer breakfast all day, and that's all they offer. The café is sandwiched between two larger buildings right on the main strip of Mandalay Avenue, so don't blink or you may miss it. The interior is much larger than you would expect from the small storefront, and there's a good amount of seating.

the Beach Shanty Café

Clearwater has a fairly dense concentration of good restaurants. But really, you owe it to yourself to go to the original **Hooters** (2800 Gulf to Bay Blvd., 727/797-4008, www.originalhooters.com, 11am-11pm Sun.-Thurs., 11am-midnight Fri.-Sat., $8-20) for some good chicken wings. Almost 25 years old, the original sports-oriented joint has spawned an international empire. It's a family restaurant, really—it's just that the waitresses are wearing flesh-colored pantyhose under orange nylon short-shorts. Use your own judgement.

Breakfast

Lenny's Restaurant (21220 U.S. 19 N., 727/799-0402, 6am-3pm daily, $5-12) is the hands-down winner for breakfast, with Jewish staple blintzes, knishes, and latkes.

Cuban/Spanish

For an upscale Cuban-Spanish lunch or dinner, head to the **Columbia** (1241 Gulf Blvd., 727/596-8400, www.columbiarestaurant.com, 11:30am-10pm daily, $20-35), which started in Ybor City and now has six locations in Florida. The menu has an excellent Cubano sandwich and mojo chicken, as well as great mojitos and sangria. The menu is remarkably large, with plenty of seafood, beef, and chicken dishes, many of them with traditional Spanish preparations. The wine list is excellent, and the *café con leche* is perfection. The dining room is exceptionally elegant, with white tablecloths, large windows that bring in the bright sunlight, exposed dark-wood beams, and tropical plants all around.

Irish

Evening partying is to be found all around, in tiki huts and outdoor decks along the Gulf beaches. One bar, though, is worth mentioning: ★ **O'Keefe's Tavern and Grill** (1219 S. Fort Harrison Ave., 727/442-9034, 7am-midnight Mon.-Fri., 7am-1am Sat., 7am-11pm Sun., $7-14). It is the bar to beat for St. Patrick's Day. The Irish pub's history goes back to the 1960s when it was O'Keefe's Tap

Room, a history still visible despite the many additions and remodelings. A white brick exterior gives way to a comfortable series of rooms decked out with lots of green accents and Irishobilia. The brogue-required bartenders are fast and furious with the beers (there are more than 100 offerings), and the all-ages crowd is unified by their affection for the place. Once known for its "seven-course Irish dinner" (that's six beers and a potato), O'Keefe actually serves really good food.

Seafood

By the way, a *cooter* is a red-bellied turtle that was historically serious eats for early Floridians. That's why **Cooters Restaurant and Bar** (423 Poinsettia Ave., 727/462-2668, www.cooters.com, 11am-11pm Sun.-Thurs., 11am-midnight Fri.-Sat., $9-20) is called that. It's a fun place with good steamed crab legs and fried grouper.

DUNEDIN
American

Located on the bike path that runs through the center of town, **Café Alfresco** (344 Main St., 727/736-4299, www.cafealfresco.com, 11am-9pm Sun.-Thurs., 11am-10pm Fri., 10am-10pm Sat., $12-20) is a perfect stop during a long walk or peddle. They serve a broad range of American, Asian, Italian, and seafood selections for lunch and dinner. With options that include gumbo, egg rolls, meatloaf, chicken curry, and Hawaiian salad, there's really something for everyone, and the food is wonderful. They have a very popular brunch on Friday, Saturday, and Sunday. The best seating, true to the café's name, is outdoors on the large and covered patio.

Grab a bite and a brew at **Dunedin Brewery** (937 Douglas Ave., 727/736-0606, www.dunedinbrewery.com, 11am-11pm Sun.-Tues., 11am-1am Wed.-Thurs., 11am-2am Fri.-Sat., $7-10), a local microbrewery with a large list of original crafts. The most popular drink is their apricot peach ale. Enjoy a casual lunch or dinner with a menu that features salads, wraps, tacos, burritos, burgers, and sandwiches. Live music happens on most weekends and sometimes on Thursdays. Happy hour is 4pm-7pm.

Just as family-friendly, **Kelly's Restaurant** (319 Main St., 727/736-0206, 8am-9:30pm Sun.-Thurs., 8am-10:30pm Fri.-Sat., 8am-9pm Sun., $8-20) has a comfort food menu that leaves no stone unturned, from baby back ribs to butternut squash ravioli. It's a kids' kind of joint, friendly and accommodating.

Café Alfresco in Dunedin

Asian

In Dunedin since 1993, **Ivory Mandarin Bistro** (2192 Main St., 727/734-3998, 11am-9:30pm Mon.-Thurs., 11am-10pm Fri.-Sat., $8-25) has slowly accrued a wall's worth of accolades and "best of" awards along with its devoted clientele. Crisp linens and Chinese floral prints make the place feel more formal, but the menu reads like a greatest-hits list of Cantonese American dishes. That means hot and sour soup, juicy pork spareribs, sweet-tangy orange beef, and pan-fried chow fun noodles.

Mexican

Downtown Dunedin has been reinvigorated with restaurants and cafés in recent years. For casual Mexican, go to **Casa Tina** (365 Main St., 727/734-9226, 11am-10pm Mon.-Thurs., 11am-11pm Fri.-Sat., 10am-10pm Sun., $7-15). It's lively, with an eye-catching color scheme, and the food is a little less heavy than many local Mexican joints—that said, try the wild mushroom quesadilla.

Seafood

A fun place to casually dine in Pinellas County is **Bon Appétit** (148 Marina Plaza, 727/733-2151, 7am-9pm Sun.-Thurs., 7am-10pm Fri.-Sat., $12-35). It's in the Best Western Yacht Harbor Inn and Suites, and owners Peter Keuziger and Karl Heinz Riedl manage to add style to the seafood-heavy menu, whether it's grilled sea scallops with a mango chutney or the season's freshest stone crabs with only a squeeze of lemon and butter. Dine at the **Marine Café** adjacent to the restaurant to watch the dolphins play as the sun sets on the water without breaking the bank. It's a different menu from the fancier Bon Appétit, but a single sheet of signature dishes from the main restaurant is available outside.

If you're looking to dine at a nouvelle restaurant, meaning a place that has high prices for small portions artistically arranged on the plates, **The Black Pearl** (315 Main St., 727/734-3463, 5pm-9pm Sun.-Mon., 5pm-10pm Tues.-Thurs., 5pm-11pm Fri.-Sat.,

$18-30) next door is perfect for you. Try the cedar-planked salmon or the crab imperial.

GREATER PINELLAS COUNTY
Fine Dining

In keeping with the glitz of the historic Vinoy, its restaurant, **Marchand's Grill** (Vinoy Renaissance Resort, 501 5th Ave. NE, St. Petersburg, 727/824-8072, 6:30am-10pm daily, $18-35), features the central Vinoy Bar with velvet armchairs around all tables. A small wine cellar provides an intimate dining space for four. The kitchen has a seafood focus, but dishes reflect a more Mediterranean approach. If you want to pull out all the stops at the Vinoy, **Fred's Steakhouse** is even more of a splurge, but you have to be a member or a resort guest to enjoy it.

The ★ **Cafe Ponte** (13505 Icot Blvd., Clearwater, 727/538-5768, www.cafeponte. com, 11:30am-2pm and 5:30pm-9pm Mon.-Thurs., 11:30am-2pm and 5:30pm-10pm Fri., 5:30pm-10pm Sat., $12-32) features chef Christopher Ponte, who trained at Taillevent in Paris and studied at Johnson & Wales and the Cordon Bleu. His upscale restaurant in the Icot Center is located in a strip mall; the setting may confound would-be diners, but a single meal will set them straight. The kitchen prepares offerings such as a rich mushroom soup with a spoon of truffle cream and a potato-encrusted sea bass.

Maritana Grille at the Don CeSar (3400 Gulf Blvd., St. Pete Beach, 727/360-1882, www. loewshotels.com, 5:30pm-10pm daily, $18-40) has a great chef's table for groups up to eight, at which executive chef Kenny Hunsberger is put through his Floribbean-cuisine paces, from pan-seared scallops served with purple potatoes to grilled filet mignon with truffled mashed potatoes and candied shallots. The restaurant's interior is incredible, with the patrons surrounded by 1,500 gallons of saltwater aquariums and indigenous Florida fish.

Seafood

If you're a fan of Jimmy Buffett, check out

the restaurant owned by his sister—**Lulu's Oyster Bar and Tap House** (500 1st St., Indian Rocks Beach, 727/333-7944, www.lulusoysterbar.com, 11am-10pm Sun.-Thurs., 11am-11pm Fri.-Sat., $6-12). The prices are low and the atmosphere is bright, tropical, and whimsical with a classic old-Florida diner feel. The menu is mostly seafood, steak, tacos, and burgers with a few Southern favorites like fried chicken. The seafood is very fresh and the shrimp and oysters are prepared blackened, grilled, fried, or beer battered.

Seabreeze Island Grill (17855 Gulf Blvd., 727/498-8688, 11am-10pm Sun.-Thurs., 11am-midnight Fri.-Sat., $9-21) offers great water views from every seat indoors and on the wraparound deck outside. The atmosphere is upbeat and beachy. The menu features burgers, tacos, steaks, and lots and lots of seafood prepared in a Key West and Caribbean style. Try the coconut shrimp, crab cakes, rum-pineapple chicken, lobster mac and cheese, or the grouper tacos. It's also a good place to just grab a cold beer or a tropical cocktail and enjoy the sunset.

Crabby Bill's (401 Gulf Blvd., Indian Rocks Beach, 727/595-4825, www.crabbybillsirb.com, 11am-11pm daily, $8-22) is a family-owned regional chain that has made a name for itself with family-style seating, group singing, seafood cookery, and flowing beverages.

Cafe Alma (111 Boardwalk Place, Madeira Beach, 727/502-5002, 11am-10pm Tues.-Thurs., 11am-midnight Fri., 9am-midnight Sat., 9am-9pm Sun., $16-25) has quickly become a favorite of Madeira Beach after it recently moved from downtown St. Petersburg. The menu underwent major changes and now features a wide variety of small tapas plates and large seafood-centric offerings. They also have wonderful tacos and a selection of tasty lunch sandwiches. If you're looking for a festive vibe, visit in the evening.

Salt Rock Grill (19325 Gulf Blvd., Indian Shores, 727/593-7625, www.saltrockgrill.com, 4pm-10pm Mon.-Thurs., 4pm-11pm Fri.-Sat., noon-10pm Sun., $15-30) is fairly mobbed every night. The menu has enticing seafood, like pan-seared scallops and mussels in white wine sauce, as well as expertly prepared steaks aged in-house and grilled over a super-hot natural oak and citrus wood pit fire. It's more formal than most beachside spots around here, and the locals love it.

Accommodations

DOWNTOWN ST. PETERSBURG
$100-200

Especially for romance seekers, **Mansion House Inn Bed and Breakfast** (105 5th Ave. NE, 727/289-2121, www.mymansioninn.com, $130-230) has 12 rooms set in two Craftsman-style houses, one of which is thought to have been built between 1901 and 1904 by St. Petersburg's first mayor, David Mofett. A courtyard between the houses is perfect for a little reading or downtime. The pool on the property is a plus.

The boutique **Hollander Hotel** (421 4th Ave N., 727/240-2560, www.hollanderhotel. com, $150-200) is in an excellent location downtown, six blocks to the Museum of Fine Arts and the Pier. The hotel also offers a free shuttle to many of the nearby downtown locations. There are queen and king rooms with a balcony option and king and queen suites with a sleeper sofa and an optional full kitchen. The heated pool and terrace area are exceptionally beautiful and full of comfy loungers, chairs, and cabanas. There's a small and stylish bar, coffee shop, bakery, and a wonderful restaurant on-site. The Tap Room serves American and Italian classics.

Find a bit of boutique charm at the **Inn on Third** (342 3rd Ave N., 727/777-6602, www.

theinnonthird.com, $90-150). This small hotel located in the heart of downtown has traditional and stylish decor. The downtown trolley stops right outside the front door, so you'll have convenient access to all of downtown. If you're visiting to see the Tampa Bay Rays, the stadium is only one mile from the hotel, and a free shuttle can be picked up five blocks from the inn. The price is a great deal considering the beautiful rooms, many of them with four-poster beds and antique furnishings, and the delicious complimentary breakfast in the morning. There is also a free wine and beer social 7pm to 9pm in the evenings. With parking and Internet access included in the rates, you can see why this cute inn is a top choice for budget travelers.

Over $300

The ★ **The Vinoy Renaissance Resort & Golf Club** (501 5th Ave. NE, 727/894-1000, www.renaissancehotels.com, $250-600) was built by Pennsylvania oilman Aymer Vinoy Laughner in 1925. At $3.5 million, the Mediterranean Revival-style hotel was the largest construction project in Florida's history. Painstakingly restored in 1992 at a cost of $93 million, the resort is incredible, with 360 guest rooms and 15 suites, many with views of the marina. The hotel also has a spa, a lovely pool with a waterfall, five restaurants, tennis courts, and an 18-hole golf course designed by Ron Garl. It hosts its own marina and is listed on the National Register of Historic Places.

ST. PETE BEACH
$100-200

If you're searching for the absolute best value on the beach, then look no further than **Gulf Tides Inn** (600 68th Ave., 727/367-2979, www.gulftidesinn.com, efficiencies $89, $650 weekly, $2,350 monthly, apartments $109, $650 weekly, $2,350 monthly). This small motel has 10 units, and you can choose between an apartment with a private bedroom or a studio. All rooms are equipped with a full kitchen. There's nothing fancy about

the Inn on Third

the place, and some may find the decor and furnishings dated, but it has an old-Florida charm that gives it a hip retro feel. The inn is on a quiet street, and there's a heated pool. There are excellent weekly and monthly rates available as well.

For families, the **TradeWinds Island Resorts** (5500 Gulf Blvd., 727/367-6461, www.tradewindsresort.com) is the way to go, with a variety of lodging at the **TradeWinds Island Grand** ($150-450) and the new **Guy Harvey Outpost** ($125-200), formerly the Sandpiper Hotel and Suites. Whichever one you choose includes playtime privileges at the other. The Island Grand is the fancier, a four-diamond property with soaring palms and a grand lobby. The whole complex offers multiple pools, a dozen places to eat and drink, multiple fitness centers, tennis courts, a pedal-boat canal, and a wide private beach. Right out back you can rent fishing or snorkeling equipment and try parasailing, waterskiing, and water scooters. The tremendous kids program, KONK (Kids Only, No Kidding!), has with seasonal programs like the Swashbucklin' by the Sea pirate package, in which you get to meet Redbeard and walk the plank. For adults there is lively nightlife at the many bars and restaurants and an on-site Beef O'Brady's Sports Bar. To meet other people at the resort, join the fun TradeWinds pub crawl and visit all five of the on-site bars. Happily, the restaurants and bars are mostly affordable.

★ **Sirata Beach Resort** (5300 Gulf Blvd., 727/897-5200, www.sirata.com, $140-350) used to be connected to the TradeWinds but is now a family-run midsize hotel with a range of kids programs and activities. It's the kind of place that locals take the family for a weekend of R&R. Of the 382 rooms, 170 are one-bedroom suites, and most have excellent views of the Gulf. The kid-friendly suites with bunk beds and entertainment centers that include video game consoles are perfect for families, and suites with jetted tubs are available for romantic visits. Enjoy the three beachfront pools and two hot tubs, as well as a relaxing beachside fire pit area.

The Vinoy Renaissance Resort & Golf Club

Nearby, is the ★ **Alden Beach Resort** (5900 Gulf Blvd., 727/360-7081, www.aldenbeachresort.com, $125-250), which is an attentively staffed, family-owned beach resort with 149 suites, especially favored by kids. It has tennis, volleyball, two heated pools (a little far from the beach, so the walk back and forth takes time for little ones), and a video game room. Rooms on the pool side are significantly cheaper than on the Gulf side. In 2013 the resort underwent a renovation that added high-speed Internet and flat-screen TVs to every room. Consider staying in one of their fully equipped one-bedroom suites with kitchenettes and water views. When you're ready to take a break from the beach, relax in their 12-person hot tub or grill up a catch of the day on the gas grills on the elevated deck.

The **Coconut Inn** (113 11th Ave., 941/960-7685, www.pagbeachinns.com, $155-365, $1,000-2,200 weekly) is a charming nonchain option on the southern end of Pass-a-Grille Beach. Located in a historic neighborhood, the inn is just a short walk from the beach. There is a small heated pool and bikes for use. Some of the rooms are rather small, so be sure to ask about the room size when making your reservation. Many of the rooms on the second floor have nice balconies that overlook the pool, but they're a bit pricier. If you're on a budget, ask about the rooms on the lower level.

$200-300

Renovated in 2016, **Inn on the Beach** (1401 Gulf Way, 727/240-2614, www.innonbeach. com, $200-450) has gathered an impressive number of accolades from CNN Travel, Yahoo Travel, and others, and for good reason. This is a classically charming and beautiful Florida seaside inn. In addition to the rooms and suites at the main inn, you can rent a one- or two-bedroom cottage with a patio, full kitchen, and living room. The rooms and cottages are bright and airy, painted in all white with colorful, stylish accents. The inn surrounds a palm tree-filled courtyard, and the beach is just steps away across the road.

Traffic noise usually isn't an issue, as the road is fairly quiet. This is a very popular place, so book in advance.

Over $300

For something more upscale, the huge, unmistakably pink **Don CeSar Hotel** (3400 Gulf Blvd., 727/360-1881, www.loewshotels.com, $250-550) is a landmark in St. Pete and a longtime point of reference on maritime navigation charts. Named after a character in the opera *Maritana,* the Don CeSar hosted F. Scott and Zelda Fitzgerald, Clarence Darrow, Al Capone, Lou Gehrig, and countless other celebrities. Originally opened in 1928, the property was commandeered by the military during World War II and eventually abandoned. These days, it's a Loews hotel, with 340 lovely rooms, fishing, golfing, tennis, and the soothing Beach Club & Spa. Even if you don't stay here, make sure to take the tour and stop in for ice cream at its old-fashioned ice cream parlor.

CLEARWATER
$100-200

In the heart of Clearwater Beach, **Frenchy's Oasis Motel** (423 East Shore Dr., 727/446-6835, www.frenchysoasismotel.com, $139-199, $805-1,095 weekly) is a boutique motel that blends modern furnishings and decor with a retro mid-century Florida vibe. There are 15 one- or two-bedroom units, each with a full kitchen, full-size fridge, and dishes and utensils. It's no more than five minutes' walk to the beach, and there are excellent restaurants, shops, and nightlife nearby. The best rooms are on the second floor at the back of the motel; they have elevated views of the bay and surrounding city lights at night. The property is owned by the Canadian restaurateur and longtime Clearwater resident Michael Preston, who also owns Frenchy's Saltwater Café just down the street.

An excellent value for visits lasting more than a week, the **East Shore Resort** (473 E. Shore Dr., 727/442-3636, www.eastshoreresort.com, $735-1,500 weekly, $2,500-4,600 monthly) is located right on Clearwater Bay, with the beach a five-minute walk away. There are 11 one- and two-bedroom units, all of which have fully equipped kitchens and private porches. Guests also have access to a heated pool as well as bikes, gas grills, and fishing gear that you can use on their pier. The furnishings are basic and beachy, with wicker chairs and tile floors. The service is excellent, and laundry service is included with your stay.

the Don CeSar Hotel

Boats up to 65 feet can also dock at the on-site marina for an additional fee.

Over $300

For beachfront resort-style accommodations, stay at the **Hyatt Regency Clearwater Beach** (301 South Gulfview Blvd., 727/373-1234, www.clearwaterbeach.regency.hyatt.com, $400-1,300). The rooms are remarkably spacious, ranging 600 to 1,100 square feet, making them the largest guest rooms on the beach, and the balconies offer stunning views of the Gulf. All rooms have full kitchens, premium amenities, and included Wi-Fi. The pool area is breathtaking, surrounded by fountains and tropical plants and featuring an elevated view of the Gulf. There is also a poolside bar as well as a spa, a fitness center, and three on-site restaurants. It's good for couples and families alike and certainly the best place to stay directly on the beach.

The first new resort to be built on Clearwater Beach in 25 years, the **Sandpearl Resort** (500 Mandalay Ave., Clearwater, 727/441-2425, www.sandpearl.com, $250-700) is extremely impressive. The combined resort and condominium project features a 253-room hotel, a full-service spa, upscale dining, state-of-the-art meeting and event space, 117 condominium units, and 700 feet of Gulf of Mexico beachfront. Rooms have an open airy feel with balconies, high ceilings, and upscale comfortable furnishings and fixtures. There are 50 one- and two-bedroom suites on the top two floors of the resort.

GREATER PINELLAS COUNTY
$100-200

Another piece of history, but I'm not sure if I'm buying this one, is claimed by **Safety Harbor Resort and Spa** (105 N. Bayshore Dr., 727/726-1161, www.safetyharborspa.com, $95-300). Many places along the Gulf Coast profess to be what Spanish explorer Hernando de Soto identified as the Fountain of Youth. Is it the mineral pools here at this 50,000-square-foot spa and tennis academy?

The waters are nice either way, filling three pools and used in the spa treatments. The resort is also home to a tennis academy, a fine-dining restaurant, and an upscale salon. The 174 guest rooms and suites are spacious and offer nice views of Tampa Bay.

Near the airport, the **Hilton Saint Petersburg Carillon Park** (950 Lake Carillon Dr., 727/540-0050, www.hilton.com, $140-220) is an excellent choice for business travelers and couples looking for quiet. The hotel offers free shuttles to and from the airport and is 10 minutes' drive to downtown. The boardwalk around Lake Carillon is a wonderful spot for a walk in the morning or a stroll at sunset. The heated outdoor infinity pool is a nice bonus. The beautiful dining room at Luna has a modern club feel, like something you may find in Miami, and serves a classic breakfast menu that includes a buffet ($15). For lunch and dinner there are yummy American and Italian entrées.

$200-300

For golfers, **Innisbrook Golf and Spa Resort** (36750 U.S. 19 N., Palm Harbor, 727/942-2000, www.innisbrookgolfresort.com, $120-550) is a 900-acre property just north of Clearwater. It has four top-ranked golf courses, 11 tennis courts, six swimming pools (including the super kids-oriented Loch Ness Monster Pool), a children's recreation center, several restaurants, and 60 acres with jogging and cycling trails. All rooms are suites with fully equipped kitchens. Its Copperhead Golf Course stretches more than 7,300 yards and is home to the PGA Tour's PODS Championship.

VACATION RENTALS

Most of the vacation rentals are found around St. Pete Beach and Clearwater, with the offerings getting thinner the farther you venture away from those two main centers of action. Most rentals in this area are condos that range from the modest to the luxurious, but private homes are available in lesser numbers. Expect to pay $150 to $300 per night, $800 to $2,000 per week. Homes generally cost about 20 percent more. Contact **Florida Beach Rentals** (516 Mandalay Ave., Clearwater, 727/288-2020, www.florida-beachrentals.com), which has extensive offerings throughout the region. For Clearwater rentals, contact **Beach Time Rentals** (800/691-8183, www. beachtimerentals.com).

Information and Services

Clearwater and St. Petersburg are located within the **eastern time zone.** The area code is **727,** but right over the causeway in Tampa the area code is **813,** so you need to dial the area code, but you don't precede the phone number with a 1.

TOURIST INFORMATION

St. Petersburg/Clearwater Area Convention & Visitors Bureau (8200 Bryan Dairy Rd., Largo, 727/464-7200, www. visitstpeteclearwater.com) has a tremendous website. **St. Petersburg Area Chamber of Commerce** (100 2nd Ave. N., Suite 150, 727/821-4069, www.stpete.com, 8am-5pm Mon.-Fri.) has a decent walk-in site with brochures and maps.

The various chambers of commerce have their own websites: **Tarpon Springs** (www. tarponspringschamber.com), **Clearwater** (www.clearwaterflorida.org) and **Clearwater Beach** (www.beachchamber.com), and **Dunedin** (www.dunedin-fl.com), among others. For outdoors information, there's **Clearwater Parks** (www.clearwater-fl. com—see Parks & Recreation under City Departments), **Florida Parks** (www.floridaparks.com), **Pinellas County Parks** (www. pinellascounty.org), and **St. Petersburg Parks** (www.stpeteparksrec.org).

St. Petersburg's largest newspaper is the **Tampa Bay Times** (www.tampabay.com); you'll see kiosks everywhere.

POLICE AND EMERGENCIES

In an emergency, dial 911. For a nonemergency police request, contact the **St. Petersburg Police Department** (1300 1st Ave. N., 727/893-7780). If you need medical assistance, the area has several large hospitals with good emergency care: **St. Petersburg General Hospital** (6500 38th Ave. N., St. Petersburg, 727/384-1414) and **St. Anthony's Hospital** (1200 7th Ave. N., St. Petersburg, 727/825-1100) in the south of the county, and **Largo Medical Center** (201 14th St. SW, Largo, 727/588-5200) in northern Pinellas County.

RADIO AND TELEVISION

Because it's a big metropolitan area, Tampa and St. Pete have an enormous number of radio stations. There's independent radio at **WMNF 88.5 FM,** variety at **WMTX 100.7 FM,** and NPR and classical music at **WUSF 89.7 FM.**

For local television programming, **Bay News 9** is Bright House Networks' 24-hour local news station, **WFLA Channel 8** is the local NBC affiliate, **WTSP Channel 10** is the CBS affiliate, **WTVT Channel 13** is the Fox affiliate, and **WFTS Channel 28** is the local ABC affiliate.

LAUNDRY SERVICES

Many of the larger hotels offer laundry service, as do most marinas in the area. If you find yourself in need of coin-operated laundry in St. Petersburg, try **Wash N' Go Laundry** (4154 Haines Rd. N., 727/522-3074) or **Washboard Coin Laundry** (4211 49th St. N., 727/521-3964). To the north in Clearwater, there's 24-hour laundry at **Thompson's Dry Cleaners and Laundry** (1713 Drew St., 727/461-2589).

Transportation

AIR

The area is served by two midsize, easily traversed airports. **Tampa International Airport** (TPA, 4100 George J. Bean Pkwy., 813/870-8700, www.tampaairport.com) is located just over the bridge and causeway from St. Petersburg and Clearwater and about 30 to 45 minutes from beachfront accommodations. It is served by Air Canada, Alaska, American, British Airways, Cayman Airways, Copa, Delta, Edelweiss Air, Frontier, JetBlue, Lufthansa, Silver, Southwest, Spirit, Sun Country, United, WestJet, and World Atlantic.

You'll probably fly in and out of Tampa, unless you're coming from Canada, but there's also **St. Petersburg-Clearwater International Airport** (PIE, 14700 Terminal Blvd., Clearwater, 727/453-7800), served by Allegiant, Sun Country, and Sunwing.

Alamo (800/327-9633), **Avis** (800/831-2847), **Budget** (800/527-0700), **Dollar** (800/800-4000 domestic, 800/800-6000 international), and **National** (800/227-7368) provide rental cars from both airports.

CAR

Pinellas County is easily accessible from major interstate highways along the Midwest (I-75) and Northeast (I-95) corridors, as well as from Orlando (I-4). I-275 serves the western portions of the Tampa-St. Petersburg area, including downtown Tampa, St. Petersburg, and Bradenton. It starts in the south at I-75 in Bradenton and extends up through St. Petersburg and Tampa, connected by two major bridges, the Sunshine Skyway in the south and Howard Frankland to the north, before reuniting with I-75 at Lutz. I-75, by contrast, skirts both cities and acts as a bypass to southwest Florida and the Gulf Coast.

Once in Pinellas County, Clearwater is in the north along the Gulf, St. Petersburg is in the south along the bay. To reach St. Petersburg from Clearwater, head south on U.S. 19A, a slow, densely trafficked mess. Farther east, the regular U.S. 19 cuts down through the center of the peninsula to St. Petersburg.

In St. Petersburg, streets are set up in a grid pattern, with avenues running east-west and streets running north-south. Central Avenue divides north and south St. Petersburg, with the numbered avenues on either side—it's tricky, though, as to the left of Central there's 1st Avenue North, to the right it's 1st Avenue South. There are some sections of town that are all one-way streets, so you may make a lot of turns while driving.

From St. Pete Beach all the way up through Clearwater, all you need to know is that Gulf Boulevard (Hwy. 699) runs right up the coast and through each little town. The city of Clearwater is on the mainland, but Clearwater Beach is on a barrier island connected by Memorial Causeway.

BUS AND TRAIN

Amtrak (800/872-7245, www.amtrak.com) offers service in nearby Tampa and other surrounding areas. Some trains even allow you to bring your car with you. Also, **Greyhound** (800/229-9424, www.greyhound.com) provides regular bus service to St. Petersburg (180 9th St. N., 727/898-1496). If you stay in Clearwater, it's easy to ditch your rental car and use the **Jolley Trolley** (727/445-1200, www.clearwaterjolleytrolley.com, $2.25) or the **Suncoast Beach Trolley** (727/540-1900, $2 per ride, $4.50 all day) to get around. **Pinellas Suncoast Transit Authority** (727/540-1800, $2 per ride, $4.50 all day) also has a fairly extensive busing system around the city.

Day Trips

© Disney

A number of worthwhile excursions can be made from Tampa and St. Petersburg. To the north, the Nature Coast has tremendous outdoor adventure opportunities. To the south, Sarasota is an upscale city with boutique shops, art

galleries, museums, and world-class beaches. To the east, Orlando, home to Walt Disney World, lures countless visitors.

PLANNING YOUR TIME

Where you choose to visit from Tampa and St. Pete largely depends on your preferences, budget, and time.

If your budget allows, **Orlando** (1.5 hours northeast of Tampa) is where most families head for a fun-filled excursion. Disney World, Sea World, and Universal Studios offer theme-park fantasyland bliss that can last for days.

At the other end of the spectrum, the **Nature Coast** (extending from North Tampa to Crystal River, about 1.5 hours) offers budget-friendly fun for outdoors enthusiasts. You can paddle spring-fed rivers and creeks, search for manatees in the first magnitude springs, fish in the flats or offshore and on

the coastline, and hike and camp in abundant the National Forest and State Park lands in the area. Kids will love the mermaid show at Weeki Wachee Springs.

South of Tampa, **Sarasota** (about 1.25 hours south of Tampa) is a large, sophisticated city with a strong arts and culture vibe and beautiful beaches. There are also many barrier islands to explore off the coast. Although the city caters more to adults, kids will enjoy the beaches and the circus attractions here as well.

These excursions can be done in a day, though one day would be stretching it for Disney World. If possible, plan on spending at least two days in any of these areas for the most enjoyable experience. Sarasota is the most day trip-friendly option, being the closest and requiring the least amount of planning.

Previous: view of Sarasota from its marina; Lido Beach near Sarasota. **Above:** fireworks at Walt Disney World.

Look for ★ to find recommended
sights, activities, dining, and lodging.

Highlights

★ **Walt Disney World:** The most visited theme park in the world encompasses four unique parks with thrilling rides, entertaining shows, world-class hotels, and your favorite Disney characters (page 106).

★ **Ellie Schiller Homosassa Springs Wildlife State Park:** Get up close to the gentle manatee on a pontoon ride down the beautiful Homosassa River (page 115).

★ **Nature Coast Canoe and Kayak Trail:** Paddle this 17-mile trail on the Salt River and you'll encounter birds, manatees, and maybe even an alligator (page 118).

★ **John and Mable Ringling Museum of Art:** This fabulous art museum houses over 600 works of art, including five enormous Peter Paul Rubens paintings. Also a part of the complex is the Circus Museum, which offers a fascinating overview of the Ringling Brothers' history (page 125).

★ **Spring Training:** Visit Ed Smith Stadium to catch a glimpse of the Baltimore Orioles training; tickets are cheap and the hot dogs are tasty (page 128).

★ **Siesta Key Beach:** This barrier island's beach is regularly voted one of the best in Florida due to its wide, white-sand shorelines and casual family-friendly feel (page 142).

Day Trips

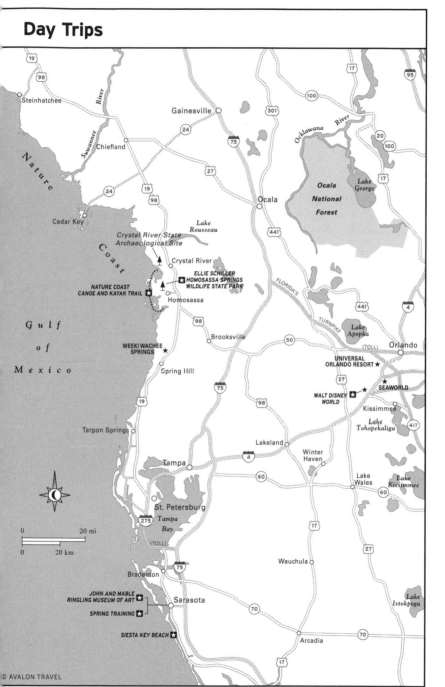

Orlando Theme Parks

The three main theme parks in Orlando are Walt Disney World, SeaWorld, and Universal Studios. Most visitors travel to Orlando to visit Disney World exclusively. However, real movie buffs and true Harry Potter fans will want to visit Universal Studios, and SeaWorld offers the best aquarium experience in Florida.

★ WALT DISNEY WORLD

Covering nearly 47 square-miles, **Walt Disney World** (407/939-5277, www.disneyworld.com) features four theme parks (Magic Kingdom, Epcot, Animal Kingdom, and Hollywood Studios), two water parks (Blizzard Beach and Typhoon Lagoon), and over 20 resort hotels. With interactive rides, animal adventures, magical attractions, dining, shopping, and nearly 60,000 cast members performing in more than 3,000 different roles, guests will be sure to feel the magic of Disney no matter where they are.

Note: the hours vary greatly from day to day for each park. Check Walt Disney World's website for detailed hours.

Magic Kingdom

The **Magic Kingdom** (1180 Seven Seas Dr.) is the heart of the park. This is where you will find the iconic **Cinderella's Castle,** complete with a fireworks show every night (usually 7:45pm). The Magic Kingdom has captured hearts and imaginations for decades with unforgettable rides featuring an endless parade of animatronic Disney images, characters, and unforgettable thrills. Climb aboard a pirate ship on the **Pirates of the Caribbean.** Zoom through space on the indoor roller coaster **Space Mountain.** Fly over Neverland on **Peter Pan's Magical Flight.** Experience a child-like perspective of an idyllic, fantastical global community on **It's A Small World.** And there are nearly 40 additional rides and attractions.

Epcot

Epcot (200 Epcot Center Dr.) is the place where you'll find that huge geodesic dome that looks like an enormous golf ball. The massive round structure houses **Project Tomorrow,** a journey through what future

Space Mountain at Walt Disney World   © Disney

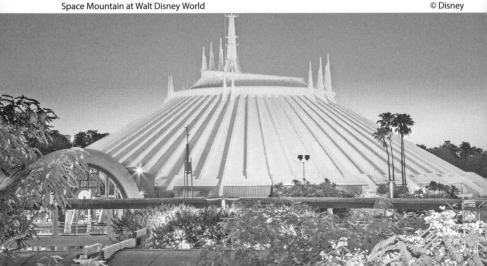

on earth may be like. Epcot explores technological innovation and cultures of the world through more than 20 exhibits, thrilling rides, shows, and educational attractions. The **World Showcase** area of the park features eleven sections that represent eleven different nations of the world, each featuring architecture, food, drinks, rides, shows, and attractions that celebrate these cultures.

Animal Kingdom

At the **Animal Kingdom** (2901 Osceola Pkwy), you can see animals from around the world, take a train ride through a recreated African savannah, and experience fun rides and attractions, all with an animal theme. The newest ride in the park is the stunning **Expedition Everest,** an exciting roller coaster that rushes through a towering recreation of the Himalayan Mountains. Along the way you'll have frightening encounters with the mythical abominable snowman, broken train tracks, and dark mountain passages before you plunge down the mountainside. It's the most fun you could ever have on Everest without subjecting yourself to a high risk of frostbite.

Hollywood Studios

Star Wars fans will be swinging their light sabers in celebration when they visit **Disney's Hollywood Studios** (351 S. Studio Dr.). You'll find storm troopers marching through the streets, explore different Star Wars worlds on a 3-D simulator, view props form the movies, and meet some of your favorite Star Wars characters. There's an array of movie-themed rides and attractions. The best show is the **Indiana Jones Epic Stunt Spectacular,** which features impressive stunts and stunning action sequences that include all sorts of gripping explosions and jaw-dropping special effects. Ironically, the ride that you should not miss has nothing to do with movies. It's the **Rock 'n Roller Coaster**, starring the music of Aerosmith. It's an unfathomably fun indoor coaster that zips and turns and loops at exceptionally high speeds through a dark

fantasy-scape of neon lights and thrilling obstacles. It's one of the best roller coasters I've ever been on, but it still takes a backseat to Space Mountain in the Magic Kingdom.

Planning Your Visit

Wait times in the lines at all the parks have reached extraordinary lengths; expect to wait for over an hour for the most popular rides, such as Pirates of the Caribbean or Space Mountain. To combat this, the park offers a **FastPass.** Look for the kiosk stations dotted all around the parks. This is where you can schedule in advance the time that you would like to experience your ride, show, or other attraction. You can even book dining times for the more popular restaurants. You can only book three rides at a time, and you're not able to book any more until you have checked in and attended the rides you previously scheduled. So if a ride is only available at the end of the day because all of the other FastPass times are full, you won't be able to utilize more FastPasses until the park is nearly closed.

You can schedule your three FastPass options up to 30 days in advance if you log onto the Disney website (http://disneyworld.com) or download the **MyExperience Disney App.** The app will give you a detailed digital map of the park with GPS capabilities to help you find where you are and how to get where you want to go, as well as give you current wait times for all attractions. The key here is to schedule the three most popular rides 30 days in advance (those staying at the resort have the 60 days advance option), and schedule them in the morning, then book the next three most popular rides after riding those ones (and hope there will be times available).

Ticket prices vary depending on the day you choose to go, which parks you would like to visit, and how many are in your party. The most popular option is the park hopper pass, which enables you to visit all four parks ($150-170 per day). Another popular option is to visit the Magic Kingdom ($100-120 per day) exclusively. The price of tickets decreases if you visit on consecutive days. For example, three-day park hopper passes are $345, and a three-day ticket with access to one park per day is $290. A ten-day park hopper pass is only $469, and a ten-day ticket with access to one park per day is only $400. Perhaps the best deal for the true Disney obsessed is an annual pass that gives you access to all four parks, 20 percent off on dining and merchandise, and free parking for $749.

Restaurants

Nearly every chain restaurant in the country is represented within a 20-mile radius of Disney, so there's no shortage of options. Each resort has its own restaurants, and inside the park you'll find food options everywhere you turn.

Beware the overpriced hot dogs and turkey legs sold nearly everywhere inside the park. Look through the descriptions of the eateries to find a place that sells something else; they're few and far between, but these places have better-quality food that offers much better value.

You can bring your own water and food in, but nothing that requires heating. Snacks and bagged sandwiches are fine. Be aware that not all rides permit backpacks, so you'll have to pay to store them in a coin-deposit locker. There are also stroller storage areas that are free and convenient.

While inside the Magic Kingdom, budget travelers will appreciate **Cosmic Ray's Starlight Café.** They have simple American choices that kids and adults will enjoy. The best deal is their cheeseburger ($15) that comes with fries and includes a trip to the toppings bar where you can unabashedly pile on stacks of tomatoes, lettuce, and other veggies to get the best bite for your buck in the entire park. It's in the Tomorrowland section, near Space Mountain. The service is often comparatively very quick. Other options include barbecue sandwiches, chicken nuggets for the kids, and the ubiquitous hot dog.

Who doesn't want to go inside Cinderella's Castle? At **Cinderella's Royal Table** (Fantasyland, $35-59 pp), you can even dine inside it. Located on the bottom floor of the castle, this exquisite dining room is decked out in coats of arms and elegant chandeliers. Guests will even have a chance to meet and take a picture with Cinderella herself. Breakfast, lunch, and dinner are served in a regal banquet style with each plate brought to your table upon request. For breakfast, it's French toast, steak and eggs, baked quiche, and pastries. For dinner, you can start with an assortment of meats and cheeses, and then choose a main course of pork tenderloin, steak and shrimp, or fresh fish. Kids options include turkey pot pie or chicken nuggets. For dessert, the sorbet or chocolate cake will satisfy the sweet tooth. The food and atmosphere create an exceptionally memorable experience for the whole family.

There are more than 52 restaurants in Epcot, but none of them can beat the fish-and-chips at **Yorkshire County Fish Shop** ($7-15). It's a small place, where you order from the window and then sit at one of the shaded tables nearby. Grab a pint of ale and you'll feel like you're in jolly old England.

Hotels

For a great value, stay at the **Holiday Inn Orlando-Disney Springs** (1805 Hotel Plaza Blvd., 877/859-5095, www.ihg.com, $140-250). It's seven miles away from the Magic Kingdom, but there's a free shuttle that runs every half hour to Disney. Alternatively, parking is $12 and gated. There's nothing too fancy about it, but the rooms are large and there's a very nice heated pool area and an on-site restaurant that serves standard American breakfast, lunch, and dinner. The restaurant prices are fairly high, but there are a large number of restaurants just 0.5 miles away along South Apopka Vineland Road.

Disney's Grand Floridian Resort (4401 Floridian Way, 407/824-3000, www.disneyworld.com, $400-900) is all about convenience, luxury, and Victorian-style class. The rooms are beautifully decorated with Victorian-style furniture. In select rooms, you're able to see the fireworks over the

Cinderella Castle from your balcony as well as their reflection in the lake that borders the property. There's a big pool area with a 181-foot-long waterslide, a "quiet pool," and an adjacent hot tub. A jazz band plays in the lobby, and there's an on-site spa. There are a few fine-dining options, some of which include a special visit from Disney characters. Transportation to and from the airport in Orlando is included, and parking at the resort and Disney World is free, but it's only one monorail stop away from Magic Kingdom.

Disney's Animal Kingdom Lodge (2901 Osceola Pkwy., 407/938-3000, www.disneyworld.com, $400–900) is the feature resort within Disney's Animal Kingdom. The rustic African themed lodge offers balcony views of the animals grazing around the recreated savannah right outside the resort. The architecture is breathtaking: high-ceiling thatched roofs with enormous exposed wood beams, exotic gardens filled with tropical plants, a huge pool tucked into a jungle styled oasis, and tiki bars dotting the property. The on-site restaurants feature African dishes as well as American choices. Free bus transportation is available to all the Disney Parks.

Budget travelers who don't mind camping can stay at the **KOA in Kissimmee** (2644 Happy Camper Place, Kissimmee, 407/396-2400, www.koa.com, $40–70). It's about 10 miles to the Magic Kingdom, which usually translates to 30 minutes in regular traffic. The campground is pet-friendly and accommodates RVs, campers, and tents. Wi-Fi is included, and there are a small gym, an on-site pool and hot tub, and laundry facilities that are open 24 hours daily. Disney has a campground in the park as well, but it costs nearly three times as much.

UNIVERSAL ORLANDO RESORT

Owned by NBCUniversal, **Universal Orlando** (1000 Universal Studios Plaza, 407/363-8000, usually 9am-9pm daily) celebrates the film industry and the many films that Universal Studios has produced. The property is the second largest theme park in Orlando after Walt Disney World. The park is divided into three sections: Universal Studios, Islands of Adventure, and Volcano Bay.

At Universal studios you'll enjoy more than 30 rides and attractions that immerse you into the imaginary worlds of some of the studio's most loved films. Ride through the sky in a flying bicycle on the **E.T. Adventure.** Journey through the world of the Minions on

Disney's Grand Floridian Resort

© Disney

the **3-D Despicable Me** ride. Explore Skull Island and have a thrilling adventure on the **Reign of Kong.** The park features roller coasters, water rides, movie-themed shows, and attractions that take you behind the scenes of the movie-making process.

The Islands of Adventure section is divided into eight islands: Port of Entry, Toon Lagoon, Jurassic Park, Skull Island, Marvel Super Hero Island, The Lost Continent, Seuss Landing, and the Wizarding World of Harry Potter. Fans of the world's favorite Hogwarts graduate will be met with wizardly delights at the **Wizarding World of Harry Potter,** which opened in 2010. You can visit the Forbidden Forest, Hogwarts Castle, and ride on the Hogwarts Express. In this section, the **Dragon Challenge** are two separate fantastic and exciting roller coasters that are intertwined at different points of the rides.

The newest addition to the park is a stunning waterpark called **Volcano Bay,** which features 15 different slides, wave pools, water rides, and even a wet-and-wild roller coaster. The attractions are all set within a tropical themed park with a massive 200-foot volcano at the center that spills out magnificent waterfalls by day and spews molten lava at night.

Ticket prices vary depending on what day you visit, how many parks you visit, and how many people are in your group. A one-day ticket to one park costs $100-120 pp; for three days it's about $200, and for five days about $225. Most people will want to visit both Universal Studios and Islands of Adventure, which I recommend. A one-day pass to both parks is $150-175, depending on the day. For three days at the two parks it's about $250; five days about $275.

Restaurants

Like Disney, there are tons of places to eat inside and around Universal Studios Resort. Inside the park at the Wizardly World of Harry Potter, you can visit the **Leaky Cauldron** (5617 Major Blvd., Diagon Alley, 407/903-5490, $12-17), a rustic British pub that serves traditional English breakfast and lunch. The food is delicious and the atmosphere is a lot of fun for fans of Harry Potter or those who love English history and culture. They serve breakfast and lunch and sling non-alcoholic butterbeer as well as the intoxicating varieties of ales and wine.

In the Islands of adventure, the **Mythos Restaurant** (Islands of Adventure, 407/224-4012, 11am-5pm Mon.-Wed., 11am-4pm Thurs., 11am-6pm Fri.-Sat., 11am-5pm Sun.,

Diagon Alley at the Wizarding World of Harry Potter

$12-18) has the best food and value. It's located on the Lost Continent section of the park. Just look for the massive rocky mountain with a face carved on the front and a waterfall rushing out of the mouth. The dining room is inside the towering structure, and the atmosphere makes you feel as if you're inside a rocky cave grotto. The mix of American, Asian, and Mediterranean options keeps everyone happy. They serve lunch and dinner only.

The Cowfish Sushi Burger Bar (6000 Universal Blvd., Suite 700, 11am-11pm daily, $12-25) is along the Orlando CityWalk, and it's as strange as it sounds, with traditional burgers and sushi as well as wacky options that combine the two. They call it burgushi—burgers made with sushi ingredients and sushi made with burger stuff. If you're unsure about this bizarre concept, try a bento box. One of the bento options comes with a mini cheeseburger, your choice of four sushi pieces, sweet potato fries, and *edamame*. It's all very tasty and has become a huge hit. Cowfish also serves spiked and nonalcoholic milk shakes as well as premium sakes, American and Japanese beers, and other cocktails. CityWalk, which doesn't require an admission ticket, is located right outside the park in the promenade that leads to the entrance.

Hotels

The five on-site resorts at Universal Studios are within walking distance of the park, and all offer complimentary shuttles and water taxis to CityWalk and the park entrance. Rates range $120-500. Outside the resort are countless hotels that offer free shuttles to the park.

The **Hard Rock Hotel at Universal Orlando** (5800 Universal Blvd., 407/503-2000, www.hardrockhotels.com, $350-600), is one such hotel, just a short walk from CityWalk. The rooms are large, modern, sleek, and very well-appointed, decorated with rock-and-roll and pop memorabilia. The pool is enormous and surrounded by palms, and its zero entry feature makes you feel like you're walking into the calm Gulf. Surrounding the pool is white sand to complete the beach

atmosphere. Included with each stay is early park admission, which allows you to enter the park one hour before regular guests. You'll also receive a Universal Express pass, which allows you to skip the regular lines and get into the fast lanes so that you can fit more rides and attractions into your day. There are several restaurants and bars on the property. It's a great choice for families, but it's not necessarily the best value, as the rates are high for what you get.

Bargain hunters will want to consider **Universal's Cabana Bay Beach** (6550 Adventure Way, www.universalorlando.com, 407/503-4000, $120-300), a colorful retro resort inspired by mid-century Florida. There's a huge pool surrounded by palm trees and multicolored umbrellas. The rooms are on the small side at 300 square feet; the family suite is a bit bigger, with a microwave, sink, and mini refrigerator. It's a top pick for families as you get to enter the Harry Potter area of the park an hour early. It's a short walk to the entrance, or take the nearby ferry or the buses that depart from the front of the hotel. There's a cool retro bowling alley that serves burgers and other American favorites, a pizza place, and a 1950s-style diner that also serves American food.

Another great deal is **The Point Orlando Resort** (7389 Universal Blvd., 877/814-9119, www.theorlandopoint.com, $120-250). It's outside the resort but less than a mile from the park and provides shuttles to all the parks throughout the day. A recent renovation updated the furniture, fitness center, and amenities. Choose from studio, one-, and two-bedroom rooms that all include flat-screen TVs and remarkably spacious baths. The suites are large, at 716 square feet, and include a balcony, a separate bedroom, a full kitchen, and a living area with a sleeper sofa. For larger family groups, the two-bedroom suites are a whopping 1,100 square feet. The pool area is beautiful and has a tropical feel. This is a family favorite, especially if you're planning on visiting all the parks but are spending the bulk of your time at Universal Studios.

SEAWORLD ORLANDO

A combined theme park and aquarium, **Sea World** (7007 Sea World Dr., 888/800-5447, http://seaworldparks.com, usually 9am-7pm daily, day pass $79, annual pass $99) is one of the most visited theme parks in the country. Famous for its Shamu shows featuring orcas that leap from massive tanks and do a variety of tricks, the park also features roller coasters, a remarkable number of marinelife exhibits, wonderful shows, other entertaining attractions, and a facility dedicated to animal rescue.

The park is separated into eight sections, called seas, including the port of entry. The **Sea of Shallows** features shallow-water creatures such as manatees, alligators, sea turtles, dolphins, and stingrays. This is where you'll find the **Manta,** an incredible roller coaster that holds you in a horizontal head-first position so that you feel like you're flying over the animal exhibits.

The **Sea of Legends** section explores mythical sea adventures like the one you'll discover on **Journey to Atlantis,** a thrilling boat ride through the mythical city of Atlantis. Also in this section is **The Kraken,** a roller coaster where you're feet dangle as you climb more than 150 feet and then zoom around the twisting tracks at high speed.

In the **Sea of Ice** area, the rides, shows, and exhibits have an Antarctic theme. On the **Antarctica: Empire of the Penguin** ride you travel through the Antarctic landscape seen through the eyes of a penguin. It's an excellent family ride and suitable for young children. After the ride is over, you exit into a fantastic live penguin exhibit and, of course, a penguin-themed gift shop.

The **Sea of Delight** section is where you'll find most of the park's restaurants. It's styled as a Mediterranean town, and it's where you'll see the **Sky Tower,** a rotating capsule that gives riders a bird's-eye view of the park from 400 feet overhead. The **Pets Ahoy** show is nearby, so after you eat you can watch this comical show featuring dogs, cats, birds, pot-belly pigs, human divers, and acrobats. Most of the animals in the show are rescues.

At the **Sea of Mystery** you'll find the **Shark Encounter** exhibit, an 85-foot tunnel that you can walk through as barracuda, venomous fish, and sharks swirl around. The park's newest ride, opened in 2016, is the **Mako** roller coaster, named after the shark. It's the fastest (73 mph), longest (nearly one

SeaWorld's One Ocean show

mile), and tallest (200 feet) coaster in Orlando. Don't miss this one if you're a coaster junkie. The **Shark's Underwater Grill** and the **Nautilus Theater** are also in this section of the park.

Kids will love the **Sea of Fun** for the little ones. Children can ride the tame **Shamu Express** coaster, meet Shamu, and play in a huge net-style jungle gym and enjoy water cannons and play fountains. Next to this area is the **Sea of Power,** the location of the Shamu Stadium, where you can enjoy the phenomenal Shamu show called **One Ocean.**

Restaurants

In the park, **Dine with Shamu** (Shamu Stadium, Sea of Power section, lunch 11:30am-1:30pm, dinner 4pm-6pm daily, $29 adults, $19 children, free under age 2) is an incredible dining experience that is geared toward children. Diners are seated at a poolside table on the edge of the Shamu tank, with fantastic views of the whales and trainers interacting. The meal is accompanied by an educational program on the importance of preserving the ocean while providing a behind-the-scenes look at the park. The menu may include sustainable seafood, chicken, and beef entrées and a selection of desserts. Make reservations well in advance as this is an extremely popular event.

For a memorable fine-dining experience, dine with sharks at the **Shark's Underwater Grill** (Sea of Mystery section, $20-40), one of the best in the park. Diners are seated next to a massive shark tank where they watch the predators circle. The food is mostly American seafood and steak dishes. the ahi tuna and filet mignon are top choices.

For the widest variety of food, stop by the Antarctic base camp-styled **Expedition Cafe** (Sea of Ice section, $15-20), with favorites such as hot dogs, fries, and chicken tenders as well as Chinese, Thai, and Italian choices. You'll be pleasantly surprised by the teriyaki chicken or the orange chicken. Order hot tea, coffee, or hot cocoa to warm you up before visiting the penguins.

Hotels

On the high-end, a good choice is the **Renaissance Orlando at SeaWorld** (6677 Sea Harbor Dr., 407/351-5555, www.marriot.com, $200-400), with a beautiful 10-story atrium less than a mile from SeaWorld. You can walk to the park in 10 minutes or take the free shuttle from the hotel. The modern and sleek rooms are well-appointed, and

the Expedition Cafe at SeaWorld

suites have pull-out sofa beds and separate living rooms. Even the smallest rooms measure 465 square feet, which makes this an excellent choice for families. There's a Starbucks on-site as well as three different restaurants, a bar, a good gym, a heated pool, and an excellent full-service spa. The hotel is six miles from Universal Studios, which makes it a great choice if you're also planning to visit that park. Kids will love the on-site waterpark, with two slides and all sorts of spraying fountains and water toys. The adult pool area is relaxing with an elegant tropical vibe that is an excellent escape from the loud and bustling theme-park environment.

The **Hilton Grand Vacations at SeaWorld** (6924 Grand Vacations Way, 407/239-0200, www.hilton.com, $100-300) is a top choice for families. The one-bed studios have kitchenettes, but the best values are the 878-square-foot one-bedroom suites and the 1,225-square-foot two-bedroom suites, both of which have fully equipped kitchens. In the separate living area is a couch with a queen pull-out sleeper and a dining table that seats six. There are excellent activities and amenities all around the property, including poolside movie nights, a jogging track, a pool table, tennis courts, and a kids activity center. The heated pool features a beautiful waterfall and is surrounded by soaring palms and private cabanas. There's also a bar and grill that serves breakfast, lunch, and dinner as well as a small deli.

Best Western Orlando Convention Center (6301 Westwood Blvd., 855/659-7049, www.bestwestern.com, $74-150) is a no-frills standard hotel that offers one of the best values in the area, with basic furnishings, flat-screen TVs, and included Internet access. In the morning they serve an included full breakfast. For a large family, this practically pays for the room, considering food prices in

the park run around $15 pp. There's a small pool area, a decent gym, and a good restaurant on-site. It's within walking distance of SeaWorld and offers a complimentary shuttle to the other parks.

GETTING THERE AND AROUND
Car

Orlando is easily accessible by car on interstate and other major highways. From Tampa, take I-4 to Orlando. From the north, I-95 runs down the east coast and intersects with I-4 around Daytona Beach. From the Florida Panhandle, take I-10 to the Lake City junction, then I-75 to U.S. 27 near the Villages, which will take you to the Florida Turnpike, where you'll join I-4 near Universal Studios Orlando. Once in Orlando, take I-4 between the theme parks; during the summer it can become extremely crowded during morning and evening rush hours. Luckily, there are shuttles to and from the parks if you're staying at local hotels. If you're driving to the parks, they generally don't open until 9am, putting you in rush-hour traffic, but the closing times of 7pm to 10pm make for an easier drive home.

Air

Orlando International Airport (MCO, 1 Jeff Fuqua Blvd., 407/825-2001, www.orlandoairports.net) is about six miles southeast of downtown Orlando. It is the second busiest airport in Florida, served by major domestic and international airlines.

Rental cars are provided at the airport by **Advantage Rent A Car** (800/777-5500), **Alamo** (800/327-9633), **Avis** (800/831-2847), **Budget** (800/527-0700), **Dollar** (800/800-4000), **Enterprise** (800/325-8007), **EZ** (800/277-5171), **Hertz** (800/654-3131), **National** (800/227-7368), **Payless** (407/856-5539), and **Thrifty** (800/367-2277).

The Nature Coast

WEEKI WACHEE TO CRYSTAL RIVER

Florida is home to 700 freshwater springs, 33 of them first magnitude, meaning they discharge at least 100 cubic feet of water per second. Several of these first-magnitude springs are along the Nature Coast, a huge draw for swimmers, divers, and paddlers.

Farther north, local cynics refer to manatees as "cash cows," and indeed the sea cows bring in a sizable revenue stream to the little towns of Homosassa and Crystal River. Upward of 400 West Indian manatees make this their winter home, drawn by the warm waters of the seven spring-driven rivers that meet here at the Gulf of Mexico.

Older than Crystal River, Homosassa has more charm and a greater reputation as a fishing destination. Today, it is home to only a few thousand people drawn by beautiful rivers, unmanicured wilderness, and fish.

Sights
★ ELLIE SCHILLER HOMOSASSA SPRINGS WILDLIFE STATE PARK

Manatees, so famous in these parts, can weigh up to 2,000 pounds and are often seen feasting on algae and barnacles. You'll catch sight of them most often during cooler months, December to March, in the Suwannee River or at Manatee or Fanning Springs State Parks. From boat or shore, look for swirly "footprints" on the water's surface or torpedo-like shapes ambling across the shallow bottom. For a guaranteed sighting, stop into **Ellie Schiller Homosassa Springs Wildlife State Park** (4150 S. Suncoast Blvd., Homosassa, 352/628-5343, 9am-5:30pm daily, $13 adults, $5 ages 6-12, free under age 6), where you can see these marine mammals several ways. Visitors are loaded onto pontoon boats and shuttled through the canopied headwaters of the Homosassa River

to a refuge for injured manatees and other animals. Alternatively, a manatee program (11:30am, 1:30pm, and 3:30pm daily) allows you to watch guides wade out to feed stubby carrots to a slow-moving swarm of these creatures, many etched with outboard motor scars from run-ins with boats. Afterward you can walk down to the glass-fronted Fishbowl Underwater Observatory and see eye-to-eye with the gentle giants and the park's other indigenous aquatic creatures. Mysteriously, the park hosts a hippo named Lu—a washed-up animal actor—that former Florida governor Lawton Chiles declared an honorary Florida citizen.

CRYSTAL RIVER STATE ARCHAEOLOGICAL SITE

In 200 BC, this was a happening spot. Native Americans came from all over to bury their dead and to participate in ceremonies and conduct trade. Archaeologists estimate that for 1,600 years, roughly 7,500 people visited these 14 acres every year. Today, **Crystal River State Archaeological Site** (3400 N. Museum Point, Crystal River, 352/795-3817, park 8am-sunset daily, visitors center 9am-5pm daily, $3 per vehicle) hosts visitors to the banks of the Crystal River who come to see the six mounds built by the prosaically named pre-Columbian mound builders. After viewing an eight-minute interpretive video and seeing the small museum's exhibit, which chronicles the archaeological excavations that were begun in 1903, you'll be better equipped to walk a paved 0.5-mile loop and marvel at the mounds, studded with shells, bones, jewelry, and pottery from earlier civilizations. The park also has an interesting dugout canoe exhibit and a Sifting for Technology interactive exhibit, which has a biweekly program in which visitors use sifting screens and other archaeological tools to recover artifacts from the spoils of a dredged boat slip.

The Nature Coast

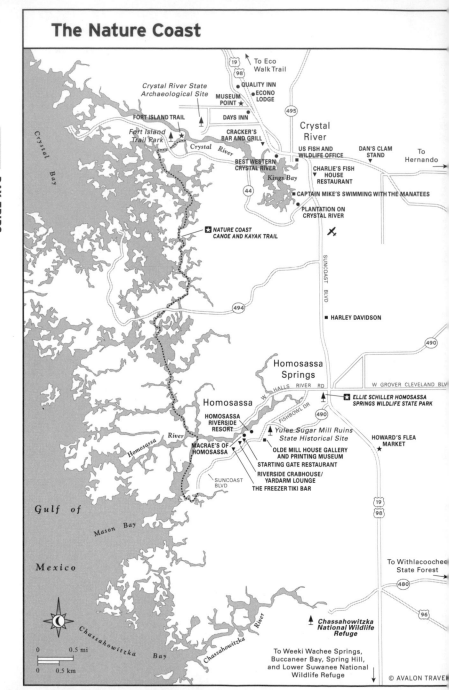

To Eco
Walk Trail

QUALITY INN
ECONO
LODGE

Crystal River State
Archaeological Site

MUSEUM
POINT ★

DAYS INN

Crystal
River

FORT ISLAND TRAIL

Crystal Bay

Fort Island
Trail Park

CRACKER'S
BAR AND GRILL

Crystal River

US FISH AND
WILDLIFE OFFICE

DAN'S CLAM
STAND

To
Hernando

BEST WESTERN
CRYSTAL RIVER

CHARLIE'S FISH
HOUSE
RESTAURANT

Kings Bay

CAPTAIN MIKE'S SWIMMING WITH THE MANATEES

PLANTATION ON
CRYSTAL RIVER

★ NATURE COAST
CANOE AND KAYAK TRAIL

SUNCOAST BLVD

HARLEY DAVIDSON

Homosassa
Springs

W GROVER CLEVELAND BLV

W HALLS RIVER RD

ELLIE SCHILLER HOMOSASSA
SPRINGS WILDLIFE STATE PARK

Homosassa

FISHBOWL DR

HOMOSASSA
RIVERSIDE
RESORT

Yulee Sugar Mill Ruins
State Historical Site

HOWARD'S FLEA
MARKET

River

MACRAE'S OF
HOMOSASSA

OLDE MILL HOUSE GALLERY
AND PRINTING MUSEUM

STARTING GATE RESTAURANT

RIVERSIDE CRABHOUSE/
YARDARM LOUNGE

THE FREEZER TIKI BAR

SUNCOAST
BLVD

Gulf of

Mason Bay

To Withlacoochee
State Forest

Mexico

Chassahowitzka
National Wildlife
Refuge

River

0   0.5 mi

0   0.5 km

Chassahowitzka

Chassahowitzka Bay

River

To Weeki Wachee Springs,
Buccaneer Bay, Spring Hill,
and Lower Suwanee National
Wildlife Refuge

© AVALON TRAVEL

WEEKI WACHEE SPRINGS

Florida is home to a variety of rare aquatic creatures, perhaps none so singular as the 20 mermaids and mermen who swim through their daily choreographed show at **Weeki Wachee Springs** (6131 Commercial Way, Spring Hill, 352/592-5656, 9am-5:30pm daily, $13 adults, $8 ages 6-12, includes admission to Buccaneer Bay). Weeki Wachee is open year-round, but Buccaneer Bay is open mid-March to October.

The audience sits in a small underground amphitheater in front of a four-inch-thick plate-glass window, behind which the blue waters of the springs teem with fish, turtles, eels, and people in oversize shimmering tails who twirl, undulate, and lip-synch on cue. Many of the mermaids have been with the show for decades, a fact that can be ascertained with a quick look through photos and memorabilia in the small Mermaid Museum (a wall of fame includes early sea nymphs cavorting with Elvis and Don Knotts), opened to commemorate the show's 50th anniversary in 1997.

After getting your picture taken with a mermaid, it's off to the rest of the 200-acre family entertainment park, Florida's only natural-spring water park. This includes a flume ride at Buccaneer Bay, a low-key Birds of Prey show, a petting zoo, and a jungle river cruise.

Sports and Recreation

FISHING

Any fly fisher will tell you that Homosassa is the place to catch tarpon, "the silver king." This little Old Florida town is where the big tarpon congregate for reasons unknown. The current world record—202.8 pounds—was caught right here. But you won't find annual tarpon tournaments broadcast on ESPN; it's a low-key endeavor, with patience often yielding nothing but sunburn. On any given day, you'll see the river dotted with 25 or 30 flat boats navigated with push poles in a hushed silence of profound concentration, everyone waiting to see one roll along the surface in water depths of 5 to 25 feet. People come from all over the world to the Nature Coast to sight-fish for these behemoths before releasing them gently into the warm, clear waters.

Regulations changed in 2013, and now only hook and line is allowed for tarpon fishing. Several other new rules have been adopted, and you can keep up to date by visiting the **Florida Fish and Wildlife website** (www.myfwc.com). Tarpon begin to run the last weeks of April and disappear in July.

fishing on the Nature Coast

What many consider the Super Bowl of fishing, tarpon fishing requires a special $50 tag to keep one as well as serious know-how. The initial jumps and runs of that hooked fish are very exciting.

If you want to try your hand at chasing giant tarpon on the Gulf or in the backwaters from Homosassa to Cedar Key, try **Captain Rick LeFiles** (Osprey Guide Services, 6115 Riverside Dr., Yankeetown, 352/400-0133, www.ospreyguides.com, $350 full day of inshore fishing for reds and trout, $450 for tarpon) or fourth-generation Homosassa **Captain William Toney** (352/422-4141, www.homosassainshorefishing.com, half-day $350, full day $400 for 1-2 people, $50 per additional person).

If you haven't planned ahead, fishing licenses can be purchased on the fly at the Kmart in Crystal River or the Walmart in Homosassa.

★ NATURE COAST CANOE AND KAYAK TRAIL

The **Nature Coast Canoe and Kayak Trail** is 17 miles long, beginning in the north on the Salt River, about one mile west of the town of Crystal River, near the Marine Science Station on Highway 44. Follow the markers on the Salt River south to the Homosassa River. From here, the trail goes east on the Homosassa River a few hundred feet to a little stretch of water called Battle Creek, and then it jags to the south through Seven Cabbage Cut to the mouth of the Chassahowitzka River. The calm, protected waters of this estuarine ecosystem, part of the Great Florida Birding Trail, are home to ospreys, cormorants, wood storks, and many other wading birds.

To rent kayaks and canoes, go to **Aardvark's Florida Kayak Company** (707 N. Citrus Ave., Crystal River, 352/795-5650, www.floridakayakcompany.com, 10am-5pm Wed.-Sat., 1pm-5pm Sun., $50 single, $65 tandem). But if paddling out on your own sounds daunting, **Riversport Kayaks** (5297 S. Cherokee Way, Homosassa, 352/621-4972, www.riversportkayaks.com) leads tours along this trail, as well as great paddling along the Halls River and even overnight camping trips with an experienced and knowledgeable guide. They also offer a lunch-and-paddle special that combines a kayak or canoe rental with a gift certificate to the Riverside Crab House for dinner, lunch, or just drinks ($45 single-seat kayak, $55 two-seat kayak or canoe).

kayaking on the Nature Coast

BIRDING

The area's salt marshes, hammocks, uplands, forest and prairie, freshwater marshes, swamps, lakes, and rivers provide a variety of habitats, which in turn draw hundreds of bird species, and birders can observe them boating along waterways, driving trails, and walking trails all over Citrus County. Roseate spoonbills, great blue herons, ibis, and other wading birds; ospreys, bald eagles, and other birds of prey; shorebirds, wetland birds, and beach birds are all on view. March through May is a good time to see colorful mating plumage.

One of the largest undeveloped river delta-estuarine systems in the United States, the **Lower Suwannee National Wildlife Refuge** (County Rd. 347, 16 miles west of U.S. 19, 352/493-0238, 8am-sunset daily, free) was established in 1979 in an effort to protect and maintain a rare ecosystem. The park is bisected by the Suwannee River, its tributary creeks fringed with majestic cypress; this part is best seen from the one-mile River Trail. Be sure to visit the upland area dotted with scrub oak and pine, and then explore some of the 26-mile stretch of tidal marshes along the Gulf.

Birders also gravitate to the **Withlacoochee Bay Trail** (east on Sunset Parkway Rd. from U.S. 19, 352/236-7143, 8am-sunset daily, free), a five-mile walking trail from Felburn Park Trailhead to the Gulf. The child-friendly, two-mile looped **Eco Walk Trail** (5990 N. Tallahassee Rd., 352/563-0450, 8am-sunset daily, free) can be reached by taking U.S. 19 north to just before Seven Rivers Regional Medical Center, then turning left onto Curtis Tool Road for the Eco Walk Trailhead, which is at the intersection of Curtis Tool and Tallahassee Road. **Fort Island Trail** (Fort Island Trail, 5 miles west of U.S. 19, 8am-sunset daily, free) is a flat, paved, nine-mile trail that ends at Fort Island Trail Beach.

SWIMMING WITH THE MANATEES

Manatee season is October 15 to March 31, but you'll spot them all year long. Kings Bay in Crystal River has the densest concentration, but the Blue Waters area of the Homosassa River is a little less trafficked by boats and thus a bit quieter. Either way, you can swim with these gentle mammals at a distance that suits you. Up close their size is unsettling—just remember they are herbivores, with blunt teeth so far back in their heads that you could, were it legal, safely hand-feed them.

Manatee Tour & Dive (36 NE 4th St., Crystal River, 352/795-1333, www.manatee-touranddive.com, tour $25-39, gear $20-30) offers two-hour manatee swim and snorkeling trips suitable for the whole family in the waters of Crystal River, and scuba trips in Crystal Springs and Kings Spring, an underwater cavern praised for its excellent visibility, size, and potential for underwater photography (thousands of saltwater fish congregate at the cavern's two exits).

Captain Mike's Swimming with the Manatees (1610 SE Paradise Circle, 352/571-1888, www.swimmingwiththemanatees.com, $10-99) has a similar range of guided ecotourism escapades in Homosassa. If a manatee swim and snorkel tour doesn't sound like a good way to take to the waters, you can try your hand at scalloping (July 1-Sept. 25), or just enjoy a boat ride to follow the river out to the Gulf of Mexico.

BUCCANEER BAY

If you've been entranced by the lip-synching mermaids of Weeki Wachee Springs, you'll be inspired to try some of your own aquatic tricks at the adjacent **Buccaneer Bay Waterpark** (6131 Commercial Way, Spring Hill, 352/592-5656, 9am-5:30pm daily mid-Mar.-Oct., $13 adults, $8 ages 6-12, free under age 6). Admission covers both the water park and Weeki Wachee Springs State Park. Pure, cold spring water laps against a tiny white-sand beach while families zoom down the flume rides and waterslides or hang out on the floating dock. It's a safe place to let kids roam free (lots of strict, eagle-eyed lifeguards make sure of that), and when they're exhausted, you can trot off to the riverboat cruise, petting zoo, and sweet animal show. Weeki Wachee Springs also hosts two-day **mermaid camps** (352/592-5656, ext. 30, $300), in which kids are taught the finer points of mermaidhood.

GOLF

The big kahuna of courses in these parts is the famous Tom Fazio-built **World Woods** (17590 Ponce de Leon Blvd., Brooksville, 352/796-5500, www.worldwoods.com, greens fees $18-178), just minutes away in Brooksville. It's a 45-hole complex with challenges for every golfer. Begin the day warming up on one of the hugest driving ranges you've ever laid eyes on (23 acres). From there you can bone up on the nine-hole short course, featuring seven par 3s and two par 4s, and then attempt either the 18-hole Pine Barrens, modeled after the great Pine Valley, or the stately and refined Rolling Oaks parkland course, an homage to Augusta National.

MOTORCYCLING

If you need a break from all that outdoor activity, you can hop on a hog and play *Easy Rider* at the **Harley-Davidson Shop of Crystal River** (1785 S. Suncoast Blvd., 352/563-9900). Sportsters, Big Twins, and V-Rods are all for rent for $150 a day for those over age 21.

Entertainment and Events
FESTIVALS

In January, Crystal River hosts the three-day **Florida Manatee Festival** (Citrus County Chamber of Commerce, 352/795-3149) with free manatee sightseeing boat tours, crafts, food, and entertainment.

The Homosassa River is home to a number of fishing tournaments worth watching: The annual **Cobia Tournament** (MacRae's Bait and Tackle, 352/628-2602) is in mid-June, and the famous **Southern Redfish Tour** (www.redfishtour.com, 478/836-4266) comes a few weeks later in July.

And on the second weekend in November, the **Homosassa Arts, Crafts, and Seafood Festival** (www.homosassaseafoodfestival.

com) whips up chowders and soft-shell crabs for the masses.

Shopping

For a real local bit of excitement, sift through the 300 or so booths at **Howard's Flea Market** (6373 S. Suncoast Blvd., Homosassa Springs, 352/628-3532, 7am-3pm Fri., 6:30am-3pm Sat.-Sun.). To safeguard against rain and muggy weather, the market is enclosed, with vendors selling leather goods, antiques, tools, fishing gear, and even pets. A bird aviary and food vendors (good barbecue and excellent old-fashioned root beer) make it fun for the whole family.

Food
WEEKI WACHEE

The town of Spring Hill, where Weeki Wachee Springs is found, has a couple of fun family-friendly places in which to refuel after a grueling day at the water park. **Richie Cheesesteak** (6191 Deltona Blvd., 352/600-7999, 10am-9pm Mon.-Thurs., 10am-10pm Fri.-Sat., $6-10) is the go-to place for lunch sandwiches, hamburgers, and cheesesteaks, of course. **Greek City Cafe** (3125 Commercial Way, 352/683-6606, 11am-9pm daily, $7-10) is a favorite for healthy lunches and dinners of Mediterranean-style salads, pizzas, wraps, and rice bowls.

For something a little nicer, **La Bella Napoli Italian Restaurant** (7386 Shoal Line Blvd., 352/556-5274, $12-25) serves up the best Italian food in town. The homemade meatballs, cannoli, and bread rolls are a favorite. The refined atmosphere is fitting for a romantic dinner.

HOMOSASSA

The south shore of the Homosassa River, accessible from Halls River Road, is host to a memorable place. Dinner at **Riverside Crab House** (5297 S. Cherokee Way, 352/621-5080, 11am-9pm Mon.-Thurs., 11am-10pm Fri., 11am-10pm Sat.-Sun., $9-30) is a relaxed and casual joint specializing in two-foot platters heaped with sweet corn, hush puppies, scallops, soft-shell crab, steamed blue crab, clams, and catfish. The attached Yardarm Lounge and the outdoor Monkey Bar tiki lounge are great places from which to spy on the four mostly tame monkeys who live on a tiny island a stone's throw away.

Dan's Clam Stand (2315 N. Sunshine Path, 352/795-9081, 11am-9pm Tues.-Sat., $8-15) is no-frills but makes a mean clam chowder, a serviceable lobster roll, and a fine fried grouper sandwich. If you don't love seafood, the buffalo wings are hot and tasty. And **The Starting Gate Restaurant** (10605 W. Yulee Dr., 352/503-2076, 6:30am-1pm Fri.-Mon., $8-10) is the place to try the local breakfast: fried cornmeal-crusted mullet with cheese grits.

For nightlife in Homosassa, locals go to **The Freezer Tiki Bar** (5590 S. Boulevard Dr., 352/628-2452), attempt a little karaoke at the **Dunbar's Old Mill Tavern** (10465 W. Yulee Dr., 352/628-2669), or have a leisurely riverside beer at **The Shed at MacRae's** (5300 S. Cherokee Way, 352/628-2602).

CRYSTAL RIVER
In Crystal River, people tend to send visitors to **Charlie's Fish House Restaurant** (244 NW U.S. 19, 352/795-3949, 11am-9pm daily, $9-16) for the views of the river and the simply prepared local fish, as well as oysters and stone crab claws (you eat only the claws because fisherfolk haul 'em up, yank off one claw, and throw them back to grow another). The restaurant has a substantial boat dock for waterborne diners.

Cracker's Bar and Grill (502 NW 6th St., 352/795-3999, 11am-10pm Sun.-Thurs., 11am-11pm Fri.-Sat., $6-13), just up the block, is a locals' hangout with a commitment to big portions and providing something for everyone. The menu is vast, with burgers and nachos alongside sautéed scallops and shrimp. Live entertainment has things hopping in the tiki bar and deck on the weekend, with karaoke many nights. Tie your boat up to one of the restaurant's 14 slips, or hop on the restaurant's water taxi and see some of Kings Bay.

For nightlife, the young folks gather at **Castaway's Bar and Grill** (5430 N. Suncoast Blvd., 352/795-3653, 7:30am-2am daily, $5-10). They also serve a wide variety of food such as hot wings, burgers, Mexican, seafood, soups, and sandwiches.

Accommodations
This swath of Florida is replete with RV parks, campgrounds, and fish camps that run from rough wooden cabins to affordable and simple motels. In nearly all the small towns that dot U.S. 19 or the little roads west to the Gulf, you can bet on finding a clean room in a casual and unique independently owned motel, where the amenities are whatever is happening out on the river, bay, or spring.

In addition, the area provides opportunities to indulge a lot of people's fantasy of endless tranquil mobility: a stay on a houseboat. Go "way down upon the Suwannee River" with a 44-foot houseboat rented from **Gateway Marina Houseboats** (90 SE County Rd. 349, Suwannee, 352/542-7349, www.suwanneehouseboats.com, $599-899 for 2 days, including weekends, $1,799 weekly). The houseboats sleep up to eight and are equipped with showers, restroom facilities, linens, full kitchens, and cookware. The owners take renters on a warm-up cruise to teach them the basics, and then you're on your own with 70 miles of river, countless springs, and an up-close view of the area's wildlife. It's a great way to pretend you're Huckleberry Finn.

UNDER $100
For RV travelers, there are 398 picturesque sites set on 80 acres at **Rock Crusher Canyon RV Resort** (275 S. Rock Crusher Rd., Crystal River, 352/564-9350, www.sunrvresorts.com, $40-47 daily, $217-263 weekly, $568-730 monthly). It contains a 7,000-seat outdoor amphitheater that has welcomed Willie Nelson, Three Dog Night, and Joan Jett, as well as some humongous RV rallies. Also in Crystal River, with lakeside and canal-side spots that include your own boat dock space,

Crystal Isles Resort (11419 W. Fort Island Trail, Crystal River, 352/795-3774, $41) is a 30-acre RV resort not far from the Fort Island Trail Beach.

In Crystal River you'll find many of the inexpensive chains, such as **Best Western Crystal River Resort** (614 NW U.S. 19, Crystal River, 352/795-3171, $90-140), with its own marina and excellent fish and dive shop; **Quality Inn** (4486 N. Suncoast Blvd., Crystal River, 352/563-1500, $60-90); **Days Inn** (2380 NW U.S. 19, Crystal River, 352/795-2111, $55-90); and **Econo Lodge** (2575 NW U.S. 19, Crystal River, 352/795-9447, $55-85). Most cater to visiting anglers and don't have many amenities beyond a computer in the lobby to check email. But for a more authentic experience, spend just a bit more and head for one of the independently owned places.

The area right around Weeki Wachee Springs has a lot of suburban sprawl, so it isn't the best vacation spot on the Nature Coast, but if you really want to be near this particular spring, the **Quality Inn Weeki Wachee** (9373 Cortez Blvd., 352/596-9000, $60-99) is the best bet. It's right across the street from the spring and its water park, with 116 rooms in a nice two-story building.

$100-200

Homosassa Riverside Resort (5297 S. Cherokee Way, Homosassa, 352/628-2474, www.riversideresorts.com, $65-210) is the oldest resort along the Homosassa River. Many rooms have full kitchens, so you have dining flexibility, but the on-site restaurant and lounge are definitely worth a visit. From the hotel you can arrange a manatee awareness tour, kayak and canoe rentals, airboat rides, and other adventures.

Presided over by Gator MacRae, **MacRae's of Homosassa** (5300 S. Cherokee Way, Homosassa, 352/628-2602, www.macrae-sofhomosassa.com, $100-150) is the rustic anglers' pick, with a series of log cabin-like squatty structures and old-fashioned rockers

on the front porches. The 12 rooms and 10 efficiencies are equipped with kitchens, and there are laundry facilities on the premises. Its riverside marina offers boat rentals, a bait shop, and fishing charters.

The **Izaak Walton Lodge** (6301 Riverside Dr., Yankeetown, 352/447-4899, www.izaak-waltonlodge.com, $150, kayaks included) is one of the few reasons to get off U.S. 19 and amble down County Road 40 to Yankeetown. The small inn has a serene setting on the banks of the Withlacoochee River, with dock space where you can tie up your boat. The on-site restaurant, **The Riverside Inn,** includes a dining room and bar on the first floor and a multitiered dining terrace. The menu has excellent local seafood choices such as oysters Rockefeller and fried gator nuggets along with entrées like New York strip and lobster.

$200-300

The Nature Coast doesn't offer the abundance of golfing opportunities available elsewhere in Florida. If you're jonesing to tee off, the **Plantation on Crystal River** (9301 W. Fort Island Trail, Crystal River, 352/795-4211, www.plantationoncrystalriver.com, $154-350, including greens fees) boasts an 18-hole par-72 championship course and a 9-hole executive course for training and practice, in addition to manatee snorkeling tours, guided scuba diving, and 145 guest rooms, 12 golf villas, and six condos. Given all the amenities and glitz, room rates are a fairly reasonable.

Getting There and Around

From south to north, Spring Hill (the town of Weeki Wachee Springs), Homosassa, and Crystal River are lined up adjacent to each other right along U.S. 19. The 27-mile drive from Spring Hill to Homosassa will take you about 40 minutes. From Homosassa to Crystal River, the 10-mile drive takes about 20 minutes. Two northbound Greyhound buses stop daily in Crystal River, but once you arrive, you'll need a car to get around.

INFORMATION AND SERVICES

Tourist Information

Citrus County Chamber of Commerce (915 N. Suncoast Blvd., Crystal River, 352/795-3149, 8:30am-4:30pm Mon.-Fri., 8:30am-1pm Sat.), stocks racks of local brochures and pamphlets. For more information about local events, pick up the *Citrus County Chronicle* (www.chronicleonline.com), the largest daily in the county.

Birders will want to check out the website of the **Citrus County Audubon Society** (www.citruscountyaudubon.org), which catalogs birding opportunities on virtually every trail in the area.

Police and Emergencies

The **Crystal River Police Department,** the largest along the Nature Coast, is in back of city hall (123 NW U.S. 19, 352/795-4241).

In the event of a medical emergency, **Seven Rivers Regional Medical Center** (6201 N. Suncoast Blvd., Crystal River, 352/795-6560) has emergency services, as does **Regional General Hospital** (125 SW 7th St., Williston, 352/528-2801). For anything major, you may want to head to **North Florida Regional Medical Center** in Gainesville or **Citrus Memorial Hospital** in Inverness.

Sarasota

The circus built Sarasota. Sure, the 361 days of sun each year and the exotic subtropical plants and animals brought people to the area. But it was when circus impresario John Ringling snapped up real estate that others started giving this rural orange grove and celery farm another look. And in the 1920s, as Ringling began amassing huge numbers of baroque paintings in his new mansion, Cà d'Zan, so too did Ringling's cohorts begin assembling collections of their own for a little winter rest and relaxation. Soon the opera, theater, and symphony orchestras took root.

Beyond Ringling's generous gift of his house and museums to the city, the Circus King gave Sarasota a tradition of arts patronage. Sarasota's population of 54,000, with a little help from twice that number of winter visitors, supports a vast number of arts events along with an equally strong restaurant and shopping scene.

The striking thing is that it's all set in an incredible natural environment. Sarasota is home to world-class beaches and all the fun beach activities, with easy access to outstanding state parks and outdoor fun.

SIGHTS

Marie Selby Botanical Gardens

If you want to see beautiful orchids, bromeliads, and other epiphytes, spend a long afternoon at **Marie Selby Botanical Gardens** (811 S. Palm Ave., 941/366-5731, www.selby. org, 10am-5pm daily, $20 adults, $10 ages 4-17, free under age 4). The nine-acre gardens on the shores of Sarasota Bay are one of Sarasota's absolute jewels. Marie Selby donated her home and grounds "to provide enjoyment for all who visit the gardens." And there's a lot of enjoyment to be had meandering along the walking paths through the hibiscus garden, cycad garden, a banyan grove, a tropical fruit garden, and thousands of orchids. The botanical gardens also host lectures and gardening classes, and have a charming shop (beginners should opt for a training-wheels *Phalaenopsis*—very hard to kill—or an easy-care bromeliad) with an exhaustive collection of gardening books (80 on orchids alone). Spend an hour gazing at epiphytes in the tropical greenhouse and you'll become a fan, I promise. Kids get fairly bored here, with a brief flurry of interest around the koi pond and butterfly garden. I would recommend not

Sarasota

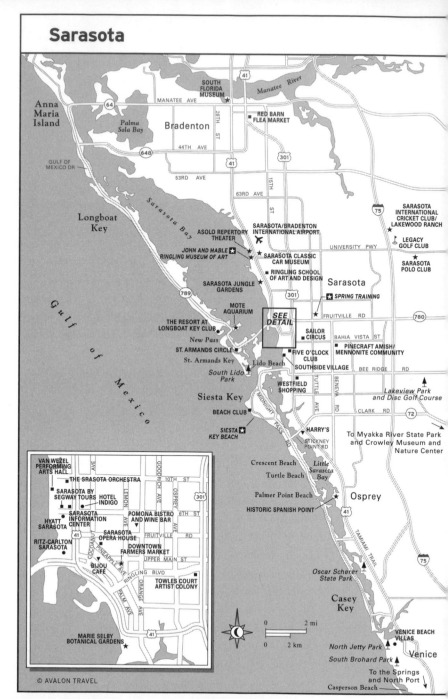

Anna
Maria
Island

Palma
Sola Bay

GULF OF
MEXICO DR

Longboat
Key

Bradenton

MANATEE AVE

SOUTH
FLORIDA
MUSEUM ★

Manatee River

RED BARN
■ FLEA MARKET

26TH
ST

44TH AVE

53RD AVE

63RD AVE

15TH
ST

SARASOTA
INTERNATIONAL
CRICKET CLUB/
LAKEWOOD RANCH

ASOLO REPERTORY
THEATER

SARASOTA/BRADENTON
INTERNATIONAL AIRPORT

UNIVERSITY PWY

LEGACY
GOLF CLUB

JOHN AND MABLE ★
RINGLING MUSEUM OF ART

SARASOTA CLASSIC
★ CAR MUSEUM

SARASOTA
POLO CLUB

RINGLING SCHOOL
■ OF ART AND DESIGN

Sarasota

SARASOTA JUNGLE
GARDENS ★

SPRING TRAINING

MOTE
AQUARIUM

SEE
DETAIL

FRUITVILLE RD

THE RESORT AT
LONGBOAT KEY CLUB

New Pass

ST. ARMANDS CIRCLE ■

St. Armands Key

Lido Beach

South Lido
Park

Siesta Key

BEACH CLUB ■

SIESTA
KEY BEACH ★

SAILOR
■ CIRCUS

BAHIA VISTA ST

PINECRAFT AMISH/
■ MENNONITE COMMUNITY

FIVE O'CLOCK
■ CLUB

SOUTHSIDE VILLAGE

BEE RIDGE   RD

WESTFIELD
■ SHOPPING

TUTTLE

AVE

BENEVA

RD

CLARK   RD

Lakeview Park
and Disc Golf Course

HARRY'S ■

STICKNEY
POINT RD

To Myakka River State Park
and Crowley Museum and
Nature Center

Crescent Beach

Turtle Beach

Little
Sarasota
Bay

Palmer Point Beach

HISTORIC SPANISH POINT

Osprey

Gulf   of   Mexico

Siesta Key

Gulf Bay

Sarasota Bay

64

648

41

301

75

789

301

780

72

41

VAN WEZEL
PERFORMING
ARTS HALL

■ THE SRASOTA ORCHESTRA

SARASOTA BY
SEGWAY TOURS

10TH   ST

GOODRICH   AVE

OSPREY

301

HOTEL
INDIGO

SARASOTA
INFORMATION
CENTER

HYATT
SARASOTA

6TH   ST

POMONA BISTRO
AND WINE BAR

LEMON
AVE

RITZ-CARLTON
SARASOTA

41

SARASOTA
OPERA HOUSE

COCOANUT
AVE

PINEAPPLE AVE

FRUITVILLE   RD

DOWNTOWN
FARMERS MARKET

BIJOU
CAFÉ

RINGLING BLVD

UPPER MAIN ST

ORANGE
AVE

TOWLES COURT
ARTIST COLONY

PALM   AVE

MARIE SELBY
BOTANICAL GARDENS ★

41

Oscar Scherer
State Park

Casey
Key

TAMIAMI TRAIL

75

VENICE BEACH
VILLAS

North Jetty Park

Venice

South Brohard Park

To the Springs
and North Port

Casperson Beach

0   2 mi

0   2 km

© AVALON TRAVEL

downtown Sarasota

all this in 1926 when the Astor mansion in New York City was scheduled to be demolished. The permanent collection is spectacular, with Van Dycks, Poussins, and lots of other baroque masters, but there are temporary shows such as a recent one on surrealism and another on the photos of Ansel Adams and Clyde Butcher that date to the 20th century.

The complex also houses the **Museum of the Circus,** a peek into circus history. It achieves a certain level of overstatement in the interpretive signs when it parallels the ascendance of the circus with the growth of the country. Still, the museum's newspaper clippings, circus equipment, parade wagons, and colossal bail rings make one nostalgic for a time and place most people today probably never knew.

The single most impressive thing about the museum, the thing that causes rampant loitering and inspired commentary like "Whoa, cool," is the Howard Bros. Circus model. It takes up vast space—the world's largest miniature circus, after all—and is a 1:16 scale replica of Ringling Bros. and Barnum & Bailey Circus at its largest. The model itself takes up 3,800 square feet, with eight main tents, 152 wagons, 1,300 circus performers and workers, more than 800 animals, a 57-car train, and a zillion wonderful details.

Fully restored in 2002, John Ringling's home on the bay, **Cà d'Zan** (House of John), can also be visited. It is an ornate structure evocative of Ringling's two favorite Venetian hotels, the Danieli and the Bauer Grunwald. Completed in 1926, the house is 200 feet long with 32 rooms and 15 baths. It is truly a magnificent mansion.

bringing them unless they're really into plants or are stroller-bound.

★ John and Mable Ringling Museum of Art

John Ringling's lasting influence on Sarasota is remarkable, but the **John and Mable Ringling Museum of Art** (5401 Bay Shore Rd., 941/359-5700, www.ringling.org, 10am-5pm daily, $25 adults, $23 seniors, $5 students, $15 active military, $10 teachers, $5 ages 6-17) makes it simply undeniable.

The whole museum complex is spectacular, but the art museum is definitely worth its hefty admission price. It was built in 1927 to house Ringling's nearly pathological collection of 600 paintings, sculptures, and decorative arts, including more than 25 tapestries. The Mediterranean-style palazzo contains a collection that includes a set of five extremely large paintings by Peter Paul Rubens, many other Spanish works of art, and the music room and dining room of Caroline Astor, widow of William B. Astor; Ringling bought

Sarasota Classic Car Museum

What's your dream car? DeLorean? Ferrari? Mini Cooper? The **Sarasota Classic Car Museum** (5500 N. Tamiami Trail, 941/355-6228, www.sarasotacarmuseum.com, 9am-6pm daily, $12.85 adults, $10.50 seniors, $7.25 ages 6-12, free under age 6) has more than 75 vehicles, from muscle to vintage to exotic cars, including a rare Cadillac station wagon, one of only five ever made. The gift shop has collectibles for most automotive preoccupations, and the museum rents out some of its cars if you want to make a grand entrance somewhere. The cars are also available for photo ops.

Historic Spanish Point

History buffs may want to visit **Historic Spanish Point** (337 N. Tamiami Trail, Osprey, 941/966-5214, www.historicspanishpoint.org, 9am-5pm Mon.-Sat., noon-5pm Sun., $12 adults, $10 seniors, $5 ages 5-12), operated by the Gulf Coast Heritage Association. Bordered on its western edge by Little Sarasota Bay and by pine flatlands to the east, the 30-acre site tells the story of life in the greater Sarasota area going back many generations. Interpretive markers and an "Indian village" show how early Native Americans fished and hunted here, building middens, or shell mounds, and a burial mound; an archaeology exhibit in the main hall provides the background on this. Then there's a restored pioneer home and chapel, revealing the story of the early settlers here, the Webb family. After that, you'll stroll the gardens of heiress Bertha Matilde Honore Palmer's winter estate on Osprey Point. The site has a butterfly garden to add to the mix, showing the larval and nectar plants for monarch, zebra longwing, swallowtail, and other butterflies native to the area.

South Florida Museum

For the history buff, the **South Florida Museum** (201 10th St. W., Bradenton, 941/746-4131, 10am-5pm Tues.-Sat., noon-5pm Sun., $19 adults, $17 seniors, $14 ages 4-12) is worth a short drive north to Bradenton. There are ice age dioramas with animals and natural history exhibits that trace the state's ancient history. The Spanish explorers are covered in detail, and the museum houses the Tallant Collection of artifacts, an assemblage of loot from Floridian archaeological sites.

Downtown Farmers Market

Every Saturday morning year-round you'll find all the sights and smells unique to the local Florida farmers market: stacked produce; the cookie lady; a band of musicians passing the hat; babies in strollers, smiling around a mouthful of gummed peach; wind chimes and handicrafts; and bromeliads, orchids, and cut flowers filling the bulging bags of nearly every shopper. The **Downtown Farmers Market** (Lemon Ave. and Main St., 7am-1pm Sat.) has been going on for 30 years.

Sarasota Jungle Gardens

My favorite family attraction in Sarasota is **Sarasota Jungle Gardens** (3701 Bay Shore Rd., 941/355-5305, 10am-5pm daily, $18 adults, $17 seniors, $13 ages 4-16, free under age 4), but then I'm a sucker for quirky Old Florida attractions. Once a boggy banana grove, the subtropical jungle was purchased in the 1930s by newspaperman David Lindsay. He brought in tropical plants, trees, and bird species. It opened in 1940 as a tourist attraction, and it puttered along through a couple of ownership changes until it ended up in the hands of the Allyn family. Every elementary school student within 100 miles has made the trek by school bus to sit and watch the short birds of prey show and then wander along the paths through the lush formal gardens, the farmyard exhibit, the tiki gardens, and the flamingo area. The zoological gardens are home to about 100 animals, many of them abandoned pets, so it's an odd assortment. Another section of the park, however, has nothing to do with plants or animals—in one back corner you'll find the Gardens of Christ, a series of eight two-dimensional dioramas by Italian-born sculptor Vincent Maldarelli depicting important events in the life of Christ.

Mote Marine Laboratory and Aquarium

The **Mote Marine Laboratory and Aquarium** (1600 Ken Thompson Pkwy., City Island, 941/388-4441, 10am-5pm daily, $19.75 adults, $18.75 seniors, $14.75 ages

4-12, free under age 4) is an enjoyable small aquarium that also serves as a working marine laboratory. For kids, the coolest parts are the 135,000-gallon shark tank and the "immersion cinema" state-of-the-art theater with a 40-foot-wide high-definition screen with Dolby Surround sound. Visitors get their own interactive consoles that change the outcome of the game or movie on the screen. Children will also like the underwater microphone in the Marine Mammal Center, which allows visitors to hear the resident manatees chirping at each other and methodically munching the heads of romaine lettuce that bob at the top of their tank. There's a touch tank, where you'll see parents cajoling their small ones to feel a sea urchin, starfish, horseshoe crab, or stingless stingray, as well as nicely interpreted exhibits of eels, puffer fish, sea horses, and extraterrestrial-looking jellies.

The more impressive part of the Mote is not open to the public—the Mote Marine Laboratory is known internationally for its shark research and more locally for its research on red tides, or algal blooms, which occasionally adversely affect Sarasota's summer beach season with fish kills.

Sarasota Bay Explorers

Sarasota Bay Explorers (941/388-4200, www.sarasotabayexplorers.com) works in conjunction with Mote Marine Laboratory and runs science boat trips out of the facility. They offer several wonderful ecotours, all perfect for a fun yet educational family outing. There are narrated **Sea Life Encounter Cruises** ($27 adults, $23 ages 4-12), backwater **guided kayak tours** ($55 adults, $45 children), and private charters aboard the 24-foot Sea Ray Sundeck *Miss Explorer* (3-hour trip $295, 4-hour trip $370, 5-hour trip $445).

Tours

One of the more popular tours in the area is a 1.5-hour ($55) or 2-hour ($65) guided tour of downtown Sarasota on a Segway with **Sarasota by Segway Tours** (1370 Blvd. of the Arts, Suite C, 941/312-2615, www.

sarasotabysegway.com, 10am and 1pm daily, participants must be at least age 12), zipping along the bay front and arts community. The electric Segway device is self-balancing and steered with handlebars. With speeds of up to 12 mph, they can be used in pedestrian areas and are a perfect way to cover serious ground at a pace slow enough to appreciate things. Tours are limited to 12 people, and there is a weight limit (300 lbs.).

If your passion is architecture, you won't need to be told that Sarasota is the birthplace of a certain strain of American modernism. The **Sarasota Architectural Foundation** (941/487-8728, www.sarasotaarchitecturalfoundation.org) hosts architectural tours, educational events, film screenings, exhibits, and parties for architecture lovers who travel to Sarasota to see its architecture up close. A list of tours is posted on the website.

Several companies offer boat tours on Sarasota Bay and into the Gulf of Mexico. **Key Sailing** (2 Marina Jack, Bayfront Plaza, 941/346-7245, www.siestakeysailing.com, $60 for 2 hours, $80 for 3 hours) offers charters and sailing instruction aboard a sleek 41-foot Morgan Classic II. **LeBarge Tropical Cruises** (2 Marina Plaza, U.S. 41 at Marina Jack, 941/366-6116, www.lebargetropicalcruises.com, 9am-6pm daily, $25 adults, $20 ages 4-12) offers two-hour cruises of Sarasota Bay. Choose from a dolphin watch narrated by a marine biologist, a narrated sightseeing cruise, or a tropical sunset cruise.

BEACHES

North Lido Beach is just northwest of St. Armands Circle, off John Ringling Boulevard on Lido Key, which itself is just a 2.5-mile spit of beach from Big Sarasota Pass to New Pass. It's a short walk from shops or restaurants, and fairly secluded. There are no lifeguards, swift currents, or real amenities. In the other direction from St. Armands Circle, southwest, you'll run into **Lido Beach,** which has parking for 400 cars, cabana beach rentals at the snack bar, playground equipment, and restrooms. It's a good hang-out-all-afternoon family beach but is more crowded than North Lido. The third beach on Lido Key is called **South Lido Park,** on Ben Franklin Drive at the southern tip of Lido Key. The park is bordered by four bodies of water: the Gulf, Big Pass, Sarasota Bay, and Brushy Bayou. It has a nature trail, and the beach offers a great view of the downtown Sarasota skyline. There's a nice picnic area with grills as well as volleyball courts. Kayakers use this area to traverse the different waterways.

SPORTS AND RECREATION
Golf

Sarasota is Florida's self-described "Cradle of Golf," having been home to the state's first course, built in 1905 by Scottish immigrant John Hamilton Gillespie. The nine-hole course was located at the center of what is now Sarasota's downtown. That course is long gone, but there are more than 1,000 holes to play at public, semiprivate, and private courses in Sarasota at all levels of play and for most budgets. Of the top Southwest regional courses as voted by the readers of *Florida Golf News* (www.floridagolfmagazine.com), many are in the Sarasota area.

★ Spring Training

Sarasota's Ed Smith Stadium has been an exciting part of professional baseball's Grapefruit League spring training program for years. The New York Giants arrived back in 1924, followed by the Red Sox and then the White Sox. These days, Sarasota's **Ed Smith Stadium** (2700 12th St., at Tuttle Ave., 941/954-4101, box seats $22-36, reserved $16-30, general $8-14, parking $9) is the spring training home of the Baltimore Orioles (the Boston Red Sox now train farther south in Fort Myers, and the Pittsburgh Pirates play in nearby Bradenton). To reach the stadium from I-75, take exit 210 for Fruitville Road.

The little 8,500-seat stadium provides intimate access to big-league play in a small-time venue. In 2010 the stadium received a major renovation that replaced all seats, moved

A boardwalk leads to Lido Beach.

bullpens, and added a Mediterranean-style facade. Cheap tickets and up-close seats make for a perfect outing on a warm Sarasota spring evening, even if baseball is not your sport. Day games start at 1:05pm and night games at 7:05pm; practices begin at 9am. Many spring training games sell out, so you might want to buy tickets in advance. For more information, visit www.baltimore.orioles.mlb.com.

Polo

There are scads of spectator sporting opportunities in Sarasota, but polo trumps a fair number of them. Games are enormous fun, the horses racing around tearing up the lush sod of the polo grounds while their riders focus fiercely on that pesky little ball. Polo is amazingly physical and exciting to watch, whether you're in your fancy polo hats or your weekend jeans. **Sarasota Polo Club** (Lakewood Ranch, 8201 Polo Club Lane, 941/907-0000, www.sarasotapolo.com, 1pm Sun. mid-Dec.-early Apr., $12 adults, free under age 13) has been in operation since 1991, with

Sarasota Golf

Call for tee times and greens fees, as they vary wildly by time of day and season.

Bobby Jones Golf Club
1000 Circus Blvd., Sarasota, 941/365-4653
6,039 yards, par 71, course rating 68.4, slope 117

Greens of Manatee Public Golf and Driving Range
101 Cortez Rd. W., Bradenton, 941/755-8888
3,521 yards, par 61, course rating 58.6, slope 96

Legacy Golf Club at Lakewood Ranch
8255 Legacy Blvd., Bradenton, 941/907-7920
semiprivate, 7,069 yards, par 72, course rating 73.8, slope 130

The Links at Green Field Plantation
10325 Greenfield Plantation Blvd., Bradenton, 941/747-9432
6,719 yards, par 72, course rating 72, slope 130

Manatee County Golf Course
6415 53rd Ave. W., Bradenton, 941/792-6773
6,747 yards, par 72, course rating 71.6, slope 122

Palmetto Pines Golf Course
14355 Golf Course Dr., Parrish, 941/776-1375
5,358 yards, par 72, course rating 68.4, slope 92

Peridia Golf & Country Club
4950 Peridia Blvd., Bradenton, 941/758-2582, www.peridiagcc.net
3,344 yards, par 60, course rating 55.0, slope 76

Pinebrook/Ironwood Golf Club
4260 Ironwood Circle, Bradenton, 941/792-3288
3,706 yards, par 61, course rating 59.9, slope 101

River Club
6600 River Club Blvd., Bradenton, 941/751-4211
7,026 yards, par 72, course rating 74.5, slope 135

River Run Golf Links
1801 27th St. E., Bradenton, 941/708-6331
5,825 yards, par 70, course rating 67.9, slope 115

Rosedale Golf and Country Club
5100 87th St. E., Bradenton, 941/753-6200
6,779 yards, par 72, course rating 72.9, slope 134

Terra Ceia Bay Golf Club
2802 Terra Ceia Bay Blvd., Palmetto, 941/729-1798
4,001 yards, par 62, course rating 67.9, slope 99

Timber Creek Golf Course
4550 Timber Lane, Bradenton, 941/794-8381
2,086 yards, par 27 (9 holes), course rating 35.1, slope 117

University Park Country Club
7671 Park Blvd., University Park, 941/355-3888
4,914-7,247 yards, par 72, course rating 67.8-74.4, slope 113-138

Waterlefe Golf & River Club
1022 Fish Hook Cove, Bradenton, 941/744-9771
6,908 yards, par 72, course rating 73.8, slope 145

professional-level players coming from around the world to play on the nine pristine fields. Bring a picnic or buy sandwiches and drinks once you're there. Gates open at 10am, and dogs on leashes are welcome. You can also take polo lessons at Lakewood Ranch.

State Parks and Nature Preserves

If you want to spend a day outdoors, the **Myakka River State Park** (9 miles east of Sarasota, 13208 Hwy. 72, 941/361-6511, 8am-sunset daily, $6 per vehicle for up to 8 people, $4 per vehicle single occupant, $2 motorcycles, bicycles, and pedestrians) has a lot of activities to offer. The 28,875-acre park offers hiking, off-road biking, horseback riding, fishing, boating, canoeing, camping, and airboating. Both part of Florida Division of Forestry's Trailwalker Program, the North Loop (5.4 miles) and South Loop (7.4 miles) are fairly easy and scenic marked trails. Beyond these, there are 35 miles of unmarked trails open to hikers, mountain bikers (rentals $15 for 2 hours, 4-person tandems $30 for 2 hours), and equestrians (BYOH—that's bring your own horse). If you just want to breeze in for a few hours, a ride on the **Myakka Wildlife Tours Tram Safari** (10151 Sommers Rd., Sarasota,

941/377-5797, Dec.-May, $14 adults, $7 ages 6-12, free under age 6 if held in lap) takes visitors on a whirlwind tour of the park's backcountry, through shady hammocks, pine flatwoods, and lush marshes.

The 14-mile stretch of the scenic Myakka River has fairly easy-to-follow canoe trails; bring your own or rent one at the Myakka Outpost ($20 for 1 hour, $5 per additional hour). Canoes and kayaks can be launched at the bridges, fishing area, other picnic areas, or at the boat ramp. During periods of low water (winter and spring), you'll have to portage around the weir at the south end of the Upper Lake. If you don't want to travel under your own paddle power, the park has a **boat tour** (941/365-0100, $14 adults, $7 children) that runs every 1.5 hours, and a couple of the world's largest airboats, the *Gator Gal* and the *Myakka Maiden,* are available for guided one-hour tours on the mile-wide and 2.5-mile-long Upper Myakka Lake, which is serious gator territory.

One unique park feature opened in 2004 in conjunction with Marie Selby Botanical Gardens. The Canopy Walkway, the first of its kind in North America, is an 85-foot-long observation-deck suspension bridge that hangs 25 feet in the air in the midst of a

Ed Smith Stadium is where the Orioles conduct their spring training.

subtropical forest canopy. Perched in the tops of live oaks, laurel oaks, and cabbage palms, your perspective on birdlife and other animals is unparalleled.

The park offers primitive camping ($5) and serviced campsites ($32.70, including water and electric), but the neatest option might be one of the five palm log cabins (800/326-3521, $70 for up to four people) built in the 1930s. They're pretty comfortable, with two double beds, linens, blankets, and kitchen facilities. These cabins are popular; reserve far in advance.

Adjacent to the state park is the **Crowley Museum and Nature Center** (16405 Myakka Rd., 941/322-1000, www.crowleyfl. com, 10am-sunset Thurs.-Sun., $5 adults, $2 ages 3-18, free under age 3 and active military), a 190-acre wildlife sanctuary and education center. A couple of hours spent here dovetails nicely with time spent hiking or paddling in Myakka River State Park—there's a short nature trail, a boardwalk across Maple Branch Swamp, and an observation tower overlooking the Myakka River. To give the area a historical context, the Crowley's core is a pioneer museum tricked out with a rustic one-room cabin, a restored 1892 Cracker house, a working blacksmith shop, and a little sugarcane mill. The museum sponsors Pioneer Days every December, an annual antiques fair, a folk music festival in October, and a yearly stargazing night with high-powered telescopes.

It won't knock your socks off with stunning topography or habitats, but **Oscar Scherer State Park** (1843 S. Tamiami Trail, Osprey, 941/483-5956, 8am-sunset daily, $5 per vehicle for 2-8 occupants, $4 per vehicle sole occupant, $2 pedestrians, bicycles, and motorcycles, $4 sunset entry) is a local hangout for birders and families who want to spend an afternoon in nature without a lot of hassle. Much of it is classic Florida flatwoods: scrub pine and sawtooth palmetto populated with animals like scrub jays, gopher tortoises, and indigo snakes. The park has several marked trails open to hikers and bikers (it's sandy terrain, most suitable for mountain bikes), and kayakers paddle around South Creek. Bring your own canoe or kayak or rent canoes ($10 per hour, $40 per day) from the ranger station, launched from the South Creek Picnic Area. Birders may want to join the informal morning bird walks (8am Thurs.), the morning ranger-led walks (8:30am Fri.), or canoe tours (9am Wed.). Check in at the park's nature center. The park also has a 104-site

Take a boat tour at Myakka River State Park.

campground with tent and RV sites ($33, $16 seniors or disabled) equipped with electricity and water. The restrooms have hot showers, and the maximum RV length is 36 feet.

ENTERTAINMENT AND EVENTS
Theater

Celebrating over 50 years of professional theater in Sarasota, the **Asolo Repertory Theatre** (5555 N. Tamiami Trail, 941/351-9010, www.asolorep.org, curtain times 2pm and 8pm Nov.-June) is a professional company that performs primarily in the 500-seat Harold E. and Esther M. Mertz Theatre at the Florida State University Center for the Performing Arts, originally built as an opera house in 1903 in Dunfermline, Scotland. The smaller 161-seat black-box Jane B. Cook Theatre is on-site for performances of the conservatory season and smaller productions of the Asolo. Students also present a series of original works known as the LateNite series, and the FSU School of Theatre presents a variety of other special events and performances. Currently, the Asolo Rep and the Conservatory perform one show each in the Historic Asolo Theatre, located in the Ringling Museum's Visitors Pavilion. All of this means more shows and more variety for Sarasota's theatergoers.

Because the Florida State University Conservatory for Actor Training's graduate-level program yields so many newly minted thespians in Sarasota, the whole theatrical playing field has been elevated. Worthwhile community and professional theater troupe efforts include the contemporary dramas and comedies at **Florida Studio Theatre** (1241 N. Palm Ave., 941/366-9000). Enjoy six annual musical productions with **The Players of Sarasota** (838 N. Tamiami Trail, 941/365-2494, www.theplayers.org), dramas in the summer with **Banyan Theater Company** (at the Asolo's Jane B. Cook Theatre, 941/351-2808), and even the small community productions on two stages of the **Venice Theatre** (140 W. Tampa Ave., Venice, 941/488-1115).

Music and Dance

The oldest continuously running orchestra in the state of Florida, **The Sarasota Orchestra** (Beatrice Friedman Symphony Center, 709 N. Tamiami Trail, box office 941/953-3434, www.sarasotaorchestra.org) offers a wide array of more than 100 classical, pops, chamber, and family concerts per year. It also hosts the internationally recognized

the Asolo Repertory Theatre

the Van Wezel Performing Arts Hall

well as being the home base for many of the local arts organizations.

The **Sarasota Ballet of Florida** (5555 N. Tamiami Trail, 941/359-0099, www.sarasota-ballet.org) splits its performances between the Van Wezel, the Asolo, and the FSU Center for the Performing Arts, offering a combination of treasured classical works and contemporary and modern dance. The ballet was founded as a presenting organization in 1987 by Jean Allenby-Weidner, former prima ballerina with the Stuttgart Ballet. Through community support, it became a resident company in 1990. The ballet often works collaboratively with other local arts organizations on productions—in 2005 it staged a ballet with Circus Sarasota that tells the story of John Ringling's life, complete with aerialists and clowns. The Sarasota Ballet also runs the Sarasota Ballet Academy; Next Generation, an award-winning scholarship program for youth at risk; and an international summer school.

The **Sarasota Opera** (61 N. Pineapple Ave., 941/328-1300, www.sarasotaopera.org) presents concerts year-round, but its much anticipated and often sold-out repertory season is in February and March, housed in the beautifully restored 1926 Mediterranean Revival-style Edwards Theatre. The opera house underwent an extensive renovation in 2007. It also offers youth outreach, and Sarasota Youth Opera receives all kinds of recognition for its productions.

It's an endurance event, one that takes grit and a good pair of opera glasses: The Sarasota Opera's **Winter Opera Festival** draws opera buffs from all over the country for a compact season of four productions, which can be enjoyed nearly at one sitting for the especially enthusiastic. The festival provides a good program of obscure operas as well as the big crowd-pleasers. While you're hanging around in the striking art deco lobby during intermission, look up: The chandelier is from the movie *Gone with the Wind*.

Sarasota also has an annual chamber music festival in April, **La Musica Festival** (rehearsals in Mildred Sainer Pavilion of

Sarasota Music Festival each June, an intense three-week event of chamber music, master classes, and concerts, with the coaching and performance of chamber music as its primary priority. Several Masterworks programs are presented by the symphony throughout the season, as well as a collection of Great Escapes programs of light classics and pops.

If you're not a huge symphonic music fan, you should try to catch a show at Sarasota's most distinctive landmark, the **Van Wezel Performing Arts Hall** (777 N. Tamiami Trail, 941/953-3368, www.vanwezel.org). Designed by William Wesley Peters of the Frank Lloyd Wright Foundation, the building riffs on a seashell found by Frank Lloyd Wright's widow, Olgivanna, near the Sea of Japan. It has an eye-popping lavender/purple color scheme, and it looks accordion-folded, like a scallop shell (supposedly to maximize the space's acoustical possibilities). Love it or hate it, the Van Wezel presents a wonderful range of Broadway productions, world-class dance, music, comedy, and popular acts, as

New College of Florida, performances in the Edwards Theatre, 61 N. Pineapple Ave., 941/366-8450, ext. 7, www.lamusicafestival.org, 8pm, single tickets $40, pass to a rehearsal $60). Before the actual evening performances there are short lectures about the pieces.

Circuses

In the 1920s, John Ringling and his wife, Mable, built a spectacular Venetian-style estate on Sarasota Bay, called **Cà d'Zan** (House of John, in the Venetian dialect). They built an **art museum** to house their bursting-at-the-seams collection of 17th-century Italian paintings, Flemish art, and works by Peter Paul Rubens. But it was 1927 when Sarasota became an official circus town—the Ringling Bros. and Barnum & Bailey Circus's winter quarters were moved here, giving the sedate Florida town a firsthand look at the oddity, eccentricity, and glamour that is the circus.

Many of the circus performers who acted in the *Wizard of Oz* and that ultimate non-PC film *Terror of Tiny Town* (a musical western starring all little people) called Sarasota home, with specially built homes in a section of town called, unsurprisingly, **Tiny Town** (you can visit this area on Ever-Glide guided tours).

Today, visitors get a sense of Sarasota's circus history at the **Museum of the Circus,** housed in the **John and Mable Ringling Museum of Art** (5401 Bay Shore Rd., 941/359-5700, 10am-5pm Fri.-Wed., 10am-8pm Thurs., $25 adults, $23 seniors, $15 military, $5 students and ages 6-17) on the Ringling grounds, but during February and March the circus comes alive with **Circus Sarasota** (140 University Town Center Dr., 941/355-9335, $15-55). Founded in 1997 by Ringling Bros. alums Pedro Reis and aerialist Dolly Jacobs (she's a second-generation circus performer—her father was the famous clown Lou Jacobs), it's a single-ring, European-style circus that changes every year. Reis and Jacobs often perform an aerial pas de deux, and there are tightrope acts, trained horses, aerial acrobats from China, clowns, tumbling, contortionists, all performed in an intimate setting.

Despite the fact that Ringling Bros. circus now makes its winter home farther north in Tampa, Sarasota is still training the next generation of circus performers. **Sailor Circus** (2075 Bahia Vista St., 941/361-6350) has been thrilling audiences for more than 50 years, educating kids ages 8 to 18 in the circus arts and then letting them put on a show. In 2004, the program was on the verge of closing. With the assistance of Sheriff William F. Balkwill, the Police Athletic League took over the Sailor Circus as one of its after-school programs. About 90 students participate in the twice-annual training sessions, where they learn circus skills like clowning, tumbling, high-wire, flying trapeze, unicycling, juggling, rigging, and costuming. Then, in March and the end of December, the students perform for the public in an exciting four-ring circus (11:45am and 7pm, $20 adults, $15 children).

Film Festivals

Sarasota supports two film festivals. By far the more famous is the **Sarasota Film Festival** (multiple venues, box office 332 Cocoanut Ave., 941/364-9514, www.sarasotafilmfestival.com), which happens every April. The fastest-growing film festival in the country, it showcases more than 180 independent feature, documentary, narrative, and short films. The event usually includes a Shorts Fest, a couple of family-oriented events, and lots of panel discussions with industry leaders and symposia with guest stars. And every November there's the Sarasota Film Society's 10-day **Cine-World Film Festival** (Burns Court Cinemas, 506 Burns Lane, 941/955-3456), which showcases Florida film artists in addition to presenting the best of the preceding Toronto, Cannes, New York, and Telluride Film Festivals.

Other Festivals

February's not a bad month to visit, because you can catch the month-long annual run of the European-style **Circus Sarasota.** Sarasota is the self-described "circus capital of the world," after all. Music lovers may want to come in February or March for the repertory season of the **Sarasota Opera,** although in April there's **La Musica Festival.** April also brings the weeklong **Florida Wine Fest & Auction.**

If you're visiting the area strictly for the white, powdery sand, you might think of coming in May for the pro-am **Siesta Key Crystal Classic Master Sand Sculpting Competition** on Siesta Key Beach. **Fourth of July** fireworks over the Gulf are wonderful from the vantage spot of Siesta Key Beach, too.

NIGHTLIFE
Bars

Downtown has a few nightspots that stand out. **Pomona Bistro and Wine Bar** (481 N. Orange Ave., 941/706-1677, 5pm-9pm Tues.-Thurs., 5pm-10pm Fri.-Sat., $15-30) has a vital bar scene with a remarkable by-the-glass wine list.

There are refreshing drinks and good times to be had many places, including the **Beach Club** (5151 Ocean Blvd., Siesta Key, 941/349-6311, www.beachclubsiestakey.com, noon 2:30am daily) in Siesta Key Village and **Sharky's** (1600 Harbor Dr. S., Venice, 941/488-1456, www.sharkysonthepier.com, 11:30am-10pm Sun.-Thurs., 11:30am-midnight Fri.-Sat.), beachfront on the Pier in Venice. **Harry's** (6606 S. Tamiami Trail, 941/922-1110, 11am-10pm daily) is a local sports bar for watching the game, and go to **8 Ball Lounge** (3527 Webber St., Sarasota, 941/922-8314, noon-2am daily) when you feel like working on your own game.

Dance and Music Clubs

When you're ready to get on the dance floor, the **Five O'Clock Club** (1930 Hillview St., 941/366-5555, concert schedule at www.5oclockclub.net, noon-2am Mon.-Fri., 3pm-2am Sat.-Sun., happy hour noon-8pm daily, small cover charge varies) in Southside Village has what the mechanic ordered. There's live music seven nights a week, with national and local rock, blues, and pop bands taking the stage at 10pm. The 5-O draws a

30s and 40s crowd and just a smattering of college kids. The **Gator Club** (1490 Main St., 941/366-5969, www.thegatorclub.com, 11:30am-2:30am Mon.-Fri., 10:30am-2:30am Sat., 8pm-1am Sun.) is another longtime nightlife haunt. There's live music every night, often of the Jimmy Buffett cover variety, plus pool tables upstairs and an impressive single-malt selection. Not recommended if you're an FSU fan. Go 'Noles.

For something totally different and not booze-centric, track down the **Siesta Key Drum Circle** on Sunday evenings, a drop-in party in which everyone adds their own beat. It all gets under way about one hour before sunset, just south of the main pavilion between lifeguard stands 3 and 4.

SHOPPING

The shops of **St. Armands Circle** on Lido Key have been a primary retail draw in Sarasota for a long time, historically known for high-end boutiques. These days the shops cover familiar ground—chains like **Chico's** (443 St. Armands Circle, 941/388-1393), **Tommy Bahama** (300 John Ringling Blvd., 941/388-2888), **Fresh Produce Clothing** (1 N. Blvd. of the Presidents, 941/388-1883), and **White House/Black Market** (317 St. Armands Circle, 941/388-5033)—and a handful of upscale independently owned boutiques. You can also explore the circle's novelty and gift-ware shops: **Fantasea Seashells** (345 St. Armands Circle, 941/388-3031), or **Kilwin's** (312 John Ringling Blvd., 941/388-3200), offering ice cream and fudge.

Towles Court Artist Colony (1938 Adams Lane, downtown Sarasota) is a collection of 16 quirky pastel-colored bungalows and cottages that contain working artists and their art. You can buy their work and watch them in action (11am-4pm Tues.-Sat.), or visit Towles Court for Art Walk (5pm-9pm 3rd Fri. every month).

Palm Avenue and **Main Street** downtown are lined with galleries, restaurants, and cute shops, and historic **Herald Square** in the SoMa (south of Main Street) part of downtown on Pineapple Avenue has a fairly dense concentration of antiques shops and upscale housewares stores. Also on Pineapple you'll find the **Artisan's World Marketplace** (128 S. Pineapple Ave., 941/365-5994, 10am-5pm Mon.-Fri., 9am-2pm Sat.), which promotes self-employment for low-income artisans in developing countries worldwide by selling their baskets, clothing, and handicrafts.

Westfield Shopping Town, Southgate (3501 S. Tamiami Trail, 941/955-0900) is a standard mall, with anchor store Macy's and many of the usual suspects (Ann Taylor, Talbots, Bare Minerals, GNCGymboree, and Chico's). For when you need to make those credit cards sizzle, you have to head north on I-75 to Ellenton to the **Prime Outlets** (5461 Factory Shops Blvd., Ellenton, 941/723-1150). There are more than 130 stores (Ralph Lauren, Gap, Guess, Tommy Hilfiger, Nike, Nautica) with deep discounts.

And if your mantra is "reduce, reuse, and recycle," you'll find all kinds of used goods at the more than 400 covered booths of the **Red Barn Flea Market** (1707 1st St. E., Bradenton, 941/747-3794), in Manatee County to the north. Go on the weekend for the greatest number of vendors and the widest variety of things, from collectibles and antiques to out-and-out junk.

FOOD
Downtown
★ **Bijou Café** (1287 1st St., 941/366-8111, 11:30am-2pm Mon.-Fri., 5pm-9pm Mon.-Thurs., 5pm-10pm Fri.-Sat., $19-36) has been a local gem since 1986, making everyone's top 10 list and bringing praise from *Zagat, Bon Appétit,* and *Gourmet.* It's what you'd call continental-American fare, presided over by chef Jean-Pierre Knaggs and his wife, Shay. Located a couple of blocks from the Ritz-Carlton Sarasota in a 1920s gas station-turned-restaurant, the vibe is special-occasion or big-business dining. A 2004 renovation after a fire brought a bar, lounge, private room, and outdoor dining courtyards. The wine list features excellent wines, and the menu contains dishes like shrimp and crab bisque, roast duck with orange or sherry sauce, and crab cakes with Creole rémoulade. Don't miss the crème brûlée.

Opened in 2003, **Mattison's City Grill** (1 N. Lemon Ave., 941/330-0440, www.mattisons.com, 11am-11pm Tues.-Thurs., 11am-midnight Fri.-Sat., 9:30am-10pm Sun., 11am-10pm Mon., $17-25) is casual and

St. Armands Circle on Lido Key

Bijou Café

A similar fun, casual seafood joint but with no water views, **Barnacle Bill's** (1526 Main St., 941/365-6800, 11:30am-9pm Mon.-Thurs., 11:30am-10pm Fri.-Sat., 4pm-9pm Sun., $15-25) renovated its downtown location in 2005. This is the chain's white-tablecloth establishment, with choices like crab cakes, fried popcorn shrimp, and stuffed flounder. Its other location is at 5050 North Tamiami Trail (941/355-7700).

Although it's slightly south of downtown, any list of important downtown restaurants has to include ★ **Michaels On East** (1212 East Ave. S., 941/366-0007, 11:30am-2pm and 5pm-9pm Mon.-Thurs., 5pm-10pm Fri.-Sat., $15-30). It has won best-of-Florida accolades from nearly everyone since opening at the beginning of the 1990s, and has kept up with all the newcomers, consistently pushing the envelope and wowing diners with its New American take and lavish interior. During the day it's a power-lunching crowd; at night, romantic dinners include grilled duck breast paired with yellow beet and potato hash and Swiss chard with a pomegranate demi-glace, all flavors showcased with a nice selection of wine.

For when you're tired of fish, ★ **Patrick's** (1481 Main St., 941/955-1481, 11am-10pm Sun.-Thurs., 11am-11pm Fri.-Sat., $10-20) gets top honors for Sarasota's best burger. It's a casual spot, with no reservations accepted, and the bar scene is fun. Patrick's has an extensive lunch and dinner menu with an exceptional variety of burgers, steaks, seafood, salads, and traditional bar-fare favorites such as chicken wings and jalapeño poppers. The burger selection is creative and original—try the Bronx bomber burger with grilled onions, Swiss cheese, and barbecue sauce. The wine list contains around 20 well-selected wines, and the beer selection focuses on stout ales and Irish varieties.

Just want a quick, inexpensive bite? Head to downtown's **Cafe Epicure** (1298 N. Palm Ave., 941/366-5648, 11am-10:30pm daily, $5-25). It's a cool bistro, deli, and market, an easy place to hang out on the patio and write

hopping, with Italian-ish small plates and pizzas. It feels more urban than many downtown restaurants, with great outdoor seating, cool wine events and cigar dinners, and live music nightly. It's been so successful that owner Paul Mattison has a virtual empire in the area now: Mattison's Riverside, Mattison's Forty One, and a catering business—all fun, fresh dining experiences.

Marina Jack's (2 Marina Plaza, 941/365-4232, www.marinajacks.com, 11:15am-11pm daily, $10-35, depending on which dining room you choose) is a longtime downtown favorite with nightly live music. It's all about casual waterside dining, with a few different ways to eat with the water in view. Choose from the second-level Bayside Dining Room, the Blue Sunshine Patio, or a cocktail at the Deep Six Lounge and Piano Bar. If you still don't feel aquatic enough, there's the *Marina Jack II* yacht, which wines you and dines you in the bay. Back on land, the menu leans to crowd-pleasers like crab-stuffed mushrooms, conch fritters, and steaks.

postcards while having a drink and enjoying a great sandwich, salad, or pizza.

Best breakfast? It's a chain, but this location is without a doubt the best of the breed. **First Watch Restaurant** (1395 Main St., 941/954-1395, 7am-2:30pm daily, $5-12) serves Sarasota's finest quick, no-fuss, inexpensive breakfasts with bottomless coffee and cheery service. Investigate the Inspired Italian omelet (roasted red peppers, tomatoes, mozzarella cheese, and Italian sausage, topped with fresh herbs) or the carrot-cake pancakes. Lines can be long, but they move quickly. If you just can't wait, walk south along Central Avenue and stop into one of the sidewalk coffeehouses.

St. Armands Circle and Lido Key

St. Armands Circle and Lido Key are often compared to Rodeo Drive and other famous shopping districts. There are a variety of shops and some of the city's best restaurants lined up around the circle.

Two of the oldest on the stretch are **Café L'Europe** (431 St. Armands Circle, 941/388-4415, 11:30am-9pm Sun.-Thurs., 11:30am-10pm Fri.-Sat., $25-40) and the **Columbia Restaurant** (411 St. Armands Circle, 941/388-3987, 11am-10pm daily, $10-25). Close together, both feature beautiful dining rooms and wonderful sidewalk dining. The Columbia opened in 1959, making it the oldest restaurant in Sarasota. (Its sister restaurant in Tampa is the oldest restaurant in Florida.) The Cuban food is authentic, and dishes include red snapper Alicante and 1905 Salad with chopped cheese, olives, and vinaigrette. The black bean soup and stuffed pompano in parchment are excellent choices. Columbia is also known for its fruity sangria. As for Café L'Europe, it's a broad collection of culinary influences that's hard to pin down: The kitchen does an equally good job with a New England lobster roll, wild mushroom ravioli, and herb crusted lamb with mint sauce.

15 South Ristorante Enoteca (15 S. Blvd. of the Presidents, 941/388-1555,

Table-Hopping

In the off-season, Sarasota's many culinary pearls are yours for the plucking—and during June that plucking gets all the more delicious with a 14-day **Savor Sarasota restaurant week** (www.savorsarasota.com). In a city with one of the highest concentrations of *Zagat*-rated restaurants in Florida, dozens have banded together to offer value-priced three-course prix fixe menus.

It's definitely a bargain, but what's in it for the restaurants? According to Michael Klauber, proprietor of Michaels on East and one of the instigators of restaurant week, "The original idea came from the local convention and visitors bureau. We thought this would be a great way to showcase the restaurants, and it gives the restaurants an opportunity to explore something different with a special menu. I hope it can become a destination event, and that hotels and resorts will see an influx of people."

Some restaurants include interactive cooking demonstrations; others feature live music. Many of the restaurants offer several choices for appetizer, entrée, and dessert, some with suggested wine pairing flights. At the core, though, it's not complicated: Pick a participating restaurant, make a reservation, dine, pay (lunch $15, dinner $29), repeat. See the website for participating restaurants, events, and pricing.

9am-2am Thurs.-Sun., 4:30-midnight Mon.-Wed., $15-35) seems to be the place to go in the area for northern Italian, and the upstairs nightclub features an excellent martini bar and diverse styles of music nightly (Latin acts, belly dancing, Caribbean tunes, big band, you name it). The restaurant's menu will be familiar, but dishes like grilled veal chop and garlic bruschetta are exceptional.

It's a chain, but **Tommy Bahama Tropical Café & Emporium** (300 John Ringling Blvd., 941/388-2888, 10am-11pm Mon.-Sat., 10am-10pm Sun., $20-30) is just plain fun, the food is excellent, and the drinks are too good for common sense to kick in. The store downstairs carries Tommy Bahama's signature mix of tropical leisure-wear and cool housewares—you have to take a flight of stairs off to the side to reach the upstairs restaurant, which has huge windows that look out on the circle. Salads and drinks are fairly pricey but good.

Cha Cha Coconuts (417 St. Armands Circle, 941/388-3300, 11am-11pm daily, $10-15) is a good place to go for a drink or to grab some island-inspired dishes like coconut shrimp or a burger topped with mango chutney. **Blue Dolphin Cafe** (470 John Ringling Blvd., 941/388-3566, 7am-3pm daily, $7-15) is where to go for cheap and delicious diner-style breakfasts. When you're ready for some great fudge, head to **Kilwin's** (312 John Ringling Blvd., 941/388-3200, 8am-11pm daily).

Southside Village

Visitors don't hit this little shopping-restaurant area with frequency, which is a shame. A few of Sarasota's most contemporary restaurants are right here. Southside Village is centered on South Osprey Avenue between Hyde Park and Hillview Streets, about 15 blocks south of downtown.

Perhaps the best place in Sarasota to pick up the ingredients for a picnic is in the same block. **Morton's Gourmet Market** (1924 S. Osprey Ave., 941/955-9856, www.mortons-market.com, 8am-8pm Mon.-Sat., 10am-7pm Sun.) has the kind of fresh salads, deli items, fancy specialty sandwiches, and cooked entrées that make you press your nose up against the glass case, leaving an embarrassing smudge. Most items are fairly cheap, and you can eat on the premises or take it all out.

Pacific Rim (1859 Hillview St., 941/330-8071, www.pacificrimsarasota.com, 11:30am-2pm and 5pm-9:30pm Mon.-Thurs., 11:30am-2pm and 5pm-10:30pm Fri., 5pm-10:30pm Sat., 5pm-9pm Sun., $10-20) takes you on a pleasant pan-Asian romp, from Thai basil curries to expertly rolled *tekka maki* sushi and beyond. You can play chef here and select your combinations of meats and veggies to be grilled or cooked in a wok.

International District at Gulf Gate

Many of the better less-expensive restaurants can be found at the **Gulf Gate neighborhood,** a tiny international district that spans a three-block area from Gulf Gate Drive to Superior Avenue, and from Mall Drive around the block to Gateway Avenue. It's where to go to get a quick meal on the fly, takeout, or just something that won't break the bank. At Gateway Avenue you'll come upon **Pasta La Pizza** (6592 Superior Ave., 941/921-0990, 11am-9pm Tues.-Thurs., 11am-10pm Fri., noon-9pm Sat., 4pm-8pm Sun., $8-15) and **Rico's Pizzeria** (5131 N. Tamiami Trail, 941/358-9958, 11am-10pm Mon.-Sat., 4pm-10pm Sun., $6-15). And once you hit Gulf Gate Drive, there are a couple of Chinese and sushi take-out places, a Russian joint, and a British tearoom.

Pinecrest and Beyond

Sarasota is a huge Amish and Mennonite winter resort. Both groups come down from Pennsylvania and the Midwest looking for sun and good Amish food. The locus of Amish activity here is in Pinecrest, where you'll see the bearded men in suspenders and wide straw hats, the women in long skirts and bonnets, all enjoying the Florida weather. While here, they eat at **Yoder's** (3434 Bahia Vista, 941/955-7771, 6am-8pm Mon.-Sat., $7-15). It's been a Sarasota institution since 1975, with wholesome, rib-sticking country ham and corn fritters, turkey and gravy, meatloaf and mashed potatoes, and pies, pies, pies. Note especially the fresh strawberry pie. **Troyer's Dutch Heritage** (3713 Bahia Vista, 941/955-8007, 6am-8pm Mon.-Thurs., 6am-9pm Fri.-Sat., $5-12) is even more venerable, dating to 1969, with sturdy, accessible buffet-style meals and a gift shop on the second floor.

ACCOMMODATIONS

Hotels and motels run the gamut from moderately priced and no-frills to truly luxurious. Generally speaking, beachside places are pricier than mainland or downtown accommodations, and winter rates are highest, dropping down usually by a third in summer. Listed here are Sarasota and Lido Key accommodations—Longboat Key, Siesta Key, and Venice are covered in *The Keys* section of this chapter.

Under $100

The **Regency Inn and Suites** (4000 N. Tamiami Trail, 941/355-7616, www.regencyinnsarasotaflorida.com, $55-95) is a clean no-frills two-story motel that was recently renovated. It's about a mile from the action of downtown, but there's a sweet little pool surrounded by palm trees to entertain you.

$100-200

Business travelers enjoy **Springhill Suites by Marriott** (1020 University Pkwy., 941/358-3385, $140-200), a moderately priced all-suites hotel fairly close to the airport. All rooms have a king or two doubles with separate sleeping, eating, and working areas. There's also a pullout sofa bed, a pantry area with a mini refrigerator, a sink, and a microwave, and a big desk with fancy chair and two-line telephones with wired Internet access. The free continental breakfast isn't an afterthought, offering items like sausage, eggs, oatmeal, and make-your-own waffles.

Courtyard by Marriott (850 University Pkwy., 941/355-3337, $149-250) is a mostly business, recently renovated three-story hotel directly across from the airport. It's convenient to both Bradenton and Sarasota. This is a great hotel for business trips or family vacations. There's wireless high-speed Internet throughout the hotel and a hot breakfast buffet.

$200-300

The three-story **La Quinta Inn & Suites Sarasota** (1803 Tamiami Trail N., 941/366-5128, $100-300) is not far from the Ringling School of Art and Design, a few minutes' drive from downtown. Rooms are midsize, some with sofa beds, and those on interior hallways have desks. There's an outdoor pool, a pleasant complimentary breakfast, and free parking, and pets under 30 pounds are accepted.

Over $300

It was controversial when it opened, but the **Ritz-Carlton Sarasota** (1111 Ritz-Carlton Dr., 941/309-2000, www.ritzcarlton.com, $500-1,000), a 266-room, 18-story luxury hotel right downtown, has managed to blend in beautifully. The chain's signature warm and efficient service, spacious rooms with balconies and marble baths, and great amenities make it the top choice among business and other travelers looking for upscale amenities. The downtown location is convenient to restaurants (although there are two laudable ones on-site) and attractions; there's a lovely pool and three lighted tennis courts, and the lounge at the Jack Dusty restaurant is always hopping.

The Ritz has a spa open to guests and members only, and the Members Golf Club, located 13 miles from the hotel, offers a Tom Fazio-designed 18-hole championship course. It is a par 72 set on 315 acres of tropical landscape with no real estate development.

One of the trendiest and hippest hotels to open in recent years is the ★ **Hotel Indigo** (1223 Blvd. of the Arts, 941/487-3800, www.hotelindigo.com, $200-400). Guest rooms have wall-size murals and fabrics in bold blues and greens—altogether it's a fun, contemporary alternative, right in the thick of things. The on-site café and little wine bar is called H2O Bistro. They have a fitness center with recently updated equipment, and the two wading pools (one hot and one cool) are a nice recent addition that will help you relax.

GETTING THERE AND AROUND
Car

Sarasota is along I-75, the major north-south corridor for the southeastern United States. Sarasota County is south of Tampa and north of Fort Myers, 223 miles from Miami (about 4 hours' drive), 129 miles from Orlando (2 hours), and about 5-6 hours from the Georgia state line. If you prefer I-95, take it to Daytona Beach, then follow I-4 to I-75 before heading south.

U.S. 301 and U.S. 41 (Tamiami Trail) are the major north-south arteries on the mainland; the Gulf-to-Mexico Drive (County Rd. 789) is the main island road. The largest east-west thoroughfares in Sarasota are Highway 72 (Clark Rd.); County Road 780; University Parkway; and (to the islands) Ringling Causeway, which takes you right to Lido Beach.

Air

Sarasota-Bradenton International Airport (SRQ, 6000 Airport Circle, at U.S. 41 and University Pkwy., Sarasota, 941/359-2770) is certainly the closest, served by commuter flights and several major airlines or their partners, including Air Canada, American, Delta, Elite, JetBlue, United, and WestJet.

Alamo (800/327-9633), **Avis** (800/831-2847), **Budget** (800/527-0700), **Dollar** (800/800-4000 domestic, 800/800-6000 international), **Enterprise** (800/736-8222), **Hertz** (800/654-3131), and **National** (800/227-7368) provide rental cars at Sarasota-Bradenton International Airport. **Diplomat Taxi** (941/777-1111) is the taxi provider at the airport.

Bus and Train

Sarasota County Area Transit, or **SCAT** (941/861-5000), runs scheduled bus service (6am-7pm Mon.-Sat., $1.25) with routes in the city and St. Armands, Longboat, and Lido Keys. **Greyhound** (575 N. Washington Blvd., Sarasota, 941/342-1720) offers regular bus service to Sarasota from Fort Myers and points north, and Miami to the southeast; **Amtrak** (800/872-7245) provides shuttle buses between the Tampa station and Sarasota.

THE KEYS

These barrier islands off the Sarasota coast are where you'll find the best beaches in the area. They also offer the relaxed atmosphere that most vacationers desire. Go into Sarasota for a taste of the city and to listen to the symphony—then head to the keys to put your toes in the sand and listen to the waves of the Gulf of Mexico lapping ashore.

The northernmost of Sarasota's stretch of keys, **Longboat Key** is a 12-mile barrier island populated mostly by extremely upscale private residences. What you can see of the residences is showy enough, but I have a sneaking suspicion that the really incredible mansions are down all those long driveways and behind those tall hedgerows. There are only about 8,000 full-time residents, but in high season (Dec.-Mar.), Longboat Key is where the rich and famous come to play golf and get a little sun. If you are interested in seeing celebrities, you can hang around at the Longboat Key Club or on the golf courses to catch a glimpse.

The island hasn't always been so swanky. The Arvida Company laid the foundation for the development of the island in the late 1950s, enabling construction on previously loose shifting soil. Visitors generally stay in the high-rises that line the well-landscaped Gulf of Mexico Drive; residents live on the bayside in discreet shielded estates.

Siesta Key is something else again. It's a similar eight-mile-long barrier island with beaches just as beautiful as those of Longboat Key. But Siesta is mostly casual and fun family-owned accommodations, none extremely upscale, with easy access to the beach from anywhere as well as fishing, boating, kayaking, snorkeling, scuba diving, and sailboarding. At night, unlike on Longboat, these people like to party. Siesta Key Village has the area's most lively nightlife.

Farther south, **Casey Key** is eight miles long, stretching from Siesta Key on the north to Venice at the southern tip. It is almost exclusively single-family homes with just a few low-rise Old Florida beach motels. Two bridges provide access to the key, including a cool old swing bridge dating to the 1920s. Parts of the key are only 300 yards wide.

The town of **Venice** is more like a real

place than a tourist destination. The residents seem to be mostly sociable and active retirees. The downtown is quaint—a handful of upscale shops and galleries, a couple of restaurants, a place to get ice cream, a couple of coffee shops, and a good wine bar. There's a little community theater, of which the residents are extremely proud. But really, the biggest draw in Venice is teeth.

Every August the Venice Area Chamber of Commerce holds the **Shark's Tooth Festival,** with arts, crafts, food stalls, and lots of little pointy black fossils. It seems that sharks of all species shed their teeth continually. They have 40 or so teeth in each jaw, with seven other rows of teeth behind that first one waiting to mature. The average tiger shark produces 24,000 teeth in 10 years. In order to find them when they wash up on Venice beaches, stop by one of the gift shops downtown and ask for a shark tooth shovel. And once you've found a few, visit www.venice-florida.com/shark.htm to identify the species.

Beaches
★ SIESTA KEY BEACH

We have a winner in the international "whose beach is better" battle. In 1987, scientists from the Woods Hole Oceanographic Institution in

Massachusetts convened to judge the Great International White Sand Beach Challenge, with more than 30 entries from beaches around the world. To this day, Siesta Key Beach remains the reigning world champ, with all other beaches too cowed to demand a rematch. Its preeminence has long been known—supposedly in the 1950s a visitor from New York, Mr. Edward G. Curtis, sent a pickle jar of Siesta's sand to the Geology Department of Harvard University for analysis. The report came back: "The sand from Siesta Key is 99 percent pure quartz grains, the grains being somewhat angular in shape. The soft floury texture of the sand is due to its fine grain size. It contains no fragments of coral and no shell. The fineness of the sand, which gives it its powdery softness, is emphasized by the fact that the quartz is a very hard substance, graded at 7 in the hardness scale of 10."

The real test can't be done with sand in a pickle jar. You need to lie on the sloping strand, run the warmed granules through your fingers, sniff the salt air, and listen to a plaintive gull overhead. For those things, too, Siesta Key Beach wins—it's been named America's Best Sand Beach and ranked in Florida's Top Ten Beaches multiple years on the Travel Channel. Dr. Beach has named it

Siesta Key Beach

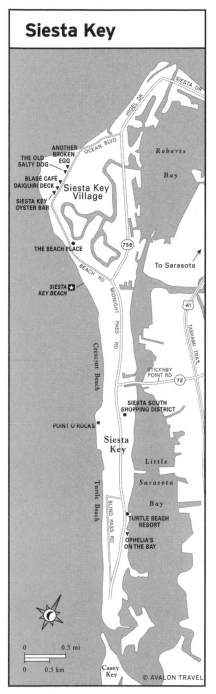

Siesta Key

ANOTHER BROKEN EGG
THE OLD SALTY DOG
BLASÉ CAFÉ
DAIQUIRI DECK
Siesta Key Village
SIESTA KEY OYSTER BAR
THE BEACH PLACE
SIESTA KEY BEACH
758
To Sarasota
Roberts Bay
HIGEL DR.
OCEAN BLVD
SIESTA DR.
BEACH RD.
MIDNIGHT PASS RD.
Crescent Beach
41
TAMIAMI TRAIL
STICKNEY POINT RD
72
SIESTA SOUTH SHOPPING DISTRICT
POINT O'ROCKS
Siesta Key
Little Sarasota Bay
Turtle Beach
BLIND PASS RD.
TURTLE BEACH RESORT
OPHELIA'S ON THE BAY
0   0.5 mi
0   0.5 km
Casey Key
© AVALON TRAVEL

in his top 10 beaches in America numerous times; *National Geographic Traveler* has also named Siesta One of America's Best Beaches. The list goes on.

OTHER BEACHES

The greater Sarasota area has lots of beaches to recommend. The beaches described here run from north to south.

Longboat Key has 10 miles of white powdery beach, but most of it is accessible only to those who live there or are staying in a resort or condo. **Longboat Key Beach** is accessible at several points—at Longview Drive, Westfield Street, Mayfield Street, and Neptune Street. It's mostly underpopulated and often offers incredible sand-dollar collecting. **Beer Can Island Beach,** at the very north end of Longboat Key and accessible by boat or from North Shore Road off Gulf of Mexico Drive, attracts a fair number of anglers and sun worshippers.

Then there's the aforementioned Siesta Key Beach, on the north side of Siesta Key (it is contiguous with another favorite beach called Crescent Beach, with good snorkeling), with white sand so reflective it feels cool on a hot day. **Turtle Beach,** on Midnight Pass Road near the south end of Siesta Key, is another popular beach, prized for its more private feel, large picnic shelter, and good shelling opportunities.

There used to be a small inlet that separated Siesta Key from Casey Key, an inlet called Midnight Pass, which was filled in, amid great controversy, in 1983. There have been disruptive environmental consequences to this choice, but for the visitor it means you can walk all the way on **Palmer Point Beach** from Siesta Key to Casey Key. The northern part of the beach was the former home of Mote Marine Laboratory. These days it's a quiet dune-backed beach, usually with just a few people walking and relaxing in the sand. There are neither lifeguards nor facilities. Casey Key also has **Nokomis Beach,** directly west of the Albee Road Bridge, a nice average beach for the area, and **North Jetty**

Park at its southernmost tip. North Jetty Park is one of the few Gulf Coast spots that draw surfers, and anglers seem to congregate here, too. Boats pass through the jetties from the Intracoastal Waterway to the Gulf.

South from here, you enter the beaches of Venice, rightfully known as the place to go when you're hunting shark teeth. The shark teeth that wash up on the beach are fossilized, floating in from a shark burial ground a few miles offshore, a deep crevice where these cold-blooded predators once went to die. In addition to these gray-black teeth, fossilized bones of prehistoric animals like camels, bison, and tapirs sometimes wash up on this beach. In local shops you can rent or buy a shark-tooth scooper, a wire rake with a mesh box that sifts the sand and shell fragments at the water's edge, leaving the teeth behind in the basket. **Venice Beach** (so different from the beach of the same name in California) is at the west end of Venice Avenue not that far from town. **Brohard Park,** at the southernmost part of Venice, is the beach of choice among anglers, with a 740-foot fishing pier for public use. Dogs are allowed at **Paw Park** at South Brohard Park, with a fenced area, a small dog beach, and dog showers. Farther south, near Venice's little airport, **Caspersen Beach** is really the locus of shark tooth mania. Truth is, it's harder to find teeth than it used to be, partly because city boosters have replenished the sand on the beach with sand from an offshore sandbar. It's a pretty beach left in its natural state, with people surf casting and red-shouldered hawks swooping above the shorebirds.

Sports and Recreation
GOLF

In the early 1920s, John Ringling purchased major acreage on the south end of the Longboat Key. He constructed a golf course and planted Australian pine trees along Gulf of Mexico Drive; he eventually abandoned the construction of a luxurious Ritz-Carlton. With this legacy, the **Longboat Key Golf Club** (301 Gulf of Mexico Dr., 941/387-1632,

greens fees $77-119) offers several remarkable golfing experiences to guests and their guests. Opened in 1960, the Bill Mitchell-designed Islandside Course (6,792 yards, par 72, course rating 73.8, slope 138) features 18 holes of crisp up-and-down shot-making through a 112-acre bird sanctuary filled with more than 5,000 palm trees and flowering plants. Water appears on 16 of the 18 fairways. The resort also has three 9-hole courses with a more country-club feel (and where more of the private members play), played in three 18-hole combinations: blue-red (6,709 yards, par 72, course rating 72.6, slope 130), red-white (6,749 yards, par 72, course rating 72.7, slope 131), and white-blue (6,812 yards, par 72, course rating 73.1, slope 132).

FISHING

Venice is a fairly well-known fishing destination—you'll see people wetting a line at the Venice jetties, Sharky's Pier, or Caspersen Beach. Expect to catch snook, redfish, Spanish mackerel, sheepshead, sea trout,

shark teeth from Venice Beach

10-mile running trail that parallels the Intracoastal Waterway, ending on Caspersen Beach, one of the most beautiful on the Gulf. It's a long, winding, wheel-friendly park, good for in-line skaters, cyclists, and even jogging strollers.

While in Venice, visit the **Venice Train Depot** (303 Legacy Trail) downtown. The Mediterranean-style depot was constructed in 1927 and is listed on the National Register of Historic Places. The depot also serves as a trailhead for the Legacy Trail, more than 10 miles of paved paths that run from just south of the city of Sarasota to Venice following the former CSX railroad corridor.

Venice Train Depot

and flounder, depending on the time of year. There are also lots of charter companies to take you deep-sea fishing out in the Gulf for grouper and snapper most of the year and kingfish, cobia, greater amberjack, and ma-himahi seasonally. At the end of East Venice Avenue on the Myakka River, **Snook Haven** (5000 E. Venice Ave., 941/485-7221, 11:30am-8pm daily) has a fun riverside restaurant, boat rides, and fishing. **Reel Fast Charters** (941/650-4938, $75 sunset cruise, $425 for 4 hours, $600 for 6 hours, $725 for 8 hours) takes groups out fishing as well as on non-fishing sunset cruises. And **Triple Trouble Charters** (941/484-3225, rates vary) takes small groups out from the Dona Bay Marina in Nokomis, just minutes from the Venice Inlet, on a 25-foot custom-rigged Parker for inshore and offshore fishing.

WATERWAY PARK
The **Venetian Waterway Park** (sunrise-sunset daily, free) in Venice is a mixed-use linear park that features a recently completed

Shopping

Shopping on Longboat Key is fairly limited: On the lush, tropically landscaped Avenue of the Flowers there's a little shopping center (525 Bay Isle Pkwy.) where you'll find a larger Publix grocery and a drugstore; at the **Centre Shops** (5370 Gulf of Mexico Dr., 941/387-3135) about mid-island, you'll find a small collection of shops selling T-shirts and resort wear as well as galleries and little restaurants.

On Siesta Key there are two main shopping areas: **Siesta Key Village** on the northwest side of the key, about one block from the Gulf, and **Siesta South shopping area,** beginning at the Stickney Point Bridge and going south along Midnight Pass Road. Both have plenty of T-shirt-and-sunglasses shops, beachy giftware shops, and a few other stores that are not quite as touristy. Neither area has high-end merchandise like galleries, antiques, or clothing.

Food
LONGBOAT KEY
Sarasota's has a long-term love affair with **Euphemia Haye** (5540 Gulf of Mexico Dr., 941/383-3633, $22-43). Hours vary depending on whether you dine in the restaurant (6pm-10pm Sun.-Fri., 5:30pm-10:30pm Sat.), dessert room (6pm-11pm daily), or the HayeLoft (5pm-midnight daily). Opened in 1975 on Longboat Key, the restaurant serves

far-reaching food in a tropical setting, including smoked salmon on buckwheat crepes and pistachio-crusted Key West snapper. The wine list is broad, with good selections at every price point. Food prices are high and dishes are rich in the restaurant; lighter and cheaper fare is upstairs in the HayeLoft. Chef-owner Raymond Arpke also offers cooking classes ($65 pp) at the restaurant.

At the **Lazy Lobster of Longboat** (5350 Gulf of Mexico Dr., 941-383-0440, www.lazylobsteroflongboat.com, 11:30am-9pm Mon.-Sat., 4pm-9pm Sun., $15-30), you'll find excellent surf and turf in a charming environment. The top-quality Maine lobster is served in a myriad of ways; if lobster's not your thing, try a juicy steak or one of many other seafood dishes. There's an indoor dining room with floor-to-ceiling windows and an outdoor patio with colorful umbrellas and tropical plants.

SIESTA KEY

Like everything else on Siesta Key, restaurants are mostly more casual here than on Longboat Key. Ocean Boulevard runs through Siesta Key Village, which is lined with loads of fun and laid-back beachy bars and restaurants. Most places have outdoor seating, and many have live music at night.

When you're looking for that special romantic restaurant, only one place on Siesta Key will do. ★ **Ophelia's on the Bay** (9105 Midnight Pass Rd., 941-349-2212, 5pm-10pm Mon.-Sat., 11am-2pm and 5pm-10pm Sun., $20-40), at the southern tip of the key, has a waterfront terrace that I swear the moon favors with an extra luminous show over Sarasota Bay and the mainland. The interior of the restaurant is stylish and romantic, but you have to sit outside. The chef prepares a distinctive and memorable collection of dishes accompanied by a unique wine list. Try the pan-roasted grouper with lobster beurre blanc and the maple pecan tarte or crème brûlée for dessert. The oyster bar next door to Ophelia's is a wonderful place to kill a little time, and appetite, if you have to wait for a table.

Another great restaurant is **Siesta Key Oyster Bar** (5238 Ocean Blvd., 941-346-5443, 10am-midnight daily, $6-15), with the acronym SKOB on the sign out front. The sandwiches are called skobwiches, and the grouper or fried shrimp skobwich is mighty fine washed down with a house margarita while listening to a live rock band. If rum is more your drink, right down the way is the **Daiquiri Deck** (5250 Ocean Blvd., 941-349-8697, 11am-2am daily, $6-17). One of the better drinks is the Siesta Tea, a mix of raspberry liqueur, light rum, gin, vodka, raspberry juice, and melon mix—tangy yet sweet, and strong.

For a great beer batter-dipped hot dog, head to **The Old Salty Dog** (5023 Ocean Blvd., 941-349-0158, 11am-9:30pm Sun.-Thurs., 11am-10pm Fri.-Sat., $5-15). Locals come for a bowl of clam chowder and a beer. It's open-air, with great views, good burgers, and saucy waitstaff. The beer bar is fashioned from the hull of an old boat, which adds a little nautical tilt to every drinker's voice. There's another location with the same hours at 1601 Ken Thompson Parkway (941-388-4311).

Best breakfast? Anyone on Siesta Key will steer you to ★ **Another Broken Egg** (140 Av. Messina, 941-552-8320, 7am-2pm daily, $7-12), one block down from its original location. The place is such a cheery and busy scene most mornings that they opened a second location at Lakewood Ranch (6115 Exchange Way, 941-388-6898, 7am-2pm daily). Try the Floridian omelet (three eggs filled with cream cheese and topped with crabmeat, Monterey jack, and onions) or cinnamon-roll French toast. The well-landscaped and shady patio is the place to sit.

Blasé Café (5263 Ocean Blvd., 941-349-9822, 4pm-1am daily, $7-23) recently reinvented itself from a well-loved breakfast spot to an even more well-loved lunch and dinner favorite with a martini bar that's hopping on most nights. They serve burgers, sandwiches, soups, salads, and a variety of entrées that feature steaks and seafood. Ask for outside seating on the wooden deck with the big palm tree in the middle, but if you're just stopping in for a drink, the bar is the seat of choice.

CASEY KEY

On Casey Key, the place to eat is **Casey Key Fish House** (801 Blackburn Point Rd., 941/966-1901, 11:30am-9pm daily, $5-15). This shambling restaurant and tiki bar does a brisk business, with diners navigating peel-and-eat shrimp while watching the sunset over picturesque Blackburn Point Marina. Casual seafood is the mainstay, and the fancier white wine-steamed mussels and almond snapper are brilliant.

VENICE

Along Nokomis Avenue (the main drag downtown) you'll find shops, diners, coffeehouses, and lunch spots—the best of which is **Venice Wine and Coffee Co.** (201 W. Venice Ave., 941/484-3667, 8am-8pm Mon.-Thurs., 8am-9pm Fri., 11am-5pm Sat.), a coffee shop by day and wine bar at night. To find Venice's Old Florida dining possibilities—all fun, all casual—you'll have to go farther afield. The **Crow's Nest Marina Restaurant and Tavern** (1968 Tarpon Center Dr., 941/484-9551, 11:30am-10pm daily, $15-30) has been feeding locals since 1976, with a fun tavern and great views of the marina, Venice Inlet, and the Intracoastal Waterway. The wine list is extensive, and the fare is fried oysters and steamed clams. Happy hour in the tavern is 4pm-6pm daily. Marina hours are 8am-7pm daily.

The **Snook Haven** (5000 Venice Ave. E., past River Rd., 941/485-7221, 11:30am-8pm daily, $10-20) has a similar vibe, only more down-home and bayou-style, right on the Myakka River (rent a pontoon boat or kayak before you eat). The burgers are good, and you can count on some entertaining fellow customers and occasional live entertainment.

Sharky's on the Pier (1600 S. Harbor Dr., 941/488-1456, 11:30am-10pm Sun.-Thurs., 11:30am-midnight Fri.-Sat., $12-24) is closer to civilization, with beach views and the day's catch offered broiled, blackened, grilled, or fried. Sit outside on the veranda and enjoy a margarita that's finished off with triple sec and blue curaçao for that dark-blue-water look.

Accommodations
LONGBOAT KEY

Longboat Key is mostly dotted with expensive high-rise condos and resort hotels that loom over the beaches. If you like a more

the relaxing view from the Casey Key Fish House

modest scale, the **Wicker Inn** (5581 Gulf of Mexico Dr., 941/387-8344, www.wickerinn. net, cottages $1,199-3,296 per week) is more like it. There are 11 casual and fun Key West-style cottages set around an inviting pool and landscaped with purple hibiscus and oleander. There's a private beach just steps away and a 16-acre public park.

★ **The Resort at Longboat Key Club** (220 Sands Pointe Rd., 941/383-8821, www. longboatkeyclub.com, from $500) is where serious golfers come for the 45 holes of the private Longboat Key Golf Club, but there are lots of other reasons to settle into one of the 210 suites (with full kitchens) or one of 20 hotel rooms. There's a fine restaurant on-site, 38 tennis courts, bike and beach rentals, great pools, and a private stretch of white-sand beach with cabana rentals and beachside service. Despite the fact that this is an extremely upscale resort, the people who work here are friendly and personable.

SIESTA KEY

There are not too many chain hotels and no huge resorts on Siesta Key—which is fine, because you're more likely to have a memorable time in one of the modest mom-and-pop house rentals or small hotels. The warm, independent spirit of many of these hoteliers is apparent in the relaxed decor and easy beachside pleasures. Many accommodations on Siesta Key adopt an efficiency approach, with little kitchens, essential for keeping vacation costs down (have a bowl of cereal in the morning, then prepare yourself a great picnic lunch for the beach).

Rented by the week, the tropical garden beach cottages of **The Beach Place** (5605 Av. Del Mare, 941/346-1745, www.siestakey-beachplace.com, $400-1,700 per week) make a nice romantic or family beach getaway. The beach is 30 seconds away and there's a pool, a tiki cabana with a wet bar, beachside barbecue facilities, lounge chairs, beach cruiser bikes, and included laundry. The cottages themselves are modest but recently repainted and pleasant, whether it's the one-bedroom Coquina or Seahorse, the two-twin-bed Starfish, the large one-bedroom Sand Dollar, or the huge studio cottage called the Dolphin.

On the south end of the island, ★ **Turtle Beach Resort** (9049 Midnight Pass Rd., 941/349-4554, www.turtlebeachresort.com, from $300) is one of the area's best-kept secrets and without a doubt my favorite place to stay on Siesta Key. Reservations are hard to

Turtle Beach Resort

come by at this extremely relaxed and casual property with 10 clapboard cottages, each individually decorated with its own porch and featuring a private hot tub. There are views of Little Sarasota Bay, Turtle Beach is a short walk away, and guests have free use of bikes, hammocks, canoes, kayaks, paddleboats, and fishing poles. Paddle a kayak from the dock of the resort to the quiet and secluded beach at Midnight Pass to enjoy the sunset. Then paddle up an appetite on the way back and eat at Ophelia's next door for a real treat. Pets are welcome.

Just down the road a few blocks from the resort, you can pull up your RV or stake out your tent and camp at the wonderful **Turtle Beach Campground** (8862 Midnight Pass Rd., 941/861-2267, www.scgov.net/turtle-beachcampground, $32-60, $178-365 weekly, $712-1,460 monthly). The 14-acre park has 40 small well-designed sites right on the Gulf. A short sandy path leads down to the beach, and the campground offers a boat ramp, a volleyball net, horseshoe pits, and a playground. The city center of Siesta Key is a short drive down the road and has plenty of fun shops, restaurants, and bars to keep you from having to rough it too much.

VENICE

If you've come to the Sarasota area with the express purpose of collecting shark teeth, then it makes sense to stay in Venice. Otherwise, Venice lacks a lot of the amenities found in Sarasota, Lido Key, Longboat Key, or Siesta Key, and the downtown pretty much closes up at night. However, a bike ride or walk along the Venetian Waterway Park trails that lead to Caspersen Beach is fun, and exploring the park and beach is the perfect reason to spend a day or two in the area. There's the fairly inexpensive **Inn at the Beach** (725 W. Venice Ave., 941/484-8471, $150-250) and a **Best Western Plus Ambassador Suites** (400 Commercial Court, 941/480-9898, $175-250), both perfectly fine. My favorite place to stay in Venice is the **Venice Beach Villas** (501 W. Venice Ave., 941/488-1580, $75-250, $500-1,700 weekly). They offer charming efficiencies, studios, and one- and two-bedroom units equipped with full kitchens. Their two locations within blocks of one another let you choose from a variety of rooms that are all centered around beautiful pools and artfully landscaped tropical grounds.

Venice Beach Villas

Getting There and Around

CAR

From downtown Sarasota, go east across the John Ringling Causeway to access St. Armands Circle and Lido Key, then continue north on Gulf of Mexico Drive (County Rd. 789) to Longboat Key. The drive from Sarasota to Longboat Key is a little over 12 miles and will take about 30 minutes in normal traffic.

To reach Siesta Key from Sarasota, head south on U.S. 41 (also called Tamiami Trail), then take a right onto either Siesta Drive or Stickney Point Road—the former takes you to the residential northern section of the key; Stickney takes you closer to the funky Siesta Key Village. The 6.6-mile drive will take about 20 minutes in normal traffic.

To reach Casey Key from Sarasota, drive south on U.S. 41, then take a right onto Blackburn Point Road. The 15-minute drive will take you about 40 minutes in normal traffic.

To reach Venice Beach from Sarasota, drive south on U.S. 41, then turn right onto West Venice Avenue. The 19-mile drive will take you about 40 minutes in normal traffic.

BUS AND TRAIN

Sarasota County Area Transit, or **SCAT** (941/861-5000), runs scheduled bus service (6am-7pm Mon.-Sat., $1.25) on routes to Sarasota and St. Armands, Longboat, and Lido Keys.

Information and Services
VISITOR INFORMATION

The **Sarasota Convention & Visitors Bureau** (Sarasota Visitor Information Center, 701 N. Tamiami Trail/U.S. 41, 941/957-1877, www.visitsarasota.org, 10am-5pm Mon.-Sat., 11am-3pm Sun.) and the **Sarasota Chamber of Commerce** (1945 Fruitville Rd., 941/955-8187, www.sarasotachamber.com, 8:30am-5pm Mon.-Fri.) both offer heaping piles of reading material on the area. The former has more useful material and a more central location.

Sarasota has its own daily newspaper, the *Sarasota Herald-Tribune,* with multiple zoned editions serving the area, along with a 24-hour television news station, **SNN.** Local weekly publications include the *Longboat Observer,* Siesta Key's *Pelican Press,* and a business newspaper, the *Business Observer.* Nine magazines cover different aspects of Sarasota County, from business to the arts and the social scene.

POLICE AND EMERGENCIES

In any emergency, dial 911 for immediate assistance. If you need the police in a non-emergency, contact the **Sarasota Police Department** (2099 Adams Lane, 941/366-8000). For medical emergencies, or problems that just won't wait until you get home, the nicest facilities are at the emergency care center at **Sarasota Memorial Hospital** (1700 S. Tamiami Trail, 941/917-9000).

Background

The Landscape

GEOGRAPHY

Florida is bounded on the north by Alabama and Georgia, to the east by the Atlantic, to the south by the Straits of Florida, and to the west by the Gulf of Mexico. The east coast of the state is comparatively straight, extending in a rough line 470 miles long. The Gulf side, on the other hand, has a more curving and complex coastline, measuring roughly 675 miles. In all, Florida's 2,276-mile coastline is longer than that of any other Lower 48 state and contains 663 miles of beaches and more than 11,000 miles of rivers, streams, and waterways. Florida is nearly pancake flat, without notable change in elevation, and young by geological standards, having risen out of the ocean 300-400 million years ago.

CLIMATE
Heat and Humidity

Florida is closer to the equator than any other continental U.S. state, located on the southeastern tip of North America, with a humid subtropical climate and heavy rainfall April to November. Its humidity is attributed to the fact that no point in the state is more than 60 miles from saltwater and no more than 345 feet above sea level. If this thick steamy breath on the back of your neck is new to you, know that humidity is a measure of the amount of water vapor in the air. Most often you'll hear the percentage described in "relative humidity," which is the amount of water vapor actually in the air divided by the amount of water vapor the air can hold. The warmer the air becomes, the more moisture it can hold.

When heat and humidity combine to slow evaporation of sweat from the body, outdoor activity becomes dangerous even for those in good physical shape. Drink plenty of water to avoid dehydration and slow down if you feel fatigued or notice a headache, a high pulse rate, or shallow breathing. Overheating can cause serious and even life-threatening conditions such as heatstroke. The elderly, small children, the overweight, and those on certain medications are particularly vulnerable to heat stress.

During the summer months, expect temperatures to hover around 90°F and humidity to be near 100 percent. The most pleasant times of the year along the length of the Florida peninsula fall between December and April—not surprisingly, the busiest time for tourism. Along the Panhandle, however, where temperatures are more moderate in the summer and chillier in the winter, the summer sees more tourist action.

The common wisdom is that the hard freeze line in Florida bisects the state from Ocala to Jacksonville. North of that, freezing temperatures rarely last long, and south of that it's just an hour here or there under the freezing point (with serious damage to tropical plants in years when the temperature dips low). The best approach for packing in preparation for a visit to Florida is layering—with a sweater for overly air-conditioned interiors or chilly winds, and lots of loose wicking material for the heat.

Rain

It rains nearly every day in the summer along the Gulf Coast—and not just a sprinkle. Due to the abundance of warm moist air from the Gulf of Mexico and the hot tropical sun, conditions are perfect for the formation of thunderstorms. There are 80 to 90 thunderstorms each summer, generally less than 15 miles in diameter—but vertically they can grow up to

---

Previous: Cà d'Zan in Sarasota; Clearwater Beach Visitor Center.

10 miles high in the atmosphere. These are huge localized thunderstorms that can drop four or more inches of rain in an hour, while just a few miles away it stays dry. The bulk of these tropical afternoon thunderstorms each summer are electrical storms.

Lightning

With sudden thunderstorms comes lightning, a serious threat along the Gulf Coast. About 50 people are struck by lightning each year in the state. Most of them are hospitalized and recover, but there are about 10 fatalities annually. Tampa is the lightning capital of the United States, with around 25 cloud-to-ground lightning strikes on each square mile annually. The temperature of a single bolt can reach 50,000°F, about three times as hot as the sun's surface. There's not much you can do to ward off lightning except to avoid being in the wrong place at the wrong time. The summer months of June, July, August, and September have the highest number of lightning-related injuries and deaths. Usually lightning occurs during daylight hours, with the highest concentration between 3pm and 4pm, when the afternoon storms peak. Lightning strikes usually occur either at the beginning or end of a storm, and can strike up to 10 miles away from the center of the storm. Keep your eye on approaching storms and seek shelter when you see lightning.

Locals use the 30-30 rule: Count the seconds after a lightning flash until you hear thunder. If that number is under 30, the storm is within six miles of you. Seek shelter. Then, at storm's end, wait 30 minutes after the last thunderclap before resuming outdoor activity.

HURRICANES

Hurricanes are violent tropical storms with sustained winds of at least 74 mph. Massive low-pressure systems, they blow counterclockwise around a relatively calm central area called the eye. They form over warm ocean waters, often starting as storms in the Caribbean or off the west coast of Africa. As they move westward, they are fueled by the warm waters of the tropics. Warm, moist air moves toward the center of the storm and spirals upward, releasing driving rains. Updrafts suck up more water vapor, which further strengthens the storm until it can be stopped only when contact is made with land or cooler water. In the average hurricane, just 1 percent of the energy released could meet the energy needs of the United States for a full year.

In Florida, the hurricane season is July to

Myakka River State Park

Hurricane Lingo

HURRICANE TERMS

- **tropical depression:** an organized system of clouds and thunderstorms with a defined circulation and maximum sustained winds of 38 mph (33 knots) or less

- **severe thunderstorm:** a thunderstorm with winds 58 mph (50 knots) or faster, or hailstones of 0.75 inches or larger in diameter

- **tropical storm:** an organized system of strong thunderstorms with a defined circulation and maximum sustained winds of 39-73 mph (34-63 knots)

- **hurricane:** a warm-core tropical cyclone with maximum sustained winds of 74 mph (64 knots) or greater

- **eye:** the calm center of a hurricane with light winds and partly cloudy to clear skies, usually around 20 miles in diameter but ranging 5-60 miles

- **eye wall:** the location within a hurricane where the most damaging winds and intense rainfall are found

- **tornadoes:** violent rotating columns of air that touch the ground; they are spawned by large severe thunderstorms and can have winds estimated at 100-300 mph (87-261 knots). A **Tornado Watch** means they're possible; a **Tornado Warning** means they're in your area.

HURRICANE WARNINGS

- **Tropical Storm Watch:** issued when tropical storm conditions may threaten a particular coastal area within 36 hours, when the storm is not predicted to intensify to hurricane strength

- **Tropical Storm Warning:** winds ranging 39-73 mph that can be expected to affect specific areas of a coastline within the next 24 hours

- **Hurricane Watch:** a hurricane or hurricane conditions may threaten a specific coastal area within 36 hours

- **Hurricane Warning:** a warning that sustained winds of 74 mph or higher associated with a hurricane are expected in a specified coastal area in 24 hours or less

HURRICANE SCALE

- **Category I:** winds of 74-95 mph with a storm surge of 4-5 feet and minimal damage

- **Category II:** winds of 96-110 mph with a storm surge of 6-8 feet and moderate damage

- **Category III:** winds of 111-130 mph with a storm surge of 9-12 feet and major damage

- **Category IV:** winds of 131-155 mph with a storm surge of 13-18 feet and severe damage

- **Category V:** winds of 156 mph and over with more than an 18-foot storm surge and catastrophic damage

November. These storms have been named since 1953. It used to be just female names, but now male names are also being used. Really powerful hurricanes' names are retired, like sports greats' jersey numbers.

The 2004 hurricane season was the last really destructive year in Florida, with Charley, Frances, Ivan, and Jeanne wreaking havoc on the Gulf Coast in rapid succession. In areas like Pensacola, it was several years before insurance and FEMA monies had been entirely paid out and blue roof tarps weren't common any longer. In the Charlotte Harbor area, hit by Charley, the reconstruction efforts have yielded an even more attractive destination for visitors. Things are finally back to normal after Hurricane Katrina's devastating effects were felt in nearby Louisiana and Mississippi, and thankfully the past few years have been, for the most part, meteorologically uneventful in Florida.

Hurricane Safety

Monitor radio and TV broadcasts closely for directions. Gas up the car and make sure you have batteries, a water supply, candles, and food that can be eaten without the use of electricity. Get cash, have your prescriptions filled, and put all essential documents in a large resealable bag. In the event of an evacuation, find the closest shelter by listening to the radio or TV broadcasts. Pets are not allowed in most shelters. There are designated pet shelters, but all animals must be up-to-date on shots. Alternatively, an increasing number of hotels and motels accept animals for a nominal daily fee.

ENVIRONMENTAL ISSUES
Oil Spills

The Deepwater Horizon oil well off the coast of Louisiana exploded on April 20, 2010, killing 11 workers and releasing oil into the Gulf of Mexico. When the well was finally plugged on July 15, it had released an estimated 53,000 barrels of oil a day into the Gulf. According to the Flow Rate Technical Group appointed by BP and the Coast Guard to estimate the extent of the spill, the total volume of oil released into the Gulf over the three months is at least 205.8 million gallons. On September 19 the Coast Guard declared the well to be officially "dead."

What the oil spill has meant for the ecosystem in the Gulf of Mexico is still largely unknown, as the long-term effects of the largest oil spill to take place in the Gulf are still being studied and documented.

On April 23, 2010, the U.S. Coast Guard began receiving reports that oil was washing up in wildlife refuges and the seafood grounds on the Louisiana coast. By June 21, about 36 percent of federal waters in the Gulf of Mexico were closed for fishing, totaling nearly 67,000 square miles and detrimentally impacting the fishing industry in the region. The oil spill has cost the fishing industry along the Gulf Coast over $2.5 billion. More than 8,000 species that inhabit the area were impacted, including more than 1,200 fish, 200 bird, 1,400 mollusk, 1,500 crustacean, 4 sea turtle, and 29 marine mammal species. According to U.S. Fish and Wildlife, 6,918 dead animals were collected, including 6,147 birds, 613 sea turtles, and 157 dolphins and other mammals.

More than 1.8 million gallons of chemical dispersants were released into the Gulf at the wellhead in an effort to break up the oil before it reached the surface. Robert Diaz, a marine biologist at the College of William and Mary, recently said, "The dispersants definitely don't make oil disappear. They take it from one area in an ecosystem and put it in another." And University of South Florida researchers are finding that the dispersed oil is having a toxic effect on the phytoplankton and bacteria in the Gulf of Mexico—the microscopic plants that make up the basis of the food chain. The EPA and NOAA have openly stated that they support the claim that dispersed oil is no less toxic than the oil alone. However, recent reports have claimed that the Corexit dispersants made the oil spill more than 52 times more toxic.

Other Environmental Issues

There are many complex and far-reaching environmental issues in Florida, from declining amphibian populations to an abundance of Superfund sites, paper mill water contamination, saltwater intrusion in the Everglades and other areas, and the quickly disappearing Florida panther population. Millions of acres have been bulldozed to make way for strip malls, condo developments, and all those beautiful golf courses and theme parks.

Recent drought in Georgia has meant that the U.S. Army Corps of Engineers has repeatedly withheld water to accommodate the needs of greater Atlanta; the Corps uses the Buford Dam to regulate water flow from Lake Lanier, which feeds freshwater into the Apalachicola River and eventually into Apalachicola Bay. Downstream along the Apalachicola River and Apalachicola Bay, the resulting salinity (less freshwater in an estuary means a greater percentage of saltwater) may mean the end of the state's oyster industry, not to mention the destruction of endangered species like Florida sturgeon and several kinds of mussels.

Still, the state's commitment to the environment elevates the situation from hopeless. There has been an enormous grassroots effort in the past decade in Florida, which has moved into the mainstream after the BP oil spill, of regular people who have stood up against offshore drilling and supported the protection of the abundant and beautiful natural resources that are so directly tied to the quality of life of everyone in the state. If their efforts are successful, the state's natural treasures, as well as its fishing and tourism industries that make up such a large portion of the Gulf Coast's economy, might be preserved, restored, and possibly even strengthened.

History

THE GULF COAST'S NATIVE AMERICANS

Twenty-seven thousand years ago, small groups of hunters crossed the Bering Strait from Asia to the Americas, moving southward through the generations until they populated what is now Florida—perhaps one of the last places in continental North America to be inhabited by humans. A warm and mild climate with waters teeming with fish, Florida was a hospitable home for early nomadic Paleo-Indians circa 12,000-7500 BC. They built small huts of animal fur and lived off the land's bounty, fishing the bays and streams. Between 1000 BC and AD 1500, these people developed advanced tools and pottery-making skills. By 1500 there were 100,000 Native Americans in what is now Florida, divided into large groupings most ethnologically and linguistically related to the Creek family. Each grouping was further divided into small independent villages.

In northwest Florida the **Apalachee people** of the Tallahassee Hills, between the Suwannee and Apalachicola Rivers, and the **Timucua people,** living in the center of the peninsula between the Aucilla River and the Atlantic and as far south as Tampa Bay, brought farming to the area, cultivating squash, beans, and corn and hunting to supplement their meals with meat. Highly organized and hierarchical nations, they lived in great communal houses and had an absolute ruler, who was assisted by a shaman and a council of noblemen, and a delineated social order. They also built elaborate burial and temple mounds, the ruins of which can still be seen.

Along the southwest Gulf Coast the **Calusa people** dominated, feared because of their fierceness. They were tall, with long flowing hair and simple garb consisting only of breechclouts of tanned deerskin. They were not farmers, living instead by fishing and hunting. Forty Calusa villages spread along the Florida Gulf Coast, with Mound Key near the mouth of the Caloosahatchee River the largest village. With simple tools, the Calusa built huge mounds of shell and deep moats to protect their villages of raised thatch-roofed huts. They practiced sacrificial worship and exhibited little interest in the Spaniards' missionary overtures.

Franciscan missionaries succeeded in bringing Roman Catholicism to the Timucua and the Apalachee peoples, just as the

Spanish soldiers were granted permission to steal from the indigenous inhabitants. The missionaries taught the converts to read and write, and they became more assimilated, leaving their villages to build houses in St. Augustine or carry corn along the Camino Real connecting St. Augustine with the Tallahassee area.

Both numbers lost population to diseases brought by the Spaniards, and then more to the British, who tried to raid the Spanish missions and gain control of Florida. The British brought the Yamasee people from South Carolina, and together they destroyed the mission buildings and took many of the indigenous people as slaves. In 1763, when the Spanish ceded Florida to the British, the Spanish departed the fort at St. Augustine and took the remaining indigenous residents to Cuba. While the Calusa people were less amenable to coexisting peacefully with the Spanish, they were wiped out in the late 1700s. Rival indigenous nations from what is now Georgia and South Carolina began raiding the Calusa territory; some Calusa people were captured and sold as slaves, and the rest succumbed to introduced diseases such as smallpox and measles.

The **Seminole people** were originally Creek, hailing from what is now Georgia and Alabama. They moved into Florida during the mid-1700s after the local indigenous people had been wiped out. They too ended up being annihilated by disease and by the Spanish, British, and American settlers. Their refusal to withdraw to reservations resulted in the Seminole Wars of 1835-1842. By the end of the war, 4,420 Seminole people had surrendered and been deported to the West. Another 300, however, defied the efforts of the U.S. government, retreating to the backwoods of the Everglades to hide. Many of their descendants still occupy the area. According to 2000 census data, 581 groups are represented in the state's Native American population of 117,880.

In recent years the Seminole nation, headquartered in Hollywood, Florida, has assumed a higher profile, with more noncontiguous reservations than any indigenous nation in North America and expansion of lucrative gaming casinos.

SPANISH EXPLORATION

The southernmost state in the United States, Florida was named in 1513 by **Juan Ponce de León,** who was clearly taken with the lush tropical wilderness. This expedition, the first documented presence of Europeans on what is now the U.S. mainland, was ostensibly "to discover and people the island of Bimini." On the return voyage he rounded the Dry Tortugas to explore the Gulf of Mexico, entering Charlotte Harbor. He soon realized that Florida was more than a large island. Near Mound Key he encountered the Calusa people, and while on Estero Island repairing his ship, he narrowly escaped capture. Eight years later he returned and headed to the Calusa territory with 500 of his men, aiming to establish a permanent colony in Florida. In an ensuing battle with the Calusa, Ponce de León was pierced in the thigh by an arrow and carried back to his ship; he never returned again.

Many of the subsequent explorers' missions were less high-profile. In 1516, **Diego Miruelo** mapped Pensacola Bay. In 1517, **Alonso Álvarez de Pineda** went the length of the Florida shore to the Mississippi River, confirming Ponce de León's assertion that Florida was not an island. In 1520, **Lucas Vásquez de Ayllón** mapped the Carolina coast, which, at the time, Spain claimed in the vast region they called Florida.

Pánfilo de Narváez was a veteran Caribbean soldier, hired by Spanish authorities in 1520 to overthrow Hernán Cortés's tyrannical rule. After a lengthy imprisonment by Cortés, Narváez went back to Spain and obtained a grant to colonize the Gulf Coast from western Mexico to Florida. Together with **Álvar Núñez Cabeza de Vaca,** an armada of five ships, and 400 soldiers, Narváez landed north of the mouth of Tampa Bay in 1527. Spanish-Native American relations deteriorated quickly during this period; the Spaniards' ruthless hunt for gold and riches

Famous Names in Florida History

- **Pedro Menéndez de Avilés:** founder of St. Augustine
- **Marjory Stoneman Douglas:** Everglades preservationist
- **William Pope du Val:** first territorial governor
- **Osceola:** Seminole leader
- **David Levy Yulee:** one of Florida's first U.S. senators and the first Jewish senator
- **Henry B. Plant:** famed late-19th-century Gulf Coast railroad baron
- **Helen Muir:** author and journalist
- **Henry Flagler:** builder of the Florida East Coast Railway, which connected the whole East Coast of Florida
- **Hamilton Disston:** bought four million acres in central Florida and created a canal system
- **Thomas Edison and Henry Ford:** inventors who lived here part-time and left a big mark
- **John Ringling:** circus entrepreneur
- **Barron Collier:** southwest Florida landowner and builder of Tamiami Trail
- **A. Philip Randolph:** labor leader

met with violent resistance on the part of the indigenous residents.

Narváez ordered his ships back to Cuba, while a band of men headed northward to the Panhandle in search of gold. Empty-handed, Narváez finally returned to the Gulf at St. Marks. Assuming Mexico to be only a few days' journey to the west, Narváez had five long canoes constructed, which capsized in a storm off the coast of Texas. Narváez drowned, and only Cabeza de Vaca and four others survived. This little band traveled 6,000 miles and in 1536 reached Mexico City to report on their ill-fated mission.

SPANISH, FRENCH, AND ENGLISH COLONIZATION

Then came **Hernando de Soto.** In the spring of 1539 he sailed for Tampa Bay with seven vessels, 600 soldiers, three Jesuit missionaries, and several dozen civilians, with the intent of starting a settlement. Where he went exactly is a topic of much debate: Some say he landed in Manatee County; others believe

it was in Charlotte Harbor. Like many of the conquistadores before him, De Soto was attracted to the stories of Native American riches to the north, so he sent his fleet back to Cuba, left only a rudimentary base camp on the Manatee River, and set off inland from the coast. He and his men never found what they sought, moving ever northward into what is now Georgia, South Carolina, Tennessee, Alabama, Mississippi, and Arkansas, where he died of fever.

There were religious missions to the state during the same time—**Luis Cancer** and three other Dominican missionaries, along with a converted Native American named Magdalene, arrived on the beaches outside Tampa Bay in 1549. Given the local population's experience with outsiders, it's no wonder that Cancer was quickly surrounded and clubbed to death. The survivors in his party promptly sailed back to Mexico.

In 1559, the viceroy of Mexico decided a settlement on the Gulf was essential in helping shipwrecked sailors and to discourage

French trading visits. He hired **Tristán de Luna y Arellano** to establish this colony. With 1,500 soldiers and 13 ships, De Luna landed at Pensacola Bay. He sent a party to scout out the interior and decided to wait until they returned to unload the supplies from the ship—a disastrous move. The scouting party returned after three weeks, only finding one Native American village, and before they were able to unload their supplies, a powerful hurricane swept through on September 19, 1559, and destroyed five of their ships and most of their cargo. The party moved inland to an abandoned Native American village, but their dwindled supplies kept the settlers on the brink of starvation through the winter and spring. In the summer of 1560, the party moved upriver and into what is now northern Georgia, where they remained until returning to Pensacola Bay in November 1560. Eventually De Luna was replaced with a new governor, in April 1561, but his impact and legacy as one of the early explorers of the Florida Panhandle remain to this day. Shortly after De Luna's expedition, King Philip II of Spain announced that Spain was no longer interested in promoting colonial expeditions into Florida. In 1992 the Florida Bureau of Archaeological Research found the remains of a colonial Spanish ship in Pensacola Bay that might have been one of De Luna's sunken ships.

French Protestant Huguenots failed in their challenge to Spain's sovereignty in Florida. **Jean Ribault,** France's most lauded seafarer of the time, set sail for Florida on April 30, 1562, establishing a colony at Port Royal, South Carolina, that year. It didn't work, and on his return to Europe, England's Queen Elizabeth I had him arrested for establishing a French colony in Spanish territory. Spaniard **Pedro Menéndez de Avilés,** a much-celebrated naval commander, took up where Ribault left off, establishing what is thought of as the first European settlement, in what is now St. Augustine, Florida, in 1565.

The history of Florida during the first Spanish administration (1565-1763) centers along the east coast, specifically around St. Augustine. The English neighbors to the north periodically attempted to capture the Florida territory; Governor Moore of South Carolina made an unsuccessful attempt in 1702, Governor Oglethorpe of Georgia invaded Florida in 1740, and in 1763 Spain ceded Florida to England. The English in turn did an incomplete job of populating the country and developing its resources, especially in light of the increasingly aggressive push-back from Native Americans. The British controlled Florida 1763-1781, at which point the Spanish occupied it again 1783-1821. But in 1821 the Spanish ceded Florida to the United States.

STATEHOOD, CIVIL WAR, AND RECONSTRUCTION

After the signing of the Adams-Onis treaty ceding Florida to the United States in 1821, Andrew Jackson was appointed military governor of the territory. Florida's present boundaries were established, with Tallahassee as the new capital and William P. Duval as its first territorial governor. It was a plantation economy, with settlers expanding ever southward and crowding out the Seminole people. Florida was admitted to the Union in 1845, the 27th state. After Abraham Lincoln's election to the presidency in 1860, Florida's proslavery stance led to it seceding from the Union in 1861 and joining the Confederacy. Florida furnished salt, cattle, and other goods to the Confederate army. Relative to population size, Florida furnished more troops than any other Confederate state, participating in the campaigns of Tennessee and Virginia. Florida was represented in the higher ranks of the Confederate service by Major-Generals Loring, Anderson, and Smith, and Brigadier-Generals Brevard, Bullock, Finegan, Miller, Davis, Finley, Perry, and Shoup. Florida was represented in the Confederate cabinet by Stephen H. Mallory, Secretary of the Navy. The most notable Civil War engagement fought in Florida was the Battle of Olustee on February 20, 1864, a Confederate victory.

After the war, a new constitution was adopted, the Fourteenth Amendment ratified, and Florida was readmitted into the Union in 1868. It took a decade or so for the state to establish social, educational, and industrial health. The state's general level of poverty led to four million acres of land being sold to speculative real-estate promoters in 1881. The discovery of rich phosphate deposits in 1889 improved the state's economy, as did its increasing popularity as a winter resort destination.

FLORIDA'S FIRST BOOM

Along with the phosphate mining in the southwestern part of the state, agriculture (especially citrus) and cattle ranching brought wealth to Florida, as did wealthy tourists who came to relax in the state's natural beauty and mild climate each winter. In the 1870s, steamboat tours on Florida's winding rivers were a popular attraction. Sponge diving around Tarpon Springs, cigar-making around Tampa—industry was booming late in the 19th century, even along the less-populated Gulf Coast.

Henry B. Plant Museum

The boom had its roots in the railroad and in road construction, industries that blossomed as a result of the state legislature's passage of the Internal Improvement Act in 1855. It offered cheap or free public land to investors, particularly those interested in transportation. On Florida's east coast, **Henry Flagler** was responsible for the Florida East Coast Railway, completed in 1912 and linking Key West all the way up the eastern coast of Florida. After making his money with Standard Oil, in retirement he realized that the key to developing the state of Florida was to establish an extensive transportation system. His biggest contribution might have been converting all of the small railroad lines he purchased to a standard gauge, allowing trains to travel the whole length without changing track.

On the Gulf Coast

Another Henry worked his magic on the other coast of Florida: **Henry B. Plant** was largely responsible for the first boom period along the Gulf, using his railroad to open vast but previously inaccessible parts of the state. The rails extended south from Jacksonville along the St. Johns River to Sanford then southwest through Orlando to Tampa. The Plant Investment Company bought up several small railroads with the aim of providing continuous service across the state, and his holdings eventually including 2,100 miles of track, several steamship lines at the port of Tampa, and a number of important hotels. The University of Tampa now occupies the lavish hotel Plant built at the terminus of his line. This new rail line not only provided passengers with easy access but also gave citrus growers quick routes to get their produce to market.

Around the same time, in 1911, **Barron Gift Collier** visited Useppa Island off the Fort Myers coast and fell in love with the subtropical landscape. Over the next decade he bought up more than a million acres of southwest Florida, making himself the largest landowner in the state. His holdings stretched from the Ten Thousand Islands northward to Useppa Island and inland from Naples into the Everglades and Big Cypress. He invested millions of dollars to convert this vast wilderness into agricultural land and a vacation paradise. His real gift, however, was his completion of the state's Tamiami Trail, a road that exists even today, linking Tampa with Miami. In gratitude, the state created Collier County in his honor in 1923, with Everglades City as the county seat.

The Roaring Twenties were good to Florida. With more Americans owning cars, visiting the Sunshine State on vacation became popular. Land speculators bought up everything, with parcels being sold and resold for ever-increasing amounts of money. Great effort was expended to drain the Everglades and Florida swampland to create even more viable land for homes and agriculture. The land frenzy reached its peak after World War I in 1925, but a swift bust followed the next year due to a major hurricane, then another one in 1928, and then the Great Depression.

CUBAN REVOLUTION

Ninety miles south of Key West, Cuba has always been closely connected with the affairs of Florida, and vice versa. Under Spanish rule in the late 1800s, Cuban relations with Spain deteriorated, and in 1868 the two countries went to war, with 200,000 Cuban and Spanish casualties. In 1898, the Spanish-American War focused the country's attention on the Gulf Coast city of Tampa, the primary staging area for U.S. troops preparing for the war in Cuba.

During the war, many prominent Cubans fled to Key West, including Vicente Martinez Ybor, who opened a cigar factory, the El Principe de Gales, in Key West in 1869. He eventually relocated the factory to a scrub area east of Tampa in 1886, once Henry B. Plant had completed rail service to aid in shipping and imports. That first factory begat a huge cigar industry in Tampa, with 200 factories at its peak.

The war lasted only a few months after U.S. involvement. Cuba was relinquished to the United States in trust for its inhabitants by the signing of the Treaty of Paris on December 20, 1898. Spanish rule ended January 1, 1899, and U.S. military rule ended May 20, 1902.

Cuban history after that continued to be fractious: Thomas Estrada Palma was the first president of the new republic, but he was ousted in 1906. Again, a provisional American government ruled, then withdrew in 1909. There was a period of prosperity, another revolt, and then General Gerardo Machado was elected president in 1925 and reelected in 1928. During his second term he suspended the freedoms of speech, press, and assembly and was forced to flee the country in 1933.

Colonel Fulgencio Batista y Zaldivar, who controlled the army, was elected president in 1940. During his term, Cuba entered World War II on the side of the Allies. Batista was defeated in 1944 by Grau San Martin, and then in 1948 Carlos Prio Socarras was elected president—but he was overthrown by Batista in 1952. Mayhem ensued, but Batista wasn't taking no for an answer. There continued to be strong anti-Batista resistance, and in 1959 Batista resigned and fled the country. Fidel Castro set up a provisional government with himself as premier. Political refugees from the Cuban revolution poured into Florida by the thousands.

Not long after came the Cuban Missile Crisis of October 1962, precipitated by the Soviets installing nuclear missiles in Cuba. Soviet field commanders in Cuba were authorized to use tactical nuclear weapons unless President John F. Kennedy and Premier Nikita Khrushchev could reach an understanding.

In 1980, more than 100,000 Cuban refugees came to the United States, mostly through Florida, when Castro briefly opened the port of Mariel to a flotilla of privately chartered U.S. ships, and in the early 1990s Florida received refugees from the military coup in Haiti and another wave of refugees from Cuba in 1994. Many of the Cuban expatriates live in Miami and environs, less on the Gulf Coast. Still, the Cuban influence is robustly felt in areas such as Tampa's Ybor City.

MODERN FLORIDA

While it was the first state to be settled by Europeans, Florida might be the last state to have entered fully into modernity. It remained more or less a frontier until the 20th century, with the first paved road not until 1920. It was really World War II that changed things in the state, prompting a period of sustained growth that lasted more than 50 years. Immigration to the state has resulted in a real diversity of ethnic groups, with a dense concentration of Cubans in the Miami area and Mexicans throughout the state.

Tourism has been responsible for much of the growth in modern times, with a serious assist from Walt Disney World, the biggest tourist destination on the planet. There are more hotel rooms in Orlando than in New York City, I kid you not. The beaches have continued to draw multitudes of tourists, and the beaches of the northwestern part of the state have seen a recent surge of interest, with locations such as Seaside and Destin becoming increasingly popular vacation destinations.

Recently the state has seen a decrease in population, partly a result of the devastating hurricane seasons of the early 2000s, the great recession, rising insurance costs, and the BP oil spill. For example, according to the *New York Times,* homeowner insurance rates in Florida have as much as tripled since the 2004 storm seasons.

In October 2010, Florida ranked second in states with highest number of foreclosures, accounting for 30 percent of home sales. It is estimated that 1 in 167 homes in Florida were in foreclosure that year. (The leader was Nevada, where an astounding 1 in 69 homes were foreclosed.) In April 2010, the Deepwater Horizon well exploded off the coast of Louisiana, killing 11 rig workers and releasing, over a three-month period, an estimated 185 million gallons of crude oil into the Gulf of Mexico. Eventually, some of the oil made its way onto the Gulf Coast of Florida. Most of the oil that impacted Florida washed onto the shores of northwestern beaches from Pensacola to just west of Port St. Joe. The well was capped three months later, and slowly the areas most impacted by the spill have recovered, but not without environmental and health impacts.

People and Culture

DEMOGRAPHICS

Florida ranks third in the United States in population, only behind California and Texas. In 2016, the population was estimated to be 20,612,439 (up from 9,746,961 in 1980). According to the 2015 population estimates, Miami is the largest single metropolitan area, with 5,929,819 residents. On the Gulf Coast, the other most populous areas are the Tampa Bay area (4,310,532), Fort Myers/Cape Coral (618,754), Sarasota/Bradenton MSA (702,281), Pensacola (52,703), and Naples (20,537). Nearly 1,000 people move to Florida every day, and the fastest-growing part of the state is in the central interior, particularly the corridor along I-4, which connects the Tampa Bay area through Orlando to Daytona Beach in the east.

Age

Florida's age distribution over the past several decades has changed very little regarding those age 65 and older. In 1990 there were 3.3 million Floridians over age 65, which was 17.7 percent of the total population, and in 2015 the census counted 3.8 million in this group, 19.1 percent of the total. This proportion is still the highest of any state in the country.

The Gulf Coast, especially the area around Tampa, has gotten younger in recent years. The population ages 0 to 19 has shown increasing growth rates over the last 30 years, from 15.5 percent in the 1970s to 22.6 percent in 2010.

The median age is at its lowest all along the northern edge of the state and the Panhandle. There's another dense concentration of youth around Miami and Tampa. St. Petersburg, famously a retirement destination, has also shifted demographically younger. The oldest parts of the state are Sarasota, Naples, and along the Nature Coast.

Race

The population of the Gulf Coast is still primarily white (77.8 percent in 2015), with the greatest ethnic diversity in the Tampa Bay area. The African American population is twice that of the Latino population along the northern border of the state and the Panhandle, while in the southern part of the state, close to Miami, the Latino population is twice as large as the African American population.

Religion

In modern times the Gulf Coast is primarily Christian. Jewish retirees don't appear to settle along the Gulf Coast, with the exception of Sarasota, which is 9 percent Jewish, compared to the east coast from Coral Gables to Palm Beach, which is roughly 13-15 percent Jewish. The southernmost part of the state is predominantly Roman Catholic, as is the area just north of Tampa through the Nature Coast. Most Floridians are Protestants, with the number increasing the closer you get to the northern border of the state.

SNOWBIRDS

First, what is a snowbird? The term means a temporary resident of Florida: someone who comes from a colder, less hospitable winter climate to bask in the Sunshine State in winter. Snowbirds are usually of retirement age or nearing it. More specifically, New Yorkers account for 13.1 percent of Florida's temporary residents, followed by Michiganders at 7.4 percent, Ohioans at 6.7 percent, Pennsylvanians

at 5.8 percent, and Canadians at 5.5 percent. The average length of stay is five months. If Florida has roughly seven million households, there are an estimated 920,000 temporary residents during the peak winter months and another 170,000 during the late summer.

CIRCUS PERFORMERS

Most people connect **Sarasota** with the circus. It was in 1927 that Sarasota became an official circus town, with John Ringling bringing his Ringling Bros. and Barnum & Bailey Circus's winter quarters to Sarasota, giving the calm Florida town a bit of spectacle. Many of the little people who starred in the circus retired in Sarasota in specially built small houses in an area known as "Tiny Town." Still, Sarasota doesn't get the title "Showtown USA"; that high honor goes to another Gulf Coast town, **Gibsonton,** or Gibtown, as it's often affectionately called, made famous as a wintering town for sideshow and circus performers as well as garden-variety carnies. Many of them retired permanently to Gibtown and have died off, but they leave the town with a colorful history. It's in Hillsborough County, south of Tampa on U.S. 41 near the town of Riverview.

Gibsonton was home to Percilla "Monkey Girl" Bejano and her husband, Emmitt "Alligator Skin Man" Bejano, billed as the "World's Strangest Married Couple" on sideshow midways. There was Jeanie the Half Girl, Al the Giant, and Grady "Lobster Boy" Stiles Jr., from a long line of people with ectrodactyly, or "lobster claw" syndrome. Stiles committed murder but got off with probation because prison wasn't equipped to handle him, only to be murdered himself some years later. The conjoined twin Hilton sisters ran a fruit stand here. Melvin "Rubber Face" Burkhart was the most recent to die, in 2001. His most famous routine was to shove an ice pick and a five-inch nail into his nose.

Gibtown has a post office counter that accommodates little people, and its zoning laws allow residents to keep elephants

Famous Floridians

An incomplete list, but these people were born and raised in the Sunshine State, or at least called it home for a long while.

- **Baseball players:** Buster Posey, Steve Carlton, Dwight Gooden, Barry Larkin, Sammy Sosa

- **Football players:** Emmitt Smith, Mike Ditka, Joe Namath, Daunte Culpepper, Mike Alstott, Warrick Dunn, Tony Dungy, Chris Simms

- **Tennis players:** Jennifer Capriati, Martina Hingis, Anna Kournikova, Ivan Lendl, Martina Navratilova, Monica Seles, Andy Roddick, Serena Williams, Venus Williams

- **Wrestlers:** Hulk Hogan, Rick Flair, Dwayne "The Rock" Johnson, Joanie "Chyna" Laurer, Randy "Macho Man" Savage

- **Actors:** Johnny Depp, Kelsey Grammer, Sidney Poitier, Butterfly McQueen, Burt Reynolds, Ben Vereen, Faye Dunaway, Buddy Ebsen, River Phoenix, John Travolta

- **Writers:** Harriet Beecher Stowe, Marjorie Kinnan Rawlings, Zora Neale Hurston, Ernest Hemingway, Carl Hiaasen, Stephen King, Helen Muir

- **Artists:** John James Audubon, Winslow Homer

- **Singers:** Jim Morrison, Pat Boone, Jimmy Buffett, Frances Langford, Gloria Estefan, Enrique Iglesias, Lenny Kravitz, Tom Petty, Bo Diddley, Backstreet Boys, some of 'N Sync, the brothers Gibb, Beyoncé Knowles, Jennifer Lopez, Scott Stapp

- **Military figures:** Joseph W. Stilwell (Army general), Daniel James Jr. (Air Force general)

and circus animals in trailers on their front lawns. It is still home to the **International Independent Showmen's Association** (6915 Riverview Dr., 813/677-3590) and a bar called **Showtown USA Lounge** (10902 U.S. 41 S., 813/677-5443) that has rollicking karaoke on the weekend. A historic eatery called **Giants Camp Restaurant,** opened by Al Tomaini (8 feet, 4 inches tall) and his wife, Jeanie (2 feet, 6 inches tall), sadly closed in 2006.

Even if you can't fit it into your trip, you can get a sense of Gibtown if you can get your hands on the "Humbug" episode of the *X-Files* (season 2), in which Mulder and Scully travel to Gibsonton to investigate the death of Jerald Glazebrook, the Alligator Man. In the episode you'll meet Jim Jim, the Dog-Faced Boy, and the Enigma, who is covered in blue puzzle-piece tattoos and eats glass. Also, there is a 65-minute documentary called *Gibtown* that is hard to find but worthwhile.

Gibsonton is also home to the largest tropical fish farm in the country, **Ekkwill Waterlife Resources** (813/677-5475, www.ekkwill.com).

MOVIES SET ON THE GULF COAST

Florida has been a film location just about as long as there have been movies. Today it is ranked third in the country for film production based on revenue generated. The climate, the scenery, and the dense tropical foliage has sparked the imagination of countless directors, cinematographers, and actors, standing in for far-flung lands on several continents. The earliest Florida films were 1898 newsreels of U.S. troops in Tampa during the Spanish-American War.

The Museum of Florida History in Tallahassee has a collection of movie posters from films shot in the state. The following are some featured in this collection, and an idiosyncratic assortment of others, all shot along the Gulf Coast.

Hell Harbor (1930), the first full-length talkie to be made in the state, was shot in Tampa and depicts the story of the descendants of pirate Henry Morgan. *A Guy Named Joe* (1944), starring Spencer Tracy as a WWII pilot who dies and becomes the guardian angel of a young pilot in love with Tracy's girlfriend, was also shot in Tampa at Drew and MacDill air fields.

The Marx Brothers' *The Cocoanuts* (1929) may well be set in Miami, it's not totally clear, but it revolves around Florida's first land boom. *The Yearling* (1946) is an absolute classic starring Gregory Peck, based on the Newbery Award-winning book by Marjorie Kinnan Rawlings and nominated for seven Oscars. Parts of the film were shot at Rawlings's homestead in Cross Creek.

Some real camp faves include *Mr. Peabody and the Mermaid* (1948), a William Powell film shot at Weeki Wachee Springs with local mermaids, and *Beneath the 12 Mile Reef* (1953), the story of a Greek sponge diver from Tarpon Springs who falls in love with a girl from the rival Key West sponge divers. The king of Gulf Coast films, *Creature from the Black Lagoon* (1954), was filmed in Wakulla Springs and Tarpon Springs and was followed by two sequels.

Directed by Cecil B. DeMille and starring Betty Hutton, James Stewart, and Charlton Heston, *The Greatest Show on Earth* (1952) was filmed at the Barnum & Bailey headquarters in Sarasota and required all the actors to do their own stunts.

Elvis spent a little time on the Gulf Coast in Pasco County filming *Follow That Dream* (1962)—not a great film. Christopher Plummer, Gypsy Rose Lee, and Burl Ives got to hang out in the Everglades for the making of Nicholas Ray's *Wind Across the Everglades* (1958), a story about the hardscrabble life in the wilds of South Florida.

Victor Nuñez has done a few excellent movies set along the Gulf Coast, from *A Flash of Green* (1988), based on the novel by J. D. MacDonald about corruption in Sarasota, to *Ruby in Paradise* (1993), a small film about a young woman, played by Ashley Judd, set on the Panhandle. Then he did the Peter Fonda pic *Ulee's Gold* (1997), a Panhandle family drama about beekeepers, and another not widely released Florida pic called *Coastlines*.

Peter Weir's *The Truman Show* (1998), starring Jim Carrey, is set in the scary-perfect Panhandle town of Seaside; Volker Schlondorff's crime drama *Palmetto* (1998) is set in and around Sarasota; and Spike Jonze's *Adaptation* (2002), a loose interpretation of Susan Orlean's book *The Orchid Thief,* takes place in the mangrove swamps of the Everglades.

John Sayles's *Sunshine State* (2002) is set in a fictional town in Florida, which might be the east coast, but it describes the conflicts of early Floridians and new developers so well that it's worth seeing. Kids will recognize Florida as the setting for *Hoot* (2006), Carl Hiaasen's environmental flick filmed in Boca Grande.

Essentials

Transportation

GETTING THERE
Air

Tampa International Airport is the largest airport on the Gulf Coast, with 550 flights per day, and was ranked in 2013 by the U.S. Department of Transportation as eighth nationwide in on-time performance for arrivals and departures. Southwest Florida International Airport in Fort Myers has also experienced enormous expansion in the past few years. Generally, the most direct routes and cheapest fares can be found through these airports, but it's worth pricing flights through Orlando, which is an hour east of Tampa (mostly from Orlando International Airport, but there is a second airport that is increasingly popular for international travelers called Sanford International Airport). Nearby airports include:

- **Brooksville Tampa Bay Regional Airport** (BKV, 40 miles north of Tampa, 352/754-4061)
- **St. Petersburg-Clearwater International Airport** (PIE, 7 miles southeast of Clearwater, 727/453-7800)
- **Tampa International Airport** (TPA, 5 miles west of downtown Tampa, 813/870-8700)
- **Sarasota-Bradenton International Airport** (SRQ, 3 miles north of Sarasota, 941/359-2770)
- **Orlando International Airport** (MCO, 6 miles southeast of Orlando, 407/825-2001)

CHEAP FARES

All the online travel resources (Kayak, Orbitz, Expedia, etc.) offer last-minute specials and weekend deals on travel. The way to get a good fare in advance on air travel or hotel rooms is by traveling outside peak season. That period is different for the different regions covered (each chapter gives the approximate peak season dates in its introduction). For instance, peak season in Orlando is the middle of the summer, when families with kids have time off from school to visit the theme parks, while in Sarasota, south of Tampa, the peak season tends to be January through March, when most of the snowbirds are there. Spring break in March and April seems to be the most expensive time to visit much of the Gulf Coast, but bear in mind that in the off-season, hours for restaurants and attractions are sometimes more limited.

Car

The main thoroughfares to Florida include I-95, which crosses the Florida-Georgia border just north of Jacksonville and hugs the east coast of the state all the way down, and I-75, which runs south from Georgia through the state's middle, then works its way west to the coast just south of Tampa. I-4 extends southwest across the state from Daytona through Orlando and then connects to I-75 in Tampa. On the Panhandle, I-10 is the big east-west road, which can be accessed from the north by U.S. 29, U.S. 231, or U.S. 19. Highway 98 is a scenic route that hugs the coast along most of the Panhandle.

Boat

If you're traveling to Florida by boat, the **Gulf Intracoastal Waterway** is a 1,090-mile toll-free East Coast channel that links Norfolk, Virginia, to Miami, Florida, and Carrabelle, Florida, to Brownsville, Texas, through gorgeous sheltered waters. There's

---

Previous: Vinoy Park in St. Petersburg; Clearwater Beach.

also a noncontiguous section of the waterway connecting Tampa Bay with the Okeechobee Waterway. The Gulf Intracoastal Waterway follows a course of sheltered bays, rivers, and canals along the Gulf of Mexico, which makes it perfect for recreational cruising.

And the **Port of Tampa** is a huge home port for a variety of cruise lines (Carnival, Royal Caribbean, Norwegian, and Holland America). Nearly a million passengers pass through its cruise terminals each year on their way to a vacation on the sea.

GETTING AROUND
Car
U.S. 98 curves all the way around the Big Bend of the Panhandle into the Florida peninsula, where it is also called U.S. 19. U.S. 19 extends along the coast all the way down to St. Pete. I-75 is the huge north-south artery on the Gulf Coast side of the Florida peninsula, stretching from where it enters the state at Valdosta, Georgia, all the way south to Naples, where it jogs across the state to the east along what is called Alligator Alley. One of the more famous north-south routes in Florida is U.S. 41, also known as the Tamiami Trail, which extends from Tampa down to Naples, where it, too, shoots east across the state (significantly south of I-75). The Tamiami Trail and I-75 run parallel, fairly close together—which you choose depends on your preference: I-75 has the speed; Tamiami Trail has the charm. I-4 runs from Tampa through Orlando and over to Daytona Beach.

CAR RENTALS
Alamo (800/462-5266), **Avis** (800/831-2847), **Budget** (800/527-0700), **Dollar** (800/800-4000 domestic, 800/800-6000 international), **Enterprise** (800/736-8222), **Hertz** (800/654-3131), and **National** (800/227-7368) provide rental cars from most of the major airports in the Tampa and Orlando area. You pay a small premium for the convenience of picking up and dropping off at the airport, and you pay significantly more if you pick up a car in one city and drop it off in another. Most rental car companies insist that the driver be at least 21 years old, some even older than that—be sure to have your driver's license and a major credit card (even if you aim to pay cash, the rental companies require a credit card), or you're walking.

Whether to accept a rental agency's insurance coverage and waivers depends on your own car insurance—before leaving home, read your own car policy to determine if it covers you while renting a vehicle. Also, some credit cards cover damages to many basic types of rental cars, so it's worth checking into that as well. If you decline the insurance, rental car companies hold you totally responsible for your rental vehicle if damaged or stolen. The rental agency's insurance may add $15-35 per day to your bill.

Bus
Greyhound (800/231-2222, www.greyhound.com) service runs from Naples up through Fort Myers, then up to Tampa and St. Petersburg, and all the way around the Big Bend of the Panhandle to Panama City and Pensacola. Greyhound buses also travel to Orlando. If traveling by Greyhound is new to you, here's some general information: There are no assigned seats (do not, under any circumstances, take the seats adjacent to the restroom—it's olfactory suicide), no smoking, no pets, and no meal service, but there are regular meal stops so you can jump out and buy something. Stopovers at any point along the route are permitted if you've paid a regular fare. The driver gives you a notation on your ticket, or a coupon, and you can get back on whenever you like. There are better ways to see the state, but few that are cheaper, and the Greyhound buses have become much nicer in recent years.

Train
Amtrak (800/872-7245, www.amtrak.com) offers service to Tampa, up the eastern side of the Florida peninsula, and to Orlando. Amtrak offers a bus service to connect travelers to Tampa and the surrounding region.

To give some idea of price, the three-hour trip from Orlando to Jacksonville is usually about $40 one-way. Amtrak service has been greatly improved over the past few years. It now offers free Wi-Fi service on some trains, and there is always more legroom on the train than on a plane. Unfortunately, much of Amtrak's service that once existed throughout the length of the Panhandle has been out of commission since Hurricane Katrina destroyed the tracks in 2005. There are plans to restore this service, but the timeline remains unclear. Make sure to check with Amtrak about the availability of any route before you make your travel plans if you need to travel through this area to get to Tampa or Orlando.

Visas and Officialdom

FOREIGN TRAVELERS
Visas

Unless you're coming from Canada, foreign travelers need a valid passport and a tourist visa (a Non-Immigrant Visitors Visa B1, for business, or B2, for recreation). Keep your passport in a safe place, and make a copy of the passport number and other critical information, keeping it elsewhere.

Money

Working with dollars is fairly simple—there's the $1, the $5, the $10, the $20, and, less common, the $50. The $100 bill is seldom used and seldom accepted without scrutiny. In coins, pennies ($0.01) are pretty much only good for wishing wells; then there's the nickel ($0.05), the dime ($0.10), the quarter ($0.25), the rarer 50-cent piece ($0.50) and dollar ($1) coins.

Money can be exchanged at a limited number of airports (Tampa, Orlando, and Fort Myers) on the Gulf Coast. Exchange money before you arrive, or use U.S. traveler's checks. For the most part, if you have a Visa or MasterCard, put all of your accommodations, restaurant meals, and attractions expenditures on that—an easy way to keep track of how you spent your money on vacation.

Electricity

The United States uses 110-120 volts, 60 hertz AC, as opposed to Europe's 220-240 volts, 50 hertz. For the most part, Gulf Coast hotels will have blow-dryers for your use, so leave yours at home. If you have other electrical devices for which you need a converter, bring one from home.

Telephone Basics

Tampa's Area code is 813, but you needn't dial it if you're calling within the area code; 727 covers Pinellas County, which includes Clearwater, St. Pete, St. Pete Beach, and Port Richey area. Most of the Nature Coast, including Crystal River and Homosassa, are in the 352 area code. Orlando has the 321 and 407 area codes. Sarasota is in the 941 area code. If you're dialing another area code, you must first dial 1 (except on cell phones), then the three-digit area code, then the seven-digit phone number. Be aware that cell phones have rendered the pay phone an endangered species. If you don't have a cell phone that works in Florida, you're better off getting a prepaid international calling card. Hotels also charge by the call, so making calling-card calls is often more cost-effective.

If calling from abroad, the international code for the United States is 1. Within the United States, the 800, 888, 877, and 866 area codes are toll-free, meaning they cost you nothing to dial.

Tipping

Service-sector workers expect a tip. It's only in name a "gratuity," meaning an elective gift. In reality it's how they make the bulk of their money. Fifteen percent is pretty much the minimum, whether it's at a restaurant, a hair salon, or in a taxi. Tip bellhops about $1 per bag; tip the valet parking attendant $1-2 every time you get your car. Tip a good waiter or bartender 18-20 percent. But here's some tricky stuff: If the hairdresser or tour operator is the owner of the business, a tip can sometimes be seen as an insult. Keep lots of small bills at the ready for all these situations, but don't ever tip at the movies, a retail shop, the gas station, the theater, ballet, or opera.

Metric Conversions

The United States failed in its attempt at going metric in the 1970s. So, you need to know that one foot equals 30 centimeters; one mile equals 1.6 kilometers; and one pound equals 0.45 kilograms. Converting temperatures is a little trickier: To convert Fahrenheit to Celsius temperatures, subtract 32 and then multiply the result by 0.555. Got it?

Travel Tips

WHAT TO PACK

Florida is casual, and what to pack is mostly about being comfortable. If you're spending time in Sarasota, or Tampa's Hyde Park, bring something a little more formal, preferably in a tropical style, to wear in the evening. Elsewhere, the name of the game year-round is layering. You will need several pairs of shoes: something for dinner, sneakers for hiking (ones that can get wet and possibly muddy, repeatedly), and swim shoes or sandals. If you're going to the theme parks, wear extremely comfortable walking shoes and possibly sandals for some of the water rides if you don't want to get your shoes wet.

Even if you're visiting the Gulf Coast in the summer, bring a sweater. Most places keep the air-conditioner going strong. You'll appreciate this when you first step inside from the relentless heat, but if you plan to spend any length of time indoors, you'll end up getting cold, especially when the cold air-conditioning is coupled with sweat on the skin. In the winter, a long-sleeved pullover with light slacks is usually fine.

Bring sunscreen, binoculars, polarized sunglasses (for seeing depth when you fish and to better spot dolphins), a bird book, a snorkel, swim flippers, a good novel, more bathing suits than you think you can use, bug spray, flip-flops or sandals, a digital camera, maybe a disposable waterproof camera, and your cell phone; it will work in almost every part of Florida these days, except a very few rural parts of the Nature Coast, especially with Verizon service.

A car is an essential tool in most of the area, but visitors can also rent bikes, scooters, skates, strollers, beach chairs, boogie boards, surfboards, skim boards, fishing equipment, motorboats, personal watercraft, kayaks, canoes, sailboards, and sailboats.

WHAT IT WILL COST

What Florida travel costs depends on what you're willing to spend. If I averaged the prices at all the restaurants in the Tampa and Orlando region, I'd say a restaurant dinner for one person costs $20. If I were to do the same thing for accommodations, I might find an average hotel room costs $120. But are those numbers really helpful? There is a range, with significant variation, on both counts.

Travel costs are most expensive during peak season, which for Tampa and the surrounding area is early spring (Feb.-Apr.) and fall (Sept.-Nov.). What's helpful to know is that Tampa is generally less expensive than most of the Gulf Coast. The more rural coastal areas to the north of Tampa such as Homosassa and Crystal River tend to be some of the most affordable places to visit in the region. Top-dollar honors go to **Sarasota,** where an average dinner for one is about $30 and an average room is about $150 mid-season.

Beaches around Tampa for the most part are free; you may spend a few dollars for parking and sunblock. What you do at them may cost more—a half-day offshore fishing trip will run at least $250, an ecotour kayak trip around $50, a brief WaveRunner rental $40. Of the attractions, everything pales financially by comparison to a day at **Walt Disney World.** Still, **Busch Gardens** in Tampa, **Asolo Theatre** tickets in Sarasota, and **snorkel-with-the-manatees** charters in Homosassa are all pretty expensive.

If you can stay for a week, which I recommend, you can cut costs: A multiple-bedroom house or condo rental in the Tampa region will cost you less per night than a swanky single room in a hotel. In a rental house, you can be even more fiscally prudent by preparing your own breakfasts and picnic lunches. Splurge on dinners.

With attractions, check the websites for free or reduced-rate days or nights. Museums tend to admit people free on Thursday evening or Sunday morning, primarily to lure locals, but you can benefit. It's worth it to visit the local chambers of commerce or convention and visitors bureaus—not only for the information but for the coupons.

VISITOR INFORMATION
Maps
Visit Florida (www.visitflorida.com) sends a great map of the whole state with its Visit Florida literature. As always, AAA members should raid the free-map smorgasbord that is their divine right. The Tampa Bay and Company's **Visitor Information Center** (401 E. Jackson St., 813/223-1111, www.visittampabay.com, 9:30am-5:30pm Mon.-Sat., 11am-5pm Sun.), in the waterfront Channelside entertainment complex at the Port of Tampa, gives out good state and regional maps. Some cities (Crystal River, Siesta Key) can be navigated with only the photocopied map the desk clerk at the hotel hands out. In other cities, including Tampa, you need a real map. And if you're traveling alone, buy the laminated flip map to the area; its ease of use in the car may keep your wheels on the road.

A portable GPS is essential for the frequent road-tripper. Unlike the built-ins, it can be stowed in luggage and plugged into every rental car. Garmin, TomTom, and Magellan all make affordable portable versions (some that have mp3 connectivity and fit in your purse or backpack).

Tourist Offices
Tourist office addresses are listed at the end of each chapter. Most convention and visitors bureaus have extremely helpful websites, and many will send you a vacation package of information, maps, and coupons free of charge.

ACCESS FOR TRAVELERS WITH DISABILITIES
The more developed parts of the Gulf Coast (Pensacola, Destin, Sarasota, Naples, Tampa) are very accessible to travelers with disabilities. As one would expect, the more remote and rural areas may not have ramps, accessible restrooms, and other amenities. You may want to consider buying a copy of *Wheelchairs on the Go: Accessible Fun in Florida,* an access guide for Florida visitors who use canes, walkers, or wheelchairs. The 424-page paperback covers wheelchair-accessible and barrier-free accommodations, tourist attractions, and activities across the state.

Society for Accessible Travel & Hospitality (212/447-7284, www.sath.org) provides recommendations and resources to help travelers with disabilities plan their vacations, and **Able Trust** (850/224-4493, www.abletrust.org) offers helpful links to disability resources throughout Florida.

Most major car-rental companies have hand-controlled cars in their fleets (give them 24 to 48 hours' notice to locate one). If you need to rent a scooter or wheelchair during your visit, **ScootAround** (888/441-7575, www.scootaround.com) is a mobility enhancement company with scooter and wheelchair rental service in a number of Gulf Coast cities.

Diabetic travelers can call the **American**

Vacation Rentals

If you're planning on staying a week or more in the Tampa-St. Pete or Orlando area, or just want more privacy than at resorts and hotels, consider renting a privately owned condo or a home. In most areas, there are companies that specialize in vacation rentals, and the offerings often run the gamut from mansions with Gulf-front views to bargain-priced studio efficiencies near the theme parks with tiny kitchenettes. Here are some tips to help you navigate the process of finding that perfect rental.

USE ALL AVAILABLE RESOURCES

There are lots of options for finding a vacation rental. Each chapter in this guide highlights some of the best local real estate companies that help match owners with renters. Since these companies are tried-and-true sources for local vacation rentals, they are often the best sources.

In recent years much of the vacation rental market has moved out of the hands of these brick-and-mortar real estate companies onto the Internet, where owners can cut out the middle man and market their rentals directly. Currently, the top website for vacation rentals is VRBO.com (VRBO stands for Vacation Rentals by Owner). Tripadvisor.com has recently dipped its toes into the vacation rental market, and its offerings are growing rapidly.

DECIDE WHAT YOU WANT BEFORE YOU START YOUR SEARCH

Determine exactly what it is that you're looking before you call the vacation rental companies, and don't dismiss the resorts, hotels, inns, and bed-and-breakfasts in the area; you might be able to find a great deal on a stay at one of these places, so check what kind of specials they are running.

Diabetes Association (800/342-2383, www.diabetes.org) to get a list of hospitals that provide services to diabetics. Log on to **Dialysis Finder** (www.dialysisfinder.com) to find dialysis centers.

The **American Foundation for the Blind** (800/232-5463, www.afb.org) provides information on traveling with a guide dog.

TRAVELING WITH CHILDREN

This area is the kind of destination suited to a rambling family car trip. But how to face the open road with a carful of antsy travelers? As with a NASA launch, it's all about careful planning and precise execution. Consider carrying a master list of all that you've packed. Although it sounds pretty meticulous, it helps to see where your gaps are, it allows you to easily keep track of things from car to motel to final destination, and if you generate this list on the computer, it can be used as the basis for future trip lists.

The list should be divided into categories: clothes and equipment (these are the things that go in the trunk, to be exhumed at your final destination), and the stuff that makes or breaks your travel time—food, entertainment, and car comfort. Older kids can each be put in charge of a category checklist as the car gets loaded.

For smaller kids, always take a change of underpants or diapers inside the car with you, rather than in the trunk with the luggage. For older kids, encourage a layered approach to dressing—when one child is chilly, donning another layer may be preferable to making everyone endure the car heater.

Think of packing foods that nature has already prepackaged—bananas, oranges, hard-boiled eggs. Avoid things with sauces or drip potential, chips coated with the dreaded nacho cheese orange goo, or things that crumb too easily. And for drinks, carry a large, plastic, spill-proof cup for each child. This way, you can get juices at convenience

The closer you get to the water, the more the rental costs. If you are going to be traveling with other families or friends, consider renting a large house that's big enough for everyone. If you want to bring a pet along, you shouldn't have a problem finding pet-friendly rentals.

CLOSELY REVIEW ALL THE LISTINGS

Not all vacation rentals are created equal. While every condo in an entire development may have the exact same layout, the owners will leave their mark on their personal unit. Always look at the pictures of each rental that you're considering.

KNOW WHEN TO WAIT AND WHEN TO BUY

If you time your purchase right, you can often save 10-40 percent. There are often more rentals available than the market can fill, so you can save if you're flexible on vacation dates. You can often save the most if you wait until

a vacation rental in Homosassa

right before you want to rent, as there are usually reduced prices offered on vacation rentals if the available dates are just around the corner. It's a bit of risk but can be a great deal.

---

stores but you won't be at the mercy of those wide-mouthed, splash-prone glass bottles in the car. Alternatively, bring a bevy of frozen juice boxes. You won't have to wait in line for sodas, and the juice boxes will be nice and cold during the first leg of the trip.

The sight of the golden arches fills most kids with joy and most parents with dread. Fast food is the most common pitfall on long car trips, a wasteland of fat, salt, and sugar. To avoid the tortures of drive-through (it's everywhere, after all), you have to stand firm. Finding other food can be an adventure on long trips. On the Gulf Coast, this is easy: Get off the highway and hunt down an old-fashioned diner, one with counter stools, a good jukebox, and a short-order cook who makes the perfect grilled cheese. In preparation for your trip, research the indigenous foods of the areas you'll be passing through. Use the Internet to print out pictures and histories of each city's culinary highlights.

When traveling in the car with small children, allow more time to reach your destination. Count on stopping every hour to stretch your legs and run around. Churches are good stopping spots if rest areas aren't available, as they often have open, grassy areas and playgrounds. Traveling at night or during nap times is a good way to make up time. Put blankets, pillows, and any necessary stuffed animals in the back seat at the ready.

Your local party goods and dollar stores are perfect places to find inexpensive new forms of amusement. Wrap each new toy as a gift, to make the excitement last. Caveat: Do not buy travel games with small pieces sure to get lost immediately under the back seat. Maze books, magic-pen books, stickers, a magnetic puzzle of the United States, even car bingo can keep everyone entertained. For long car trips, the book *Miles of Smiles* is filled with car games. Picture-puzzle books (like *I Spy* and *Where's Waldo*) can be made into games as well: One person names an object for the rest to find in the picture.

Even if you dislike the plugged-in feel of video games, iPods, or DVDs in the car, bringing a stereo headset for each child allows everyone to listen to their first choice. You can even make your own books on tape: Record your child's favorite stories on audiotape, and then they can have the stories "read" to them in the car.

Bring lap desks and art supplies for projects. Dated spiral-bound drawing pads can be a nice way to chronicle a trip, with each child keeping the finished pad (parents can annotate as instructed). Encourage older kids to journal with a cool pad and a set of gel pens.

TRAVELING WITH PETS

More and more hotel chains are accepting people's canine companions; other pets are a harder sell. Best Western, Motel 6, Holiday Inn, and even swanky chains such as Four Seasons often accept pet guests for an additional fee. To get good information, visit www.petswelcome.com.

Flying with your pet to and from Florida can be problematic, as most major airlines have an embargo against pets as checked baggage during the summer months (any day in which the outdoor temperature might reach 90°F), and even for small pets that fit under an airplane seat, the airlines only allow one pet per cabin. The ASPCA strongly discourages pets traveling as checked baggage.

Dogs are prohibited on many walking trails in Florida, as well as most beaches. There are designated dog parks and dog beaches all over the Gulf Coast. Tampa, St. Petersburg, and Sarasota all have designated dog beach parks with amenities such as fenced play areas, dog water fountains, and poop bags. Be aware that in much of the Gulf Coast's wilderness areas, poisonous snakes and alligators pose more of a threat to your dog than to you.

TRAVELING ALONE

Most activities on the Gulf Coast are well suited to traveling alone. The only exception to that is backwoods camping in the Everglades or deep wilderness, and traveling around high crime areas of the cities on the Gulf Coast. Consider giving rangers your schedule and detailed whereabouts when camping, and be vigilant when traveling in urban areas. Look up crime data for the cities you are visiting and avoid the parts of town where most of the crime occurs. I wouldn't hesitate to recommend the Gulf Coast as a spot for quiet solo travel—except during college spring break, and then I would recommend it for loud, lively, socializing and partying.

LGBTQ TRAVELERS

While Tampa and St. Petersburg aren't comparable to Miami or Key West, these cities are both LGBTQ-friendly. While neither can boast terrific nightlife, there are some great LGBTQ bars, and both cities host their own pride festivals.

A good resource is the **Gay, Lesbian & Bisexual Community Services of Central Florida** (407/228-8272, www.thecenterorlando.org) for welcome packets and calendars of events, or the **International Gay & Lesbian Travel Association** (954/630-1637, www.iglta.com, membership $99 annually) for a list of gay-friendly accommodations, tours, and attractions.

Alligator Safety

Florida residents have learned to be blasé about gators. They're an everyday part of living in this subtropical climate. The problem with gators is not just a function of their large numbers; people feed the gators and thus they have gotten chummy and less fearful of humans, and vice versa. New policies are being put in place. In many spots along the Gulf Coast, if gators get large (over eight feet), they are culled. Smaller ones get relocated. The jury is out on this interspecies relationship.

Here are a few safety tips to keep in mind:

- Don't feed the gators. If you see others doing so, give them a hard time.

- Don't bug them during their cranky spring mating season.

- Don't bother the babies or come between a mother and her young.

- Closely supervise kids playing in or near fresh or brackish water. Never allow little kids to play by water unattended. The same goes for pets; don't let your dog swim in fresh or brackish water in Florida, period.

- Alligators feed most actively at dusk and dawn, so schedule your lake or river swim for another time.

- They don't make good pets. They are not tamed in captivity, and it's illegal.

- If you are bitten, seek medical attention, even if it seems minor. Their mouths harbor infectious bacteria.

- If you see a big one that seems especially interested in humans, call the local police nonemergency number.

- Don't throw your fish scraps and guts back into the water when fishing. This encourages gators to hang around boats and docks.

Health and Safety

Despite what it might look like in the backcountry of the Everglades, Florida is a modern, developed kind of place, with good emergency services and medical care pretty much all over the Gulf Coast. From Tampa to Sarasota you'll see more medical facilities, pharmacies, and billboards for MRI scanners than nearly anywhere else, a remnant of the area's recent past as a mostly retirement-age destination (as the Bob Dylan song says, "it's younger than that now").

The sun is probably the biggest underestimated danger. **Sunburn** can be debilitating, so be sure to slather with at least an SPF 30 sunscreen, and because you'll be in and out of water, and sweating in the steamy humidity, opt for waterproof or water-resistant cream such as waterproof and sweatproof

Banana Boat Sport Sunblock Lotion. Even better, one of my favorite finds on the Gulf Coast, Avon now makes an SPF 30 Skin So Soft cream with a DEET-free bug repellent in it to cope with the Gulf Coast's other big bully, the **mosquitoes.** DEET-based products are more effective in preventing mosquitoes from landing on you, but I hate to have that poison sitting on my skin all day. Lather up with the Avon product, then apply a DEET-based spray only if the mosquitoes are bad. Mosquitoes in Florida don't carry any diseases such as malaria, but their itching bites can certainly be preoccupying.

Another burning subject is **fire ants.** If you see loose, sandy mounds on the ground, do not stand in them. These little devils get incensed at the foot in their house and swarm up your shoe and beyond to bite, leaving raised white or red welts that really hurt and itch for days. There is no known treatment for their bites, but I have found that if you douse the bites with aftershave or just plain alcohol, it helps reduce the itching substantially, though maybe not the burning.

The **water** in this area of Florida is perfectly safe to drink, although it tastes a little funky in some areas. In terms of **food,** throughout this region you'll find one great seafood restaurant after another. Make sure to try some of the most adventurous local foods when you're traveling, as they are usually the most memorable and tasty: Try the oysters and clams raw on the half shell with a splash of Tabasco. For some, though, this is dangerous; pregnant women, young children, the elderly, or anyone with an immune system problem should order all seafood baked, broiled, steamed, or fried. The bacterium *Vibrio vulnificus* can, at the very least, ruin your vacation. For a list of safe and sustainable flatfish, California's Monterey Bay Aquarium's website (www.montereybayaquarium.org) has a useful Seafood Watch section.

Many travel articles suggest getting **medical travel insurance.** If you have medical insurance, though, that's probably all the coverage you'll need. The best emergency rooms are listed in each chapter, and you can always dial 911 (a number used nationwide to contact local emergency medical, fire, or police personnel) or the **Centers for Disease Control and Prevention** (800/232-4636, www.cdc.gov) for information on health hazards by region.

Resources

Suggested Reading

TAMPA
Travel Guide

Murphy, Bill. *Fox 13 Tampa Bay One-Tank Trips With Bill Murphy*. St. Petersburg, FL: Seaside Publishing, 2004. An offshoot of a television segment Murphy does, the books showcase 52 Florida-based adventures that are all within a full tank of Tampa. It's got lots of off-the-beaten-path attractions, all worthy of your time, from Pioneer Florida Museum in Dade City to the excellent camping at Fort De Soto Park in Pinellas County.

Drama

Cruz, Nilo. *Anna in the Tropics*. New York: Theatre Communications Group, 2003. This play won Cruz the Pulitzer Prize for drama in 2003. Loosely a retelling of Tolstoy's *Anna Karenina*, it depicts a Cuban-American family of cigar makers in Ybor City, Tampa, in 1930, and the factory's new lector, a person hired to read aloud great works of literature and the day's news to the cigar workers. It is a beautiful stage play— keep your eyes open for performances during your visit to Florida.

ST. PETERSBURG AND PINELLAS COUNTY
Nonfiction

Klinkenberg, Jeff. *Seasons of Real Florida*. Gainesville: University Press of Florida, 2004. *St. Petersburg Times* writer Klinkenberg may have invented the term "Real

Florida," which means the Old Florida, without Disney, fancy golf courses, or really anything glamorous. This book is an assemblage of largely humorous essays he's written for the paper that tell great stories about the people, flora, and fauna in west-central Florida. Another collection of essays titled *Pilgrim in the Land of Alligators* was published in 2008 by the University Press of Florida.

THE NATURE COAST
Nonfiction

Warner, David T. *Vanishing Florida: A Personal Guide to Sights Rarely Seen*. Montgomery, AL: River City Publishing, 2001. I love this book, written by a guy who sounds like a dead ringer for Ernest Hemingway (Papa features occasionally in the book, so maybe Warner fancies a resemblance himself). Some of this book appeared as features in *Sarasota* magazine—mostly it's chapter-long ruminations and odes to small towns along the Gulf Coast (especially good chapters on Cedar Key and other parts of the Nature Coast), with lots of drinking and womanizing thrown into the mix.

Fiction

Cook, Ann. *Trace Their Shadows*. New York: Mystery and Suspense Press, 2001, and *Shadow Over Cedar Key*. New York: Mystery and Suspense Press, 2003. As a baby the author was the model for the original Gerber baby (daughter of cartoonist Leslie Turner, who drew the famous portrait in 1928), but as an adult she has turned to mystery writing. The cool thing about these books is the setting—they are easy, beachy reads with plucky reporter Brandy O'Bannon having exciting adventures all over charming Cedar Key.

SARASOTA COUNTY
Photography

Evans, Walker. *Walker Evans: Florida.* Los Angeles: J. Paul Getty Trust Publications, 2000. Everyone knows Walker Evans's gutsy, gripping Depression-era photographs. But for six weeks in 1942, Evans focused his lens on Sarasota for *Mangrove Coast,* a book by Karl Bickel. These are some of the wonderful photos he took during that time of the circus's underbelly, old people, railroad cars, and decrepit Florida buildings. The text is by novelist Robert Plunket.

Nonfiction

Apps, Jerry. *Tents, Tigers, and the Ringling Brothers.* Madison: University of Wisconsin Press, 2006. Apps writes pretty much exclusively about Wisconsin, and this story started in Baraboo, Wisconsin. It's a wonderful history of the Ringling Circus and the seven brothers who made "The Greatest Show on Earth" from scratch. It's got great photos of early circus life.

Internet Resources

GENERAL FLORIDA
Visit Florida

www.visitflorida.com

For a good introduction to Florida, contact the state's official tourist information organization, Visit Florida (or call 888/735-2872), for a copy of its excellent annual *Visit Florida* guide, the *Florida Events Calendar,* or *Florida Trails.* Online resources include a number of electronic travel guides, for which you can order printed versions if you prefer. Visit Florida also has a 24-hour multilingual tourist assistance hotline (800/656-8777).

Florida Secrets, The Insider's Guide to Unique Destinations

www.floridasecrets.com

The graphics have a cheese factor and it's heavy on the advertising, but the site is a treasure trove of little-known destinations in Florida, divided up on the Gulf Coast by southwest, west-central, eastern, and western Panhandle.

FISHING
Florida Fishing

www.floridafishing.com

It's a clearinghouse of fishing guides, fishing charters, and fishing captains in the state, divided by region.

CAMPING
Florida Association of RV Parks & Campgrounds

www.campflorida.com

It's an easy-to-use comprehensive database of Florida campgrounds, including amenities information for each site. You can also go on this website and order a print version of the guide. To make reservations at a Florida state campground, however, you must use Reserve America (www.reserveamerica.com).

PARKS AND FORESTS
Florida State Parks Department

www.floridastateparks.org

Find a park, its affiliated camping and lodging, or get a bead on what events are coming up along the Gulf Coast. The site also has maps and directions to Florida's state parks, and it runs an amateur photo contest of state park photography.

Florida Trail Association

www.floridatrail.org
The Florida Trail Association is a nonprofit that builds, maintains, promotes, and protects hiking trails across the state, especially the 1,400-mile Florida Trail. From this site you can download all kinds of trail maps and park brochures.

SPORTS
Florida Sports Foundation

www.flasports.com
The foundation usually posts the "Grapefruit League" Florida spring-training baseball schedules on its website late in January. Another way to find out about spring training for your favorite team is by visiting the website of Major League Baseball (www.mlb.com).

TAMPA
Tampa Bay Convention & Visitors Bureau

www.visittampabay.com
This is a good site for background on the Bay Area as well as travel strategies and accommodations.

Creative Loafing

www.cltampa.com
The local alternative weekly newspaper has a great website. The writing is provocative and witty and covers politics, arts and entertainment, local events, and regional news.

ST. PETERSBURG AND PINELLAS COUNTY
St. Petersburg/Clearwater Area Convention & Visitors Bureau

www.visitstpeteclearwater.com
Similar to the Tampa Bay Convention and Visitors Bureau site, this one focuses, not

surprisingly, on the beaches. It's easy to book a room from this site, and it features excellent downloadable maps.

Tampa Bay Times

www.tampabay.com
The daily metro paper covers local as well as national news. It has a great website, and the paper's movie, book, and pop music reviews are notable. The paper's food-critic column by Laura Reiley is also worth the read for her outstanding, mouthwatering descriptions of the area's best eats.

THE NATURE COAST
Citrus County Tourist Development Council

www.visitcitrus.com
This is an interactive site with a wealth of information on Homosassa, Crystal River, and environs. It's a good site from which to choose a manatee snorkeling trip or fishing charter.

Steinhatchee Landing Resort

www.steinhatcheelanding.com
Steinhatchee is one of the Gulf Coast's least-known destinations, and generally the web doesn't help much to illuminate. This is the best site about the area, a site brought to you from the most popular upscale resort on the Nature Coast. The recreation section is helpful in planning a trip.

SARASOTA COUNTY
Sarasota Convention & Visitors Bureau

www.visitsarasota.org
This award-winning site is as user-friendly as they come, with easily sortable menus of restaurants, accommodations, outdoor attractions, and more. The excellent feature stories on the area's lures are written by local travel writers. The site is offered in English, Spanish, and German. A second site, www.discovernaturalsarasota.org, focuses exclusively on the natural draws of the area, including beaches, parks, gardens, and historic sites.

Anna Maria Island Chamber of Commerce

www.annamariaislandchamber.org

Too far from Tampa in the north and too far from Sarasota to its south, Anna Maria Island doesn't really get covered in other, bigger regional websites. This one doesn't have as many bells and whistles, but it's got all the basics of where to stay, what to do, and where to eat.

Index

List of Maps

Also Available

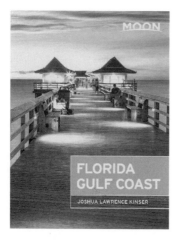

MAP SYMBOLS

▭▭▭	Expressway	★	Highlight	✈	Airfield	⛳	Golf Course
▭▭▭	Primary Road	○	City/Town	✈	Airport	P	Parking Area
▭▭▭	Secondary Road	◉	State Capital	▲	Mountain	🛆	Archaeological Site
- - - -	Unpaved Road	✪	National Capital	✚	Unique Natural Feature	⛪	Church
- - - -	Trail	★	Point of Interest			⛽	Gas Station
⋯⋯⋯	Ferry	●	Accommodation	🜚	Waterfall	⬭	Glacier
⋯-⋯-	Railroad	▼	Restaurant/Bar	▲	Park	▨	Mangrove
▭▭▭	Pedestrian Walkway	■	Other Location	⬛	Trailhead	▨	Reef
▥▥▥	Stairs	⋀	Campground	🎿	Skiing Area	▤	Swamp

CONVERSION TABLES

°C = (°F - 32) / 1.8
°F = (°C x 1.8) + 32
1 inch = 2.54 centimeters (cm)
1 foot = 0.304 meters (m)
1 yard = 0.914 meters
1 mile = 1.6093 kilometers (km)
1 km = 0.6214 miles
1 fathom = 1.8288 m
1 chain = 20.1168 m
1 furlong = 201.168 m
1 acre = 0.4047 hectares
1 sq km = 100 hectares
1 sq mile = 2.59 square km
1 ounce = 28.35 grams
1 pound = 0.4536 kilograms
1 short ton = 0.90718 metric ton
1 short ton = 2,000 pounds
1 long ton = 1.016 metric tons
1 long ton = 2,240 pounds
1 metric ton = 1,000 kilograms
1 quart = 0.94635 liters
1 US gallon = 3.7854 liters
1 Imperial gallon = 4.5459 liters
1 nautical mile = 1.852 km

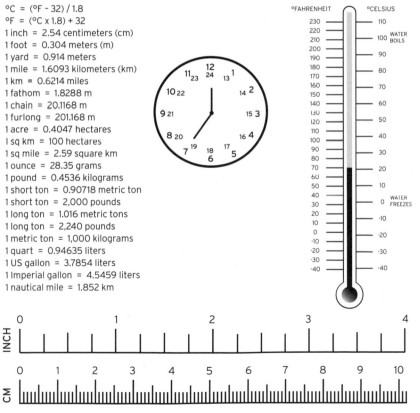

TAMPA & ST. PETERSBURG

Avalon Travel
Hachette Book Group
1700 Fourth Street
Berkeley, CA 94710, USA
www.moon.com

Editor: Rachel Feldman
Series Manager: Kathryn Ettinger
Copy Editor: Christopher Church
Graphics and Production Coordinator:
  Lucie Ericksen
Cover Design: Faceout Studios, Charles Brock
Interior Design: Domini Dragoone
Moon Logo: Tim McGrath
Map Editor: Kat Bennett
Cartographers: Kat Bennett, Brian Shotwell
Indexer: Greg Jewett

ISBN-13: 978-1-63121-710-4

Printing History
1st Edition — October 2017
5 4 3 2 1

Front cover photo: sea oats on a St. Petersburg beach © Slow Images/Getty
Back cover photo: fishing pier at Clearwater Beach © Jon Bilous | Dreamstime

Title page photo: Vinoy Park © Joshua Kinser
All interior photos © Joshua Kinser, except: page 5 © The Manta rollercoaster at SeaWorld Orlando/SeaWorld; page 6 (top) © mariakraynova/123RF, (bottom) © Ginosphotos | Dreamstime.com; page 8 © Universal Orlando Resort; page 9 (bottom left) © Disney, (bottom right) © dustyboots photography/123RF; page 11 © sepavo/123RF; page 14 (right) © Jocrebbin | Dreamstime.com; page 16 © andylid/123RF; page 20 (top) © Disney, (bottom) © Icholakov | Dreamstime.com; page 21 (top) © sepavo/123RF; page 57 © The Epicurean Hotel; page 102 (bottom) © Npgal77 | Dreamstime.com; page 103 © Disney; page 106 © Disney; page 109 © Disney; page 110 © Universal Orlando Resort; page 112 © SeaWorld; page 113 © SeaWorld; page 142 © Todd Arena /123RF.com

Printed in Canada by Friesens